THE POLITICAL BIOGRAPHY OF AN EARTHQUAKE

EDWARD SIMPSON

The Political Biography of an Earthquake

*Aftermath and Amnesia
in Gujarat, India*

HURST & COMPANY, LONDON

First published in the United Kingdom in 2013 by
C. Hurst & Co. (Publishers) Ltd.,
41 Great Russell Street, London, WC1B 3PL
© Edward Simpson, 2013
All rights reserved.
Printed in India

The right of Edward Simpson to be identified as the author of
this publication is asserted by him in accordance with the
Copyright, Designs and Patents Act, 1988.

A Cataloguing-in-Publication data record for this book
is available from the British Library.

ISBN: 978-1849042871

www.hurstpublishers.com

This book is printed using paper from registered sustainable
and managed sources.

Let none admire
That riches grow in hell; that soil may best
Deserve the precious bane.

John Milton, *Paradise Lost*, 1, 690–92.

'The Blind Men and the Elephant' is a poem based on an Indian fable. It is often regarded as a condensation of the Jain religious principle of *anekantavada*: pluralism and multiplicity of viewpoints. This is an old idea which preceded the 'reflexive turn' in anthropology by some millennia. Truth and reality are perceived differently from different positions. No single point of view is the complete truth.

It was six men of Indostan
to learning much inclined,
who went to see the elephant
(though all of them were blind),
that each by observation
might satisfy his mind.

The first approached the elephant,
and happening to fall
against his broad and sturdy side,
at once began to bawl:
'God bless me! but the elephant
is very like a wall!'

The second, feeling of the tusk,
cried,—'Ho! what have we here
so very round and smooth and sharp?
to me 'tis mighty clear
this wonder of an Elephant
is very like a spear!'

The third approached the animal,
and happening to take
the squirming trunk within his hands,
thus boldly up and spake:
'I see', quoth he, 'the Elephant
is very like a snake!'

The fourth reached out his eager hand,
and felt about the knee.
'What most this wondrous beast is like is mighty plain', quoth he,
'Tis clear enough the Elephant
is very like a tree!'

The fifth, who chanced to touch the ear,
said: 'E'en the blindest man
can tell what this resembles most;

deny the fact who can,
this marvel of an Elephant
is very like a fan!'

The sixth no sooner had begun
about the beast to grope,
then, seizing on the swinging tail
that fell within his scope,
'I see', quoth he, 'the Elephant
is very like a rope!'

And so these men of Indostan
disputed loud and long,
each in his own opinion
exceeding stiff and strong,
though each was partly in the right,
and all were in the wrong!

Moral:
So oft in theologic wars,
the disputants, I ween,
rail on in utter ignorance
of what each other mean,
and prate about an Elephant
not one of them has seen!

John Godfrey Saxe (1816–1887)

CONTENTS

CONTENTS

ACKNOWLEDGEMENTS

While researching and writing this book I have spent long periods of time around people who have suffered. I have been inspired by their fortitude, but also by their ability to turn to laughter and cynicism for catharsis. I have spent more than ten years thinking, reading and talking about mass death and ugly politics. If this was dark for those around me, then I apologise.

My arguments were both refined and abandoned during interactions with seminar and lecture audiences at the universities of East Anglia, Oxford, St Andrews, Edinburgh, Manchester, Cambridge, East London, Aarhus, Syracuse, Iowa, as well as Goldsmiths College, the School of Oriental and African Studies, the London School of Economics, Free University (Berlin), Jawaharlal Nehru University (New Delhi), the Goethe Institute (New Delhi), the Tata Institute of Social Science (Mumbai) and the Centre for Ethnic Studies (Colombo).

Ideas appearing in the following journal articles have made their way into the text:

2011. 'Blame narratives and religious reason in the aftermath of the 2001 Gujarat earthquake'. *South Asia: Journal of South Asian Studies*, 34 (3): 421–38.

2008 (with Malathi de Alwis). 'Remembering natural disaster: Politics and culture of memorials in Gujarat and Sri Lanka'. *Anthropology Today*, 24 (4): 6–12.

2006 (with Stuart Corbridge). 'The geography of things that may become memories: The 2001 earthquake in Kachchh-Gujarat and the politics of rehabilitation in the pre-memorial era'. *Annals of the Association of American Geographers*, 96 (3): 566–85.

2006. 'The state of Gujarat and the men without souls'. *Critique of Anthropology*, 26 (3): 331–48.

2005. 'The "Gujarat" earthquake and the political economy of nostalgia'. *Contributions to Indian Sociology*, 39 (2): 219–49.

In 2005, Anil Mukim, former collector of Kutch, and then an advisor to the chief minister of Gujarat, gave me an hour or so of his time. An eloquent and considered man, what he said inadvertently shaped the general drift of what I have written. I thank Chandrika Parmar for reminding me not to get too caught up in the drama of it all.

Johnny Parry and Chris Fuller initially encouraged me with this project and have remained interested throughout. Chris asked me the first question about this research that I was not able to shake. A.F. Robertson and Mattison Mines were also influential at the start.

The research was funded by the Nuffield Foundation (New Career Development Fellowship, 2002–2005, NCF/00103/G), ESRC (Non-Governmental Public Action Programme, 2006–2008, RES–155–25–0065) and British Academy Small Grants (2008). While holding the Nuffield New Career Development Fellowship, I was fortunate to be mentored by Stuart Corbridge. Stuart visited me in Bhuj and I have been influenced by what he saw there. While I was funded by the ESRC, I worked under Jude Howell, who was a great source of support and encouragement. She also stood up for my long-termism and general approach.

UNNATI in Bhachau and Ahmedabad and Abhiyan in Bhuj generously gave me access to their resources and experiences. The staff of the *Kutch Mitra* newspaper in Bhuj have always been welcoming and opened their archives for me.

In Kutch, I am grateful for the time and friendship of Pragmulji, K.S. Dilipsinhji, Nana and Ivan Koschmider, Anderson Bakewell, D.V. Maheshwari, Kirti Khatri, Rajesh Jethi, Umesh Jadia, Gafoor Jamadhar, Jainul Pir, Dr Shyam Sundar, Pramod Jethi, Majid Khatri, Devendra Vyas, Sohag Vyas, Bhushan Vyas, Anis Khatri, Ratnakar Dholakia, Mohammed Hussain Khatri, the Colonel, Saleem Ahmed Khan Pathan and the late Ranjuben of Senorita. I am also grateful to the many other people in Kutch, Ahmedabad, Gandhinagar, Mumbai and London who shared their thoughts about the earthquake.

Sandeep Virmani and Sushma Iyengar were generous with their time and ideas. Had I focused only on their work in Kutch with Abhiyan then this book would have been different—but then so would have been the research questions. Srinivas Chokkakula, B.R. Balachandran and Azhar Tyabji, who then worked for the Environmental Planning Collaborative (EPC), tried to encourage within me an appreciation of the complexities of regional and urban planning. I was not, I fear, a good student. I remain thankful to them for trying, and for the access they gave me to their documentation.

A long time ago now, Rachel Dwyer, Jagdish Dave and Dinesh Katira started to teach me Gujarati. More recently, Pushpa Vaidya instructed me on the irregular verbs and Sanskrit roots.

Nikolai Tannen worked as an assistant during my research in Bhuj. He unravelled a lot of what I thought I knew about Gujarat, before leaving for Dubai and then for an American military base in Afghanistan. The late Kundanlal Dholakia made me aware of how much I had to learn about the post-colonial history of Gujarat. He also demonstrated some of what he knew about acting with principles in mind. Aditya Dogra, the much-loved innkeeper of Diu (www.resorthoka.com), visited Kutch on a number of occasions and shared his thoughts and humour. I started and (nearly) finished this book in the shade of his forked palms. I have to thank the forbearance of Isabella, Jack, Henry and Albert for the period of writing that came in between.

Undergraduate and Masters-level students at SOAS in the 2007, 2008 and 2009 cohorts took some of my ideas seriously and to task. The publisher's anonymous reviewers made a number of important suggestions which have been firmly incorporated into the text. Elsewhere, I have enjoyed extended conversations with Miwa Kanetani, Shiv Visvanathan, Rita Kothari, Alpa Shah, Farhana Ibrahim, Jennifer Hyndman and Manuela Ciotti about this work. Discussions and a touch of fieldwork with Malathi de Alwis in Gujarat and Sri Lanka have also strongly informed some of the ideas presented here. Peter Gow knows little about this research but my anthropology owes a lot to him. Aparna Kapadia organised a conference on the 'Idea of Gujarat' with me at SOAS in 2008, I am grateful for her efforts and for the experience. I thank Indira Varma for allowing me to go around in circles and insisting that there must be a point.

David Mosse, Kanchana Ruwanpura, Magnus Marsden, Richard Axelby, Maddalena Chiellini, Patricia Jeffery and Alice Tilche kindly and critically read previous versions of the manuscript. I have benefited from their comments and suggestions and consider myself fortunate to have them as colleagues and friends. Lucia Michelutti also read a draft and gave me a number of pointers which helped to determine the final shape and tone. I am particularly thankful to her for her efforts and care.

Ian Lacey, Christopher Dance, my parents, Enrico Lepri, Isabella Lepri Simpson and Jack Simpson visited me in Bhuj. The things they saw and the questions they asked fill the pages that follow. At an important stage of writing, I was given the courage to say what I thought by Shaina Anand and Ashok Sukumaran. My wife, Isabella, has been with me through the highs and lows of this research and everything else of the last ten years.

Dilip Vaidya has been my greatest friend and instructor in Kutch—my encounters with him have often made me feel happy to be alive. He may tut at my prose and judgements, but I dedicate this book to him nevertheless. The opinions expressed here are my own.

NOTE ON THE REGION

This note is 'tone setting'. It is written for those without specific knowledge of western India. It serves as an introductory and discursive glossary for names, ideas and organisations appearing frequently in the text. Readers may find it useful to refer back to some of the detail as they move through the book.

India is often represented as a chaotic and unregulated country, where anything goes and corruption and nepotism reign. There is, of course, a trace of truth in the stereotype, but the country also hosts a vast government, sophisticated (although generally slow) legal system, and state departments to regulate most aspects of human life. The government is federal, tiered at national, state, district, sub-district and village levels. Democracy and party politics are entrenched, with high voter turnout when compared to Western Europe. Despite illiteracy, the consumption of newspapers and news is high. There is an extremely active civil society. There are societies for most conceivable causes and activities, public and private libraries, gymkhanas, theatre groups, laughter clubs, campaign associations and religious and nationalist organisations.

Gujarat is the only part of India to border both Pakistan and the western Indian Ocean. If you imagine India as a diamond shape, then Gujarat forms the left or western corner. Someone from Gujarat is generally known as a Gujarati; Gujaratis is the plural form. Gujarati is the official language, but other languages are also spoken. Therefore, in Gujarat the Gujaratis speak Gujarati (the same as saying that in England the English speak English). According to the census of 2011, Gujarat has a population of around sixty million people. In addition, many millions of Gujarati-speaking people live in Mumbai, the largest city in western India in the neighbouring state of Maharashtra. Hundreds of thousands of Gujarati-speaking people have migrated to East Africa, Britain and the United States of America.

The capital of Gujarat is Gandhinagar, a leafy and planned city built soon after Gujarat state came into existence in 1960. The name of the city is taken from Mohandas Karamchand Gandhi, or Mahatma Gandhi, who was born in the region in 1869. The major cities of Ahmedabad, Baroda and Surat are also in the east of the state. The large peninsula at the centre of Gujarat is known as Saurashtra or

Map of Kutch District

Kathiawad, the main city here is Rajkot. However, the term Central Gujarat refers to a region in the east of the modern state, harking back to an era when what was counted as Gujarat was much smaller than today.

The westernmost part of Gujarat is known as Kutch. In the Roman alphabet, Kutch is also known as Cutch (a curly legacy of the British colonial period), Kachchh (a consonant-heavy transliteration from Gujarati) and Kachh (common in continental Europe, as is the Kachh). I will use 'Kutch' throughout, which rhymes with Dutch, not hooch or catch. It was Kutch that bore the brunt of the earthquake in 2001 and is the region on which this book primarily focuses. In Kutch, the Kutchis speak Gujarati; but more commonly they speak Kutchi, which is a separate language, rather than a dialect of Gujarati, as is sometimes said. Kutch has a population of around two million, around 3.3 per cent of the total for Gujarat. Kutch covers an area of around 46,000 square kilometres (half of which is desert), representing nearly a quarter of Gujarat's total landmass. Kutch is between Estonia and the Dominican Republic in size. The population density in Kutch is low, at around 43 people per square kilometre (like New Zealand or Maine); it was 34 at the time of the earthquake in 2001 (between Oman and Belize and like Utah). There has been a rapid rise in the population density due to immigration from other parts of India following the earthquake.

Until India gained independence from British colonial rule in 1947, Kutch was a semi-independent kingdom, a tributary of the colonial government. The capital of that kingdom was the town of Bhuj (which rhymes with the sound that falls between scrooge and huge). Bhuj is now the administrative centre of Kutch District, one of twenty-six districts in Gujarat. Most of the research for this book was conducted in Bhuj, with additional research undertaken in and around the towns of Mandvi, Mundra, Anjar and Bhachau. There are 949 villages in Kutch. Those which feature most prominently in the text are Adhoi, Indraprashta, Jawaharnagar, Jiyapar (Narayan Nagar) and Lodai (New Keshavnagar Township).

In Kutch, and Gujarat more generally, the majority of the population is Hindu. They are divided into a large number of sectarian, caste and regional interest groups. There are also significant populations of Muslims, Christians and Tribals. Caste means many things, but in a broad sense is a named group that ideally inter-marries, shares a style of life, perhaps an occupation, and a place within a local hierarchy of other castes. Caste is a strong organising principle. There are hundreds of named caste groups in Gujarat, many with their own traditions and practices.

I now turn to the broader political currents in Gujarat. The Bharatiya Janata Party (commonly called the BJP) is a national political party formed in 1980 from the remnants of the earlier Janata Party and its forbearer the Bharatiya Jana Sangh. The BJP represents the interests of politicised Hinduism in electoral politics, although it does not have exclusive rights. Hindu nationalist ideas have spilled well beyond the confines of a single political party, as they have become parts of mainstream Hindu culture. The BJP has held uninterrupted power in Gujarat from 1998, some three years before the earthquake.

At the time of the earthquake, the BJP advocated Hindu nationalism and conservative social policies, self-reliance, free market capitalism, foreign policy driven by a nationalist agenda, and strong national defence. The party's platform is generally considered to be to the right of centre in the Indian political spectrum, especially when set against its main rival, the Indian National Congress (commonly known as 'the Congress' or 'Congress'). Congress emerged in the campaign against British colonialism and became the dominant party for decades after Independence. As a family dynasty, it was led by Jawaharlal Nehru, his daughter Indira Gandhi, her son Rajiv, his wife Sonia, and her son Rahul. In Gujarat, the Congress has lost its earlier influence, partly perhaps due to poor organisation and more certainly to the spread of sentiments such as this: 'coz Congressi pimps ate India for 50 yrs ... now it should be someone else's turn', which recently did the rounds on mobile phone messaging systems. As we will see, after the earthquake, much effort was put into popularising the symbols and ideas of the BJP over those of the Congress.

The cultural ideas which legitimate the politics of the BJP have been strongly promoted in Gujarat. Many of the principal organisations of civil society in western India are inspired by religious and nationalistic ideals.[1] The Rashtriya Swayamsevak Sangh (RSS) is part of a group of Hindu organisations collectively known as the Sangh Parivar ('family'). The RSS came into existence during the struggle against colonial rule in the first half of the twentieth century. Its vision of the nation is one in which the principles of Indian civilisation, as the organisation sees them, should form the basis of individual subjectivity, collective identity and political life in the country. Hindus are seen as the authentic and natural inhabitants of India. Muslims, Christians and obstinate colonial ideas, such as secularism, are seen as alien and unfitting. The aim of the organisation is to instil suitable moral values in the population and to produce leaders for renascent Hindu India. In this sense, the RSS was born with a fight on its hands and was organised accordingly. Its members are trained to be strong willed and disciplined, running camps and campaigning on various social and cultural issues. The organisation has a vast network of schools and offices throughout Gujarat; its influence runs deep.

The Vishwa Hindu Parishad (VHP) is a cultural society, founded in 1964 to campaign for the revival of the ancient signs of Hindu might and amity across India—it too played an active role in the aftermath of the earthquake. The VHP also promotes the idea of a Hindu race, and a natural unit of territory known as Bharat (India), a land of former glories. In this view, the ancient symbols and temples of Hindu power have been weakened by past invaders. Foreign ideas have entered and corrupted the country, such as 'pseudo-secularism' and 'minority appeasement'. For the VHP, Indian culture is a civilisational condition, and it is from such principles that governance and morality should flow.

The VHP is deeply concerned about the conversion of Hindus to other religions in India, which it describes as an 'anti-national' activity. It has campaigned for all foreign funding to be stopped, in order to prevent missionary activity. At the same time, it argues that Indians living overseas should be protected by the Indian government and treated as Indian citizens, and, therefore, donations from Indians overseas to the VHP in India are acceptable. The VHP has global ambitions, and one of its aims is to open offices throughout the world to 'consolidate, strengthen and make invincible the global Hindu fraternity by following the eternal and universal life values'.[2]

The VHP runs a monthly newspaper in Hindi and English from offices in Mumbai. The following extracts give a sense of the editorial position of the publication. Following the arrest of a well-known actor for the illegal possession of firearms in May 2013, the lead article read: 'Bollywood, that cesspool of depravity and moral corruption has perverting the social, cultural and family values of this country. It is powered by the Khans and is mostly fuelled by funds from the Muslim underworld. Most of the glamorous Khans have seduced and married Hindu girls'.[3]

On the controversial decision to dredge a shipping lane between India and Sri Lanka, where, in Hindu tradition, a bridge was constructed by Hanuman for Ram to rescue his wife from Lanka:

In a calculated, callous conspiracy to hurt the religious sentiments of … Hindus across the globe … We consider this a Christian conspiracy orchestrated by the female Italian immigrant Sonia Gandhi in collusion with her Christian and Muslim lackeys and her Hindu slaves … We will not allow destruction of a Hindu heritage. We will not allow Lord Shri Ram to be blasphemed. We call upon every single Hindu to rise against this international Christian conspiracy hatched by the female Italian immigrant to destroy Hindus and Hinduism.[4]

On Rahul Gandhi taking over the leadership of the Congress from his mother, Sonia Gandhi:

Over a thousand years ago, the Muslim barbarian Babur barged into India and founded the Mughal dynasty. The Muslim rule established then was the darkest period in the history of the world's most civilized, cultured and peace loving race. A thousand years later, Rajiv Gandhi, the grandson of the British educated barrister Nehru brought in an Italian bride. This bride, an Italian Roman Catholic known as Antonia Maino. Through manipulation, intrigue, scheming and control over the immeasurable wealth looted by the Congress over sixty years of its corrupt rule established her dynasty which we now can call the Maino dynasty.[5]

These extracts show the type of discursive realities promoted by the VHP against the politics, history and personalities of the Congress. The VHP has previously campaigned for a uniform civil code (Personal Law for Muslims would be abolished) and the removal of legislation and commissions protecting minority communities. Sanskrit is to be introduced as a compulsory language taught in schools; Urdu, a language associated with Muslims and Pakistan but commonly spoken in North India, is to be dropped as an official language. Activities associated with Hindu worship and temple construction are to be exempt from taxes. Non-vegetarianism and the consumption of alcohol will be 'discouraged' by the state, abattoirs will be closed and a ban will be placed on meat exports. Prominent Hindu festivals will be national holidays. The old and glorious names of towns, roads and places will be restored to what they were before invaders altered or mispronounced them.

Such ideas are buoyant in western India, but it is worth pointing out that a great many Hindus are meat eaters, drink alcohol, do not speak or read Sanskrit, and have very different ideas about the future of their country. The chauvinistic and xenophobic ideas about language, history and cultural diversity inherent to the VHP's agenda may surprise some in the West, where Hinduism often continues to be viewed as a religion of quiet spirituality and fate. In Europe and North America, Hindu organisations have remained very careful about how they represent themselves. Overseas, such organisations go to some lengths to distance themselves from the aggressive politics with which they have clear affinities in India.

Among some sections of the Hindu population in western India, the aims and objectives of the VHP are so well known that they usually appear simply as good sense, rather than as the discriminatory politics of a particular organisation. Many of these ideas emerge strongly in the everyday life of post-earthquake reconstruction, not always presented in the name of the VHP, but by organisations and individuals which share similar ideas about history and civilisation, the naming and renaming of things, and temple building, whether they are aware of the intellectual history or not.

These organisations promote strong religious nationalism from the grassroots, along with free-market policies. With the BJP in power in Gujarat throughout the aftermath of the earthquake, the VHP and RSS were among the main organisations to build and extend their support bases, working first with 'relief' and later with reconstruction, permeating all aspects of everyday life with their ideas as they did so.

INTRODUCTION

The earthquake took place in January 2001, a time when many things in India were changing fast. I had conducted research in Gujarat before the disaster. Partially because of this, my attention was drawn to my friends who had survived. When I first visited after the earthquake in the second half of 2001, it was obvious that the overwhelming concern of those I knew was the endemic sense of uncertainty about the future. They were also struggling to interact with those who had come from elsewhere to use the moment of shock to profit and to change the order of things. This initial focus gradually became my general approach: an exploration of the everyday life of post-disaster reconstruction.

Reading this book will lead you to think about sudden death. And, what it means to live when others have died. The earthquake will shout at you: 'in the midst of life, we are in death'. You may allow these simple words to carry your thoughts for a short while. But the loss of life is only part of it. It is the living, their actions and reactions to mass death, which will shape your impression of what happened and what people are capable of in the name of disaster.

This book is about the chaotic war of ideas prompted by a disaster, and the various kinds of cultural entrepreneurship that came to characterise life. I describe the ways in which those affected by the earthquake experienced the aftermath, and what those who came to intervene brought with them. It is an account of how abstract political ideas are made into concrete realities. It is also about memory, and the uses of history, hope and forgetting.

The desire to come to the aid of those suffering usually appears only as a proper moral imperative.[1] It is, therefore, a delicate matter to critically address the 'good works' of others in the aftermath of a disaster.[2] I do not think for one moment that 'good work' is inherently bad, but it is never as neutral or innocent as people often claim and sometimes appear to believe. 'Good work' is a form of politics and intention, just as it is, more obviously, in non-disaster times. I have not focused on particular people or organisations in my analysis for any reasons other than that their works were controversial, interesting, or they had drawn my attention through deliberate publicity. Consequently, there are no descriptions of incriminating corruption, aid comedy, double funding or other forms of endemic naughtiness, for it is not that kind of book.

Much of what I have written explores the politics of intention in the following spirit: what is given is generally not what is received; love is not always understood as such, sometimes it is stifling or unrequited; ideology can either be seen as a mask which hides the true realities of exploitation and domination, or as a cultural system through which we understand and embrace the world. I have tried to write as if ideology inconsistently takes both forms.

I now strongly feel that most of what is known about disasters is produced by those who have a stake in presenting the clear-up and reconstruction as rip-roaring successes. The reports produced by development agencies and governments are generally not about failure, any more than they are about the lives of ordinary people. As Michel Foucault succinctly put it, 'discourses are practices which systematically form the objects of which they speak'.[3] Conventional discourses and ways of speaking and writing about disasters serve particular ends, and have made disasters appear in particular ways. These ways are not always the most beneficial to those suffering, nor perhaps are they the most logical, if indeed the aim of humanitarian assistance is to aid others. My focus on the everyday life of the aftermath goes someway to counter these routinised biases.

This book presents a disaster from a novel perspective: we look out of the ruins and into the faces and at the ideas of those who came to intervene. What if we take this perspective seriously? What if we look at the activities of the humanitarians as if they are powerful strangers or trespassers? Then, their actions no longer seem so routinely sensible or so morally untouchable. On the contrary, what they do may often appear as self-interested impositions on those suffering. When we focus on how ordinary people understood the catastrophe and the aftermath, whom they blamed and cursed, how they perceived the interventions of the government, and how they went about restoring passable conditions in which they could live out their own lives, then the story of the disaster has a different feel and logic.

The research for this book was conducted amid the dust, thumps and the nerve-jangling tapping sounds of reconstruction, for periods ranging from two weeks to six months each year between 2001 and 2012. My longest stays were in 2003, 2004 and 2005, and, consequently, the material I have for this period is richer than for others. In Bhuj, I variously rented a house or stayed in a hotel. I occasionally employed research assistants to translate Gujarati newspapers and to broker new introductions and meetings. I speak Gujarati well enough to conduct interviews myself. My friend Dilip often accompanied me, primarily because he enjoys travelling and meeting people. He is a retired government employee, and well-known locally as a scholar and a gentleman.

I have attempted to describe the general sociological processes that were at work in the aftermath. Consequently, I have not focused on any particular demographic, although there is an obvious emphasis on what men say in public—but given the arrangement of gender politics in western India, there was always something of the inevitable about that. It is not that I do not know women in Kutch, but I do not know them well.

My general approach draws on anthropology, philosophy and history. I have used allegory and varying styles of language in order to engage your empathy and to convey something of the confusion and open-endedness of a contemporary disaster. The text will make more sense if read from beginning to end, rather than rebelliously. I have preferred English words to Indian terms or jargon. Grey literature is cited with as much detail as possible in endnotes; other references can be traced through the notes to a list of references at the end. I have mostly paraphrased people, while remaining loyal to their meaning. The voices of many people are subsumed into my narrative. The result is succinct and requires less context-setting work in the text. This was a conscious decision on my part from the outset. Many of the issues discussed in the book are, or have been, controversial locally, and following the general ethical guidelines of the Association of Social Anthropologists I have been keen to write so that particular individuals cannot be readily identified, unless they are public figures or have expressly given their consent.

The structure and tone of the material reflect my experience of conducting the research. There are very few digressions outside the themes and ideas I encountered during fieldwork. I have presented ideas as they were given to me in Gujarat. I have generally and deliberately not provided a systematic and context-setting literature review for each strand of political thought I touch upon—because that would have been to impose order where there was no order and an overview where no overview was ethnographically possible. I have attempted to allow discomfort to protrude in the text when discomfort was apparent. Likewise, when things were partial, incomplete or poorly apprehended, I have generally let them remain such. This coin has many flip sides, and I am well aware of that. An alternative strategy would have been to write a bookish and formal account of the main currents of Indian political thought, and to provide 'genealogies' of the ideas presented here.[4] But this is not how the people I know in Gujarat experienced the aftermath—for them there was chaos and conflict, and things were often raw.

Academic theory is treated briefly, and mostly between the lines and in notes—but it is there for those who want it. There are some rather practical and obvious lessons in the material on how aftermaths might be better managed, information effectively conveyed and intentions shared. The analysis reveals a number of emergent trends in Indian political thought and practice, most notably how a neo-corporatist ideology has come into being in which societal interest groups participate directly in the decision-making of the state. At another level altogether, this book is an account of humanity in the face of disaster.

The text is divided into thirty-four chapters, distributed over seven sections. Each section has a theme, and each chapter within that section addresses a particular issue relating to that theme. The drift of the book is chronological, moving from the moment of the disaster forward in time, with some rather obvious digressions to other periods and regions of the world. Section 1 reconstructs the disaster, and out-

lines the spirit of the aftermath and the principal changes brought about by reconstruction policies. Section 2 describes the political context in which the earthquake
took place. For various reasons, towns and villages were treated differently when it
came to rebuilding. Therefore, Section 3 looks at what happened in rural areas. The
following two sections focus primarily on the provincial town of Bhuj, with Section
4 exploring how the reconstruction of the town was conceived and organised. Section
5 narrates some of the sociological currents which accompanied the rebuilding.
Section 6 analyses various manifestations of hope in both rural and urban areas.
Section 7 describes the amnesia of those who live with the threat of earthquakes. An
Afterword discusses what the point of it all might be. Below, I add flesh to this
skeleton of an outline.

In Gujarat, change has run deep. The different scales and types of policies co-opted
to restructure the region have allowed for the formation of new kinds of citizens and
consumers, as well as religious and cultural subjects. A phoenix of industrial sprawl
has risen from the desert. Against this backdrop, the transformation of the once
commonplace in the aftermath, the 'everyday', was, in many ways, as dramatic as the
rapid loss of the conspicuous and noteworthy in the moment of ruin brought about
by the earthquake. In sum, the aftermath had greater consequences for life in the
region than the earthquake itself.

Section 1 addresses the big picture: governmentality, industrialisation and the
dynamics of intervention. I also lay out my theoretical and conceptual approach to
the aftermath. The 'aftermath of the mind' is a notion loosely derived from the
eighteenth-century philosophy of Immanuel Kant. For him, when the mind is
humiliated by scale (really big things, like earthquakes) then self-contemplation and
self-admiration emerge in the recoil. From the nineteenth-century political economy
of John Stuart Mill, we have the provocation that disasters are moments of hyper-
consumption, which may give rise to a booming economy as entropy is accelerated.
In this study, the ideas of these two grand theorists are brought together as the
principal structuring themes. The story of the Gujarat aftermath is one in which
self-admiration and ecstatic citizens emerge from humiliation and shock against the
backdrop of hyperbolic capitalism—and, as a whole, the structure of the book narrates this passage.

Before the emergence of the ecstatic citizen, we also have the arrival of a great
many people from elsewhere, mostly from other parts of Gujarat, but also from other
parts of India and the world. These people came with their own ideas of what should
be done and how. Their interventions might have been presented as 'help' or 'aid' or
'development'. Many of these interventions required that those affected by the disaster be altered in some way. The change might simply have been to their standard of
living or to the way they disposed of their household waste. Other interventions
required more fundamental religious and cultural change, through which broader
notions of society and the self were manipulated. Generally too, and necessarily so,
there was a sense among those who intervened that they were gifting improvement

of various kinds. In other words, the moral imperative to help also contained within itself other moral imperatives.

The extensive literature on humanitarianism, aid and post-'bad things' reconstruction emphasises the culture and corruption of an international circus of institutions in 'Aidland', the colonial and imperial associations of intervention, and the common mismatch between what is given and what is required.[5] While I have been influenced by some of the pointed conclusions of this literature, in Gujarat the aftermath was a largely domestic affair, the twists and pinches of which need to be understood in the local idiom. The competition to impose meaning was not a straightforward battle between modernity and tradition, or Eastern and Western civilisations. Looking at the ensuing conflicts from the outside, the stakes might seem rather parochial and slight. From the inside, however, there was a tangible sense of violence and imposition, as older and deep-rooted struggles were brought to bear on the population in the form of contemporary cultural politics. In other ways, it was the identity of India's recent past and immediate future which was being fought over, and, in this regard, the stakes were rather high.

Other scholars, notably Naomi Klein, have observed how new doctrines are often introduced after a population has suffered the shock of an invasion or a natural disaster.[6] Governments around the world commonly use catastrophe as a time to bury other forms of bad news. In Gujarat too, we have a range of doctrinal interventions in the aftermath, as the state of shock of the population was exploited to push new ideas and ways of doing things. My focus is more firmly on the gifting of ideas and ideology than it is on sewing machines or tents. As we will see, ideas can also take the concrete form of houses and urban plans, but they are often also ethereal and initially rather hard to discern.

Section 2 explores the political landscape shaken by the disaster, and describes how the earthquake induced a consequential regime change. It considers how Gujarat was put together in history in order to explain why some people attempted to shake the state to pieces in the aftermath. I also describe elements of the high-level politics that characterised life at the time to give a sense of the atmosphere in which reconstruction took place.

Notwithstanding the earthquake, Gujarat has been in the international news a great deal over the last decade. There have been dramatic and fatal attacks on temples and trains, and there was more widespread violence in the state in 2002. These events have attracted volumes of critical attention, far more so than the earthquake, which received little after the dust had settled.[7] These incidents took place primarily in the east of Gujarat, but deeply coloured earthquake reconstruction in the west. It was not as if the earthquake was such a terrible thing that everyone forgot about their usual squabbles in order to focus on remaking the world. State-level politics, 9/11, the 'war on terror' and other big events found their ways into the language of the aftermath. The brief window of international focus on the region reminded the affected that they were part of a broader world: America's apparent hostility to

Muslims and its support of Israel found particular approval among certain sections of the population.

The chief minister of Gujarat, Narendra Modi, has described how the 'backward region' demolished by the disaster now resembles Singapore. While the comparison is jingoistic, the sentiment it contains is revealing because it plays on a widespread and growing sense in Gujarat that intensive infrastructural and industrial development is straightforwardly super. A recent celebratory book on this new Gujarat, financed by some of the leading figures of the Gujarati diaspora in London, dedicates more than half its considerable volume to the details and images of industry in the state. In the past, similar productions have contained images of temples, palaces and other cultural glories. The land in which Gandhi was born and developed his ideas, the 'land of will and wisdom', has become a land of 'unstoppable growth', 'development' and smoke stacks.[8] In India, this form of industry-led development has become known as the 'Gujarat model'. This is a political model, forged largely (but not only) during the period of post-earthquake reconstruction, in which the state focused on building new infrastructure and expanding the industrial sector.

In the words of an economist enthusiastic about the Gujarat model:

It is one of freeing up space for private initiative and enterprise and the creation of an enabling environment by the State. It is one of decentralisation of planning and empowering people. It is about targeted public expenditure through specific schemes. It is one of bureaucratic empowerment and improving the efficiency of public expenditure. It is one of feedback loops from the government machinery to people and from people to the government machinery. It is one of delivering public goods (water, roads, electricity, schools, education). Stated thus, this is a standard development template that any State ought to adopt and implement.[9]

At the time of the earthquake, the language and aims of high politics in Gujarat were very different. Then, 'hatred' and 'terror' were watchwords, rather than 'industry' and 'progress'. India was still a few years away from 'shining'.[10] Muslims were routinely demonised because of their supposedly anti-national spirit. From other perspectives, the demonisation of the Muslim minority (about 10 per cent of the state's population) created a unified Hindu vote bank, a majoritarian polity, and a convenient scapegoat for all manner of ill. In the ten years I have taken over this research, the entire language of public politics in Gujarat has altered, and, in no small part, I think the destruction of the earthquake was one of the principal catalysts or 'enablers' of this shift, from the watchword 'Muslim' to those of 'development' and 'growth'.

These days, there is a concerted effort to promote the chief minister from his provincial seat of power in Gujarat to the leadership of India. As part of this move, Narendra Modi has lurched from the far right to the centre right of politics—the place where there are most votes at a national level. The firebrand moments of his rise are slowly being forgotten. Amid the things that might have been done well in Gujarat, it has largely been ignored that, due to deliberate neglect, state enterprises are making losses to the favour of private-sector profit, undue and gross favours have been granted to particular industrial houses, and the distribution of wealth is increasingly unequal. The United Nations Human Development Index (HDI), which is a highly respected measure of life expectancy, education and standard of living, shows the situation in Gujarat to be improving only slowly when compared to other states in India. The focus on industrial growth has led to a relative decline in investment in basic services for the poorer sections of society.[11] There is little public discussion about industrialisation as a means of organising social life.

The story of the earthquake might also be read as an allegory of ten years of politics in the region. As I discuss in Section 2, the earthquake brought the chief minister directly to office. In a variety of ways, he and his advisors have successfully harnessed its reverberating powers. Political and moral ideas, which make it appear only sensible to vote and think in particular ways, have been ground hard into the fabric of society through the institutions of a democratic state in the name of post-earthquake reconstruction. In this, the supine aid of international financial institutions such as the development banks has been instrumental. While the book I have written is unequivocally about the aftermath of a 'natural' disaster, it might also be read profitably as an alternative political biography: the 'Gujarat model' at the grassroots.

As I have said, the aftermath brought a range of people to the region whose aim was to alter what the local population believed and how they behaved. Some of these came to attract people to their religion; others came to present their political vision of an ideal society. The greatest of these efforts was led by the government itself, which attempted to provide Gujarat with a new political hero to replace Gandhi. Gandhi was born in what is now known as Gujarat. He led many of his most successful anti-colonial campaigns in the region. Today, he is regarded by some sections of political society as an effete figure of historical note, whose main political messages of self-sufficiency and non-violence are out of kilter with the times. In the aftermath, a man called Shyamji Krishnavarma was heavily publicised.

Before the earthquake, Krishnavarma was little known. His birthplace in Kutch housed a fond, but crumbling, museum. In the aftermath, amid an orchestrated hullabaloo, an airport and a university were named after him, and a wonderful memorial park was built in his name. Today, schoolchildren are bussed to the site to learn about his ideas and to get to know his face. Although he had lived in Europe for much of his life, Krishnavarma campaigned energetically for a free India. His methods, most unlike those of Gandhi, involved strategic assassination, weaponry and a strong libertarian mandate. In the shock of the aftermath, the state has incorporated a new hero into history. The act contributes to the formation of new kinds of political citizens, fit for a competitive, aggressive and industrial society.

In Section 3, I turn to explore the ways in which religious and nationalist philosophies were operationalised as planning paradigms in the reconstruction of rural areas. Swiftly after the disaster, a public–private partnership arrangement was introduced to rebuild villages. This scheme allowed private organisations to 'adopt' villages for reconstruction. Rural Kutch became a haven for those who wished to give things and ideas to the region. The reconstruction of villages was handed over to religious organisations, the naively generous, toothpaste and tobacco manufacturers, and other kinds of fantasist. As with most other dimensions of post-earthquake life, there was also room for sincere and sensitive interventionists, but their efforts were mostly harder to see as they worked quietly to build what they thought would be a better world. Not all were in it for the publicity.

People of Gujarati origin living overseas built villages for the beleaguered, projecting through the new architecture their own nostalgic sense of what village India was like. Others, mostly from metropolitan India, came to build what they thought a progressive Indian village should be. In Section 3, I focus on a number of these initiatives to highlight the kinds of notions imposed on those affected by the disaster in the name of post-earthquake reconstruction and improvement.

Throughout, I have interwoven the intimacy of individual emotions and experiences with broader stories of reconstruction policies and different ideological interventions. This approach is similar to that adopted by Robert Jay Lifton (1968) in his exploration of the survivors of the Hiroshima bomb and by Barbara Bode (1989), who described the experience of those in highland Peru who lived in the aftermath of a dramatic earthquake in 1970. Both writers (psychologist and anthropologist respectively) attempt to place the intimate and personal aspects of survival within a broad landscape of policy and social change. They write of worlds in which categories and boundaries are blurred, where rival ideas and persons interact and produce unintended outcomes. Anger and rehabilitation policy, budgets and shame, and targets and joy live together. In this regard, their writing is honest and humane in a strict and admirable sense.

Bode recounts how changes in individual mentality and structure were affected in the aftermath of the earthquake in Peru. The disaster occurred two years after a coup in which General Velasco Alvarado took over the revolutionary leadership of the country. His 'Inca socialism' or 'Peruanismo' strove for freedom from the shackles of America and the doctrines of socialism and capitalism. Alvarado saw it possible to make a new human morality, resurrecting the Indian past, and elevating suitable national heroes. Part of his vision was to integrate the marginal sierra culture of Indian peasants (of which the earthquake-affected region was part) into the coast-dominated national sphere. Bode suggests that Alvarado seized upon the disaster as a springboard for his vision of the future. The Catholic Church too had expanded its presence in the valley in the years before the earthquake. Marxist-inspired, the political hermeneutics of the gospel also came down squarely on improving the lot of the oppressed. Revolutionary and religious forces interpenetrated and stood united in an attempt to overturn the old hierarchical structures and to build a new egalitarian state.

Bode sees deliberate political will and the spread of bureaucracy as the key to explain the transformation of the valley in the aftermath of the disaster. The disaster came to be seen as a providential mandate for further redesigning all that had been. The state formed new offices and departments to oversee reconstruction and to bring about a new social order and modernisation. Urban space was expropriated and the new plan redistributed the population over a greater area.

Neo-liberal economic and political policies were implemented in Latin America long before they came openly to South Asia. Thus, in the 1970s, as in Gujarat today, the 'marginal' population was integrated into the finances of the nation through soft loans and obligatory insurance policies. In Peru, the Catholic Church took 'progress' to mean that false and sinful religious practices, such as the worship of local deities, were to be extinguished. In response, the survivors repeatedly protested, fearing the foreign aesthetic and design being given to their town. In Gujarat, political and religious forces also interpenetrated in their attempt to vanquish older hierarchical structures in favour of a new egalitarian order over which they had power. What Bode saw in Peru is remarkably similar to what I have seen in Gujarat, as those surviving the earthquake have been taken up by the challenges and comforts of the new ideologies presented to them.

Lifton's more psychological approach suggests that links between survivors and those who spectate (or perhaps indeed also read about disasters) is not metaphorical; rather, we are linked by psychological components in which the growing spectacle of the holocausts of the twentieth century has imposed on us all a series of immersions in death which mark our existence. We have all been marked by images of great waves rolling onto tropical beaches and smoke rising from melting nuclear plants. We have also seen cracked and broken towns, huddles of people in tents, and blankets and ruins. We know what disasters look like, but the subjective responses to these images, as destruction intermingles with the contours of personality and experience, is something quite different again. I suggest it is worth pausing for a moment to consider what you bring to reading a book on the aftermath of an earthquake. What do you expect? More importantly, how have you learned to know what to expect? What will this do to the way you read this book?

Lifton's 'death imprint' or 'death spell' relates to imagery and the conditions of death: the jarring awareness of the fact of death, in his case, the grotesque and sudden burning and then slow disintegration of A-bomb bodies. In Chernobyl, the interaction of the disaster, the state and survivors of the nuclear explosion created 'biological citizens'.[12] A survivor of Nazi concentration camps wrote, 'In every stiffened corpse I saw myself'.[13] The tsunami of 2004 encouraged us to imagine what it is to drown, but with our minds alone we could never quite reach the end of the fantasy. The death imprint of those in earthquakes, as we shall see, is characterised by crushing, falling, the fear of falling again, and the kind of gasping anxiety produced as certainties move under our feet: madness, submission and images of collapsed things that should be standing.

Lifton describes the impossibility for the survivor of catastrophe of completing what Freud called the 'work of mourning' because there is no time to prepare for the theft of life.[14] Survivors of Hiroshima mourn for their dead as well as the dead of others, inanimate objects and lost symbols, but also for beliefs that have been shattered, for a way of life that has been killed. Yet they mourn in vain. The survivor mourns for their former self, for what they were prior to the intrusion of death and the emergence of a life impaired by mourning and the guilt of survival. The consequence of the survivor's defence against death anxiety and the guilt of survival is the cessation of feeling. We may characterise this lack of feeling as an affective anaesthesia and as a key element in a broader disaster syndrome.[15]

Lifton observes tendencies among survivors of the A-bomb to feel special neediness, but also to mistrust others. Those around them begin to appear as disingenuous (what he calls 'counterfeit nurturance'). In addition, they suffered 'contagion anxiety', which I interpret to mean: if I come too close to you, I will experience your experience of annihilation and later your death, and I do not want that. I do not want to suffer more.

I take from Lifton then the idea that individual survival carries with it the structural conditions which lead to a more general social fragmentation.

Throughout, we will see examples of how the aftermath became a providential mandate for redesigning all that had been, not always in a coordinated manner, but often so. We will see in Sections 4 and 5 how encounters in the aftermath of the earthquake in Gujarat annihilated a general sense of life's coherence. By getting close to those who lived through the earthquake, we will recognise Lifton's survivor, the seeds of social fragmentation, and the ideological imposition of a new egalitarian order akin to that eloquently described by Bode in Peru.

Section 4 describes the reconstruction of the town of Bhuj and the consequences of plans and planning for notions of citizenship, belonging and history. For a while, a sense of predation was endemic as the town was knocked around to be improved. The townsfolk learned about maps, planning and compensation schemes. They struggled to come to terms with what was being done to them and the new ways in which they had to understand the world. In the end, they uneasily began to appreciate the new ways.

Section 5 looks at the dynamics of a society in mourning, alienated from the familiar by both the disaster and reconstruction. I present a series of personal narratives relating to nostalgia, grief and opportunism. These narratives complement and confuse the broad narrative of urban planning—to show how the longitudinal march of reconstruction also had a turbulent and discontinuous emotional life. Together, these sections form an ethnographic exploration of the social fragmentation inherent to survival.

The French cultural theorist Henri Lefebvre has argued that the ideological project of bureaucratic capitalism is obscured in the routine nature of 'everyday' life.[16] The everyday has been drained of historical meaning because it seems to be constituted by the endless production of newness: development, innovation and fashion. The everyday comes to seem natural and inevitable, without origin or direction. Everyday life is the recurrence generated by economic and bureaucratic systems, which disguise their artificiality by aligning themselves to the daily and seasonal cycles of nature. Consequently, the everyday appears as natural or self-evident, and history as a transcendental reality. While the everyday appears as domestic and familiar, the big events of history appear as the disruption of the everyday, as exceptional and strange. In this arrangement, we are left with the historicity of history and the timeless repetition of the everyday. The everyday remains, and history changes the order of things.

This arrangement can only be partly correct, for fundamental change also takes place in the everyday of the commonplace. We are reminded of this by hair and dress styles in old photographs, as well as by the colour and texture of objects themselves, which recall for us gradual shifts in technology. Change is not only top down, from the macro structures of state or nationalist history, but is also to be found in the small moments and actions of everyday life.

Writing about natural disasters often tends to abstract and intellectualise the event. The disaster is turned into policy or the language of development or the endless production of newness. In contrast, Lefebvre's everyday is the residual and what is left over after all distinct, superior, specialised and structured activities have been singled out by analysis. In my analysis, I have mostly neglected the distinct structures of policy documents and the statistics associated with the disaster. Others have already tallied those up.[17]

They estimate that the earthquake killed around 14,000 people (a huge number, but many times less than died in the 2005 earthquake in Pakistan or in the Indian Ocean tsunami of 2004). Of these, 12,221 died in Kutch district, on which my analysis focuses. In this district, 178 villages were classified as 'totally collapsed', 165 suffered more than 70 per cent destruction, and four major towns (Bhuj, Bhachau, Anjar and Rapar) were damaged enough to have emergency measures imposed. Shy of 300 people were unaccounted for. The earthquake produced between 25 and 50 million tonnes of rubble. In Bhuj, there was an oil spill. Highly toxic chemicals escaped into the air at Kandla port. Coal dust and fluorspar spilled into the inter-tidal waters at Navlakhi.

Huge amounts of relief and aid were donated. Government of Gujarat figures suggest 600,000 blankets and 250,000 tents were distributed; in Kutch alone, the state provided 21,000 tonnes of grain, 4,500 kilogrammes of kerosene. Based on figures available for immediate relief, Australia gave Au$2.5 million, the European Union collected over €100 million from member states, the Disasters Emergency Committee in the United Kingdom found £24 million, and the government of the United States contributed $12.8 million.[18] The policies for compensation and gratuitous relief cost the government of Gujarat over $1 billion. Additional borrowing from development banks reached over $2 billion. Scores of non-governmental organisations planned to reconstruct a total of 49,913 houses in 473 villages. Private funds, for which no amalgamated figures exist, flowed generously in the region. After the initial relief period, the three largest private organisations (out of the eighty-two registered) working in Kutch returned budgets of between $7 million to $8 million for their contribution to rehabilitation works.[19] In other words, there was no shortage of stuff. This is not a story of disaster neglect, but glut.

Following Lefebvre, I have moved towards the everyday of gesture, routine, narrative and habit to tease out the changes that have taken place to the everyday during the long drag of the aftermath. People greet one another, complain, move house, cheat, go on walks and picnics, and worry about dust. In this, I have also been influenced by the work of the anthropologist Veena Das, who has explored the relationship between the extraordinary violence and the everyday.[20] In her writing, the boundaries between the ordinary and the eventful are drawn in terms of the failure of the grammar of the ordinary. By this, Das means that what is put into question is how we ever learned what kind of object something like grief or love is. In Gujarat, the earthquake also encouraged people to think much more broadly about how they had learned things, how particular kinds of sense and sensibility had become embodied through their interactions with the landscape. When things fell down, or were demolished because of new plans, it was frequently jarring to have such object lessons in just how entwined the landscape and the contours of the mind were.

Importantly, for Das, the eventful is not distinct from the ordinary, for daily life buries within itself violence and other catastrophes which provide a certain force within everyday relationships. The ordinary is not the mundane, for through routine acts there is healing and the ability to tame great events. The thoughts and presence of violence, Das suggests, become part of the everyday. This formula is the antidote to the divorce of the everyday and the exceptional: we can find history being made in the everyday of the aftermath.

The disaster is not the big, bad state of exception to which all and everything can be attributed. I present my ethnography in this spirit—with two caveats. First, the 'ordinary' and the 'everyday' were not exempt from the meddling of those who intervened in the aftermath. The 'everyday' of thought, horizons and expectations has been gradually transformed. Today's 'everyday', has a fading resemblance to the 'everyday' of the time I had spent researching other things in Kutch before the earthquake.

Secondly, I see the need to distinguish catastrophe from communal violence in this analysis. In Gujarat, we have both catastrophe in the form of the earthquake, but we also have the mass violence of 2002 for comparison. The everyday aftermaths of these events have very different psychological structures, not simply because a house collapsing has a different death spell to the attack of an angry and anonymous mob; rather, and as I further explain in Chapter 28, the structures of blame which commonly congealed after the earthquake focus on failings of the self, while in the case of violence, blame is cast upon an 'other'. Blaming others for an earthquake would be to grant their gods power over nature and therefore legitimacy—and that would never do. It is better to say that your own god did it, however difficult the consequences of such a claim might be for your own behaviour.

Although the earthquake occurred in 2001, the aftershocks have continued. In 2012, it was estimated that over 700 people had only recently been arrested for corruption relating to post-earthquake funds.[21] Among them was Pradeep Sharma, an important figure in the administration of the aftermath. He was arrested in 2009 for earlier irregularities in the distribution of land. He countered with an affidavit containing florid allegations about an architect commissioned to work on the Hill

Garden in Bhuj and the otherwise chaste chief minister. Journalists working for BBC East Midlands have not yet given up the hunt for the £100,000 unaccounted for by the Leicester Earthquake Relief Fund.[22] The British man we encounter in Chapter 5 is currently being prosecuted by children from Gujarat, who claim they were sexually abused by him in the name of post-earthquake reconstruction.[23] Arvind Thaker, former president of the Bhuj Chamber of Commerce (the town at the heart of my analysis), was arrested at the same time as Pradeep Sharma, but later released. In the early days of 2011, shortly before the tenth anniversary of the earthquake, he swallowed rat poison and died in his bed next to his sleeping wife. In this miserable and memorable act, he became the earthquake's latest victim. He will not be the last.

Throughout, the earthquake in Peru I have already described and another one that occurred in Lisbon, Portugal, in 1755 serve as comparative foils. The comparisons are mostly open ended, but are drawn most clearly in Section 6 where I extend an ethnographic analysis of hope in the aftermath. Comparing the thoughts provoked by the earthquake in Gujarat with the ones in eighteenth-century Lisbon reveals certain commonalities. The great philosophers of Europe, who were encouraged into healthy debate by the Lisbon disaster, wrote things which are very similar to things people in Gujarat told me about their earthquake. Do we live in a world where god (however named and conceived) wants the best for humanity? Are we able to communicate with god though our actions? What place do death and destruction play in god's design of the universe? Why did I live and he die?

Quite probably, these are the thoughts that earthquakes provoke, almost regardless of the cultural and historical context. Religious traditions are often seen as providing frameworks for interpreting natural disasters. At some level this is true of course. Different religious traditions use their own terms and concepts to understand the relationship between human beings, god and causation. However, religion does not exist in isolation from lots of other social stuff. In the aftermath of disasters, religious discourses often leave behind the theological and universalistic explanations for the existence of suffering and evil. Instead, religious narratives become context-bound commentaries on the state of morality of local communities, with the aim of defining and reaffirming social boundaries.[24] In this way, in both Lisbon and Gujarat, what masqueraded as an explanation for the disaster was, in fact, part of the experience of being humiliated by something incomprehensible. Explanations for the catastrophe confirmed to people who they were, rather than addressing or putting in order the unknown greatness of the forces that animate the universe.

Following on from this, Section 7 explores the various ways in which amnesia allows people to live with the ever-present threat of an earthquake. We look at the history and associations of earthquakes in the traditions of Gujarat. Earthquakes in 1819, 1956 and 2001 killed many people on the exact same spot in the town of Anjar. After each disaster, promises were made to build it back better or not to build it back at all. Yet, after each earthquake, life slowly returned to that particular spot. I trace some of the ways in which the area was re-inhabited after the

2001 earthquake, using both images and text in order to make some sense of this seeming perversion.

Since the earthquake, relevance has been gradually reintroduced to a broken land. As people went about making things stand up again, they also knew of the lurking sadism of catastrophe. Disaster is waiting for things, even ruins, to reassume beauty and meaning.[25] We can assume that future earthquakes lie in wait. How do people live with this truth?

SECTION 1

CHAI WALLAHS AND THE CARPETBAGGER

An earthquake came unexpectedly at breakfast time. It shook buildings and personal certainties. Those who survived were hurtled into a time of comic tragedy in which everyday life was exposed as absurd. Men from powerful organisations identified what had collapsed and how the world was to be remade. Without exception, the earthquake destroyed only what would have eventually been destroyed anyway. Consequently, the moment of accelerated consumption gave way to a hyperbolic economic boom. The government cut tax to attract investment. Industries flocked to the ruins. Others came to present their doctrines as part of their aid. A sadist came and went, but was not forgotten.

Homeless asleep among broken idols, 2002, Anjar.

1

SUBLIME

The image is pixelated, rushed, but I can make out that the woman is standing in open ground, seemingly certain of the direction she is facing. Eyes closed, her supplication lacks the fluidity of movement usually seen in well-practised prayer. Terror and sincerity are naked as she takes us into the moment of the 2001 earthquake. Through mushrooming dust, people run frightened with the noises of fear. Amid strewn rubble lie dead bodies. Stripped of the head covering she probably normally wore in public, and certainly wore for prayer, she goes through the sequence of familiar movements. The conventions of dress and modesty have gone—this is a woman submitting to Allah, as if utterly alone, and there is nothing and no one else left.

The scene is remarkable and haunting. An unveiled woman, at the moment of disaster. A woman through a lens, unaware, I think, that the cameraman and the men who watched it later, were seeing something usually concealed behind elaborate codes of gender segregation and public behaviour. The cameraman moved on, later gaining celebrity status for the arresting images he captured shortly after 8.46 am on 26 January 2001. It was Republic Day, a national holiday. For the nation, it was an occasion to raise the tricolour, parade, and to sing patriotic songs. As a holiday, it was also a day for a slow start and a leisurely breakfast. On that morning, the plates of a geological fault slipped somewhere deep in the earth, causing the ground to convulse and contort. These movements brought about widespread, but highly irregular, patterns of damage to property and life across Gujarat. Hundreds of villages were flattened to varying degrees, badly built tower blocks collapsed in the faraway city of Ahmedabad. The worst affected areas were the older parts of Bhuj, Anjar and Bhachau in Kutch.

In the town of Anjar, a couple of hundred children participating in a parade to mark Republic Day were crushed to death. This loss sat poignantly at the centre of the heart-wrenching national tragedy. Elsewhere, the open spaces around flagpoles saved the crowds from death by masonry, electrocution and suffocation. Patriotism brought mixed blessings. Some thought the unusual rumbling they could hear was caused by passing helicopters, others thought it was a distant flour mill or that war had broken out again with Pakistan and bombs were falling from over the border, others still reported a thunderous 'boom, boom, boom', almost as if the land were talking. A seemingly large number of those treating the day as a holiday were in the bathroom at the time, which gave rise to disastrous toilet humour: when the shit hit the pan and the earth started to shake I wondered what I had unleashed.

In his 'Analytic of the sublime', the German philosopher Immanuel Kant suggested that the sublime is the pleasure produced by the mind as it reaches its own limits.[1] In the case of natural disasters, the sublime enters the frame when the imagination recognises the body's physical impotence. This is what Kant calls the 'dynamic sublime', a sublime distinct from the 'mathematical', which arises from gazing at stars at night. The imagination is rescued from pain by reason. The mind restores its own power by calling on its own superiority to nature. This is, I hope you agree, deft work, indeed. Reason produces the idea of infinity to soothe the pain of a starry night and of a natural disaster by reminding itself of the irreducible dignity of the human calling to live as free moral agents who make the laws of their own reason.

Earthquakes intrude on the cosy arrangement men make with nature. Earthquakes, we might say, humiliate the mind. Slowly, after the math (and here we follow rather than paraphrase Kant), pleasure and self-admiration restore humanity to a position above nature and beyond the quake. However incomprehensible the event may have been, and despite the fact it was experienced first-hand, terror and humiliation pass to indulgent self-contemplation.

Although Kant does not mention an earthquake in his account of the sublime, the language used suggests he had in mind his earlier fascination with the one that occurred in Lisbon, Portugal, in 1755.[2] Kant's sublime moves the mind with tremors or deep shudders. Amidst all the vibrating, gushing and shaking, this natural object defeats the imagination. Yet, at the same time, from the perspective of reason's idea of the 'supersensible', this object does not gush or effuse at all; rather, it conforms to reason's law for the imagination to strive in this way. Thus, the object becomes attractive to the same degree to which, before, it was repulsive to mere sensibility. Through the power of reason and its moral law, the great evil of natural catastrophe is elevated and transfigured into a foil for human dignity.

If we recast the emphasis within Kant's account slightly, we can say that the mind too has its moment of shock, but it also has an aftermath through which the effects of the initial shock cause something quite different to be brought into being: the humiliation of the earthquake, to push the idea further, gradually passes to self-indulgent contemplation. We might think of this as the 'aftermath of the mind'.[3] This is an idea that runs through this book, not as a strict clinical concept, but as an ethnographic and heuristic device. This broad sense of a passage from humiliation to self-indulgent contemplation sits rather comfortably alongside the contours of collective experiences of rejuvenation and reflection in the public aftermath of the Gujarat earthquake.

The sublime probably derives from the Latin for 'under the door' or 'lintel'. Echoing Kant, Robert Brown, a historian of violent nature imagery in Germany, has noted: 'A sublime experience slips past borders and barriers to confront life itself in unadulterated form, which may prove frightening. By way of compensation, something familiar tends to be projected in the foreground of the sublime view … in order to protect from nature's menacing reaches'.[4] Kant traces the passage from humiliation to self-contemplation. Brown adds to this sequence that the mind grasps something in the foreground, perhaps something trivial or commonplace, which guards against the enormity of nature. We have already heard of bombs and flour mills.

At the same time as the unknown woman turned in prayer to Allah, some miles away, Shivang was in the bath. He is an entrepreneur, a Brahmin, and at the time in his mid-twenties. We have been friends for many years, and speak frankly with one another. I asked him what happened to him at the time of the earthquake. This was his reply:

Then I did not know what was happening. The water started to run backwards and forwards. I had soap in my eyes, it hurt and I could not see. Then I thought that I had gone mad. I was all alone and my mind had taken over; it had become more powerful than my own will; it was playing with the world. I had entered a tunnel and would never come out again. I was terrified. I thought a hundred thousand thoughts in that minute. In films, they show lives flashing before those who are about to die, or lose their minds. It was not like that for me. I thought, of course, about my family and grandparents, and how they would treat me now that I was mad. I did not think of god. I found myself instead thinking about the blue plastic pen holder in my office. It had fallen to the floor and broken the day before. I had sent the peon out to buy strong glue. I was going to repair it when I reached my office later that day. I clung to the image of that broken blue pen holder. It seemed to save me. It gave me a reason not to die. I wanted to make it whole again.

I washed away the soap, and the water stood still. The house was quiet. I got dressed, brushed my hair, and went downstairs. Then I heard my father shouting from outside about an earthquake. I rushed out to the street but everything looked normal, apart from our neighbours who were standing on the road in their pyjamas.

When I think back, I have always been afraid of madness. I get terrible headaches, and I think madness will take me one day. The earthquake made this fear stronger. It gave me an experience of madness that I cannot forget. But the real thing is my family, my father, mother, brother and his wife. When it came to it, they ran outside to save themselves. They did not come for me. They left me in the bath.

I ask you, reader, to hold on to the image of the broken blue pen holder and the power of this mundane object to save Shivang, both from himself and the earthquake. Within the intimacy of this kind of conversation, helplessness and solitude is what people most readily recall (at least in the early years of this project). But alongside these powerful sensations there was nearly always something ordinary, such as a pen holder. For others, the commonplace of the pen holder was a clock, a collection of Jews' harps, metal cupboards standing with noblesse in the rubble, ceiling fans protruding at odd angles from ceilings which had collapsed to form walls.

A man in his late fifties, a journalist, Harijan or Dalit (an Untouchable in an older language), and then a self-proclaimed pessimist, recalled trying to find someone in a position of authority in the moments after the earthquake. Perhaps because it was a holiday, but more certainly because most of the government buildings in Bhuj had fallen down, he was unsuccessful in this quest for some time. He wandered further to find that the municipal hospital had collapsed on its patients. A dusty head, not obviously wounded, protruded neatly from the rubble. The head asked my friend for help. My friend approached the buried man, drawing close enough to look into his eyes, before realising there was no help he could offer. My friend moved on. The stranger's face, caught in that moment, went with him, and occasionally manifests itself in confounding rage. This man was my landlord for a while and I know the stranger often bothered him in the still of night.

I was not in Kutch at the time of the earthquake, so I cannot write about its terrifying convulsions or the appearance of familiarities with personal conviction. I cycled through an earthquake in Pakistan in 1991, so I am not unacquainted with the vertiginous feeling, which, with hindsight and subsequent experiences, seemed like grief in accelerated form. In the case of Gujarat, too, I am convinced of the importance of trying to understand something of what that moment did to those who experienced its ravage in order to understand their subsequent anguish and musings. Moments of catastrophe influence the ways in which people know the world and what its certainties are. These experiences have fed into social life in the aftermath, perhaps as an antidote to ambivalence, and more certainly, as we shall see later, to explain and blame.

Over the years, I have spoken to a great many people I knew well from before the disaster about their own experiences of life and death. I have read short stories and viewed art inspired by the earthquake, and seen a highly disturbing and improbable amateur film of the terrifying moment in which a woman prays without other cares. My opening earthquake vignettes represent quite different relations between people and the earthquake. But all, significantly, involve some form of radical personal transformation, and, as far as I can know, necessitate engaging with the familiar: motions of prayer, an everyday object, and the professional curiosity of a journalist. At the same time, the shock also forced novel thoughts and associations, which have had enduring consequences. The earthquake set people free from their usual moorings, in a horrid way. The marks left by the earthquake have, however, proved seductive, and people have been repeatedly drawn back to them, often in the search for sense and explanation.

In addition to the shocking grief and long-term disruption to life that the earthquake brought, many people now have to live with themselves and others quite differently. An unknown woman gave herself indecently, head uncovered, to god (and she was televised). A business man experienced madness and saw his abandonment by his family, all at the same time. How does he stop curiosity drawing him back to lunacy or contempt from forcing him away from his family? The face of a dying stranger took up residence in my friend's head, and has accompanied him on and off for many years.

These are some of the things the earthquake did, giving birth to various 'aftermaths of the mind'. As we shall see, all around these people the earthquake had also shaken the broader structures of history and politics that had made Gujarat.

Damaged sculpture from a Jain temple as rubble, 2006, Adhoi, photograph courtesy of Isabella Lepri Simpson

2

RETROSPECTIVE ANATOMY

On the morning of the earthquake, Suresh Mehta, then the industrial minister for Gujarat, was in Bhuj. Realising what was happening, he took shelter in a door frame, as he had been told to do since he was a child in the event of an earthquake. After the shocks had subsided, he made his way first by car, until falling houses obstructed him, and then on foot to hoist the national flag, as was his official duty to the country for the day. He recalled how the air was full of dust, the town was wrecked, and how fallen buildings impeded his passage, but he was one of the lucky ones. Over two thousand people died in Bhuj, or about 1.7 per cent of the town's population.

On the morning of the earthquake, Naranbhai, a tea trader, later recalled through welling eyes how he had put down his newspaper to investigate the 'rumble' outside (no one had ever told him to shelter in a door frame in the event of an earthquake). As he did so, his feet were crushed by a slab of concrete as the house tumbled around him. Unknown rescuers arrived some hours later and laid him on the roof of a neighbour's house, which was now much lower than it had been early that day. For a few hours, he lay alone, in pain, and wondering what was to become of him. A few hours later, masked rescuers appeared with two injured women, one of whom was a local primary schoolteacher whose family was known to him. He talked to them, but just before dusk, he sensed that both women were dead.

On the morning of the earthquake, Umashankar was out of town on business. When the earth started to shake it took him some time to realise what was happening. He decided to head back to Bhuj. The roads were damaged but passable. When he entered the old town he began to find it difficult to make his way. The way he knew from years of walking familiar streets no longer allowed him to return. His house had stood in the worst-affected part of Bhuj, adjacent to an area called Soniwad. He found it easier to climb over buildings than to attempt to walk where there were once roads and alleyways. Bodies were lying on and in the rubble. He tried not to go near them, but he could not avoid the sounds of injury so easily. Eventually, he found his house, which had partially collapsed. The milk buffaloes that lived in the courtyard were crushed, bloody and dead. Flies buzzed. His possessions were scattered. He stood on the debris, staring at the rearrangement. He listened hard for any sounds. Inexplicably, he found himself saying 'my rubble'. His rubble was silent. He headed for open ground with an 'unconscious mind'. For some reason, his mother and brother had found their way to the same open ground. They sat together until some religious men from the local temple came to help them.

Everyone can remember where they were and what they were doing on that ill-fated morning. They can recall the smells, sounds and images of the days following the disaster. These were terrifying times when no one could be sure of exactly what had happened and what might happen next. Much later, when I asked, people also called to mind particular snapshots of the disrupted landscape. It was not simply that things were not as they normally were; rather, while some areas of the town were in complete disarray, in other parts very little had changed. The normalcy, the everyday, was now made to appear odd, rendered visible and conspicuous by the adjacent ruination.

The day after the earthquake, *Kutch Mitra*, then the best-selling and most influential local newspaper, shifted production to its publishing group's offices in Rajkot. The issue it produced on 29 January led with the telling understatement, 'Gujarat, including Kutch, has experienced a major earthquake: further shocks expected'. The rhetorical partitions of geography in the headline were also to prove telling. A few days later, as lines of communication were restored and the extent of the tragedy became clear, the tone of the coverage began to change. Of Bhuj, it was noted, 'the town, like a ghost, is beginning to stink'.[1] A front-page editorial asked 'Why is the god of death [variously in its pages Yamraj or Kal Devta] so annoyed with Kutch? Why, after two years of drought, has Kutch given its children death instead of water?' The editorial ended with the plea: 'Amid the ruins of our thoughts we are reduced to nothing, we are living for today; we should live the religion of humanity, work together and pray for the souls of those who have lost their lives'.[2]

In the aftermath of the Latur earthquake in the neighbouring state of Maharashtra in 1993, many bodies were hastily placed in mass graves. This caused considerable retrospective consternation, especially among Hindu cultural organisations, and for those who remained living in the haunted and inauspicious areas. Local cadres of these organisations from across Gujarat were well prepared to pay close attention to the correct cremation of the dead in Bhuj. The management of mass death was mostly well ordered, and, aside from the usual conjecture of the media, there was no contagion from corpses. Supplies of wood quickly arrived. At least one truck made the long trip to North India to submerge ashes in the purifying waters of the Ganges. Muslims buried Muslims, and I am unaware of any great controversy over the 'incorrect' disposal of the dead, other than that in the haste some corpses were not properly identified, which led to certain bureaucratic and compensatory ambiguities further down the line.

When asked about the time of the earthquake, a great many people recalled the mass rites performed for the dead (called *shraddh*) by the Rashtriya Swayamsevak

Sangh (RSS) and Vishwa Hindu Parishad (VHP) in the first week of February 2001. Many also remembered struggling to gather the necessary clarified butter and Indian basil. Also present at these events were a number of local political leaders, and they took the opportunity to say that rebuilding Kutch would be a fitting tribute to those who had lost their lives. A number of people who were there remembered this sentiment, but rather more remembered the words of the speaker who said Kutch rocked its people to death as a mother might rock her child to sleep.

This turn of phrase was repeated to me an astonishing number of times in the early years of this research, sometimes as a way of remembering the rites for the dead, and at others as a general discursive strategy for talking about the earthquake. Later, while reading the archive of *Kutch Mitra*, I found that this statement had been reproduced in the newspaper's original coverage of the death rituals. Both from the press, then, and from simple attendance at the ceremony, the metaphor grew in stature and became a popular way of talking about the earthquake.

Private organisations were at the forefront of the initial relief operations in Bhuj, often before the state, whose functions they took over in some places.[3] They distributed aid, opened relief camps, and oversaw rescue and cremation operations. Their well-organised systems of communication and hierarchy, as well as the dedication and discipline of their volunteers, meant that many people in Bhuj associate the arrival of the organisations of Hindu nationalism with the initial relief after a major trauma. They became heroes, their work deeply valued by all. It is hard to say equivocally whether the organisations such as the RSS left such an impression on people because they were one of the first groups to make their presence felt in Bhuj or because the cremation and ritual services they administered were so important to those who survived. Either way, their presence in Kutch strengthened and expanded thereafter.

In the first weeks after the earthquake, local newspapers contained page after page of death notices. Death was the news, and the announcement of death in the pages of a newspaper was part of the last rites, a public announcement that the person was no more. In other ways, too, death became a public spectacle as the deceased and dying were placed on the ground for scrutiny and identification. Others were burned where they were excavated. Teams of masked men came with a magic spray that made the dead smell like lemons. A surprising number of people told of the hasty field amputations that were performed by emergency rescue crews to allow victims to be freed from the rubble. Many lives were saved, while others were lost in especially tragic circumstances. Eighteen members of a family from Mumbai, who had come to attend a marriage party in Bhuj, were killed when the apartment block they were staying in collapsed.

Five days after the earthquake there were still corpses littering the ground in the old court area. The press reported that the army sealed off the old town to prevent looting and contagion. Some people heard that bodies were lying unclaimed in the rubble of temples in the village of Dudhai (later to become Indraprastha, as we shall see) up to a week after the disaster. There were heart attacks and suicides, and deranged people blind with grief wandered hopelessly through the debris. The police fired warning shots over the heads of the crowd that gathered to protest over the unfair distribution of relief materials. Angry men discussed what action they might take against the contractors whose buildings had collapsed. The contractors fled town. In Ahmedabad, court and police cases were very quickly lodged against those thought to have built shoddy tower blocks.

Foreigners began to arrive in large numbers with cutting equipment and wonderful machines that could see through buildings. Journalists also came from around the world, finding miracles of survival and sorrow in the ruins. Dhows set sail from Dubai laden with relief, including tins of the highest quality fish, which were later donated to a temple known for the strict vegetarianism of its Hindu followers. Pakistan gave aid to India. The event attracted considerable press coverage, and there was a scramble in Bhuj for the donated tents. The leader of India called his counterpart in Pakistan to offer his thanks. The correspondent for the UK's *Guardian* newspaper reported: 'Looting has begun. In Bhachau, the town worst affected by the earthquake, survivors have started combing through the market, removing—among other things—odd shoes. Since almost everyone died here, there is no one around to complain'.[4] The Italian Episcopalian Conference pledged to give more than $1 million in aid, but the government of Gujarat said it did not want or require the donation—such was the negative feeling towards Christians in the state at the time.

Within a week of the disaster, there was discussion about the collapse of heritage buildings, which were said to have given Bhuj its identity and pride. These included the cremation memorials for the former kings of Kutch, the royal palaces, and the town's ancient gates, walls and temples. It was widely agreed that multi-storey culture, and cement and concrete jungles, were not part of the 'true' heritage of the region. From the beginning, then, and before the intervention of foreign agencies and development banks with their own policies relating to catharsis, there was talk of heritage, identity and what had been lost.

Idols were shifted from temples and placed in the safe custody of the police. Businesses advertised free services; temples and schools organised mass meals and supplied provisions. Departures for the *haj* for local Muslims were postponed. There was a flurry of visits by high-profile politicians. Bill Clinton would later come (bootlegged copies of the account of his activities with Monica Lewinski had sold well in Kutch in the late 1990s, and he remained a popular figure). The state opened its coffers and distributed money in the form of emergency cash doles to all, regardless of their need or status. The postal service was unable to deliver letters addressed to people who no longer lived at houses that no longer stood. A temple in which the names of the Hindu deity, Lord Ram, had been chanted day and night for eighteen years closed its doors. These were highly unusual times.

Elsewhere, fresh water was seen to burst forth from the land and salt water emerged from a cemetery in the village of Faradi in the south of Kutch. There was speculation that the Indus River had changed its course away from Pakistan to irrigate the parched soils of western India. It was rumoured that the sea had retreated and that large quantities of dead fish were appearing on the beaches. Many recall

K.K. Shastri of the VHP saying that the presence of sweet water in the soil was a sign that the mythical Saraswati River had resurfaced after 5,000 years of pursuing a subterranean course. The river is praised as a goddess in a number of ancient texts. The supposed reappearance was intended to be interpreted as an indication of the resurgence of lost Hindu glory.

In December 2000, *Aaj Kal*, a Gujarati-language daily newspaper based in Rajkot, had published a report in which the astrologer Liliya claimed an earthquake would ravage Gujarat on 26 January 2001.[5] After the earthquake, many astrologers and seismologists predicted further tremors. Some of the former were arrested for rumour-mongering, which is a violation of the Indian Penal Code. It was said that 3 February was to be 'doom day', to match the day of the earthquake itself. Seismologists published their own versions of doom-mongering in the press without sanction.

The state started to operate free bus services. It is said this policy brought unknown and frightening faces in search of booty. In Bhuj, a convicted murderer walked free from a mental hospital when the building collapsed. He was later seen by other people helping the injured to safety. In the town of Rapar, another prisoner escaped from jail to help with the rescue operations and saved the life of a police inspector's wife. A Sikh furniture dealer from Maharashtra was also seen wandering in the rubble with a board which said something along the lines of: 'Dear people of Bhuj do not be chased away by fear. Chase away fear and earthquakes, love your homeland, love your motherland and do not desert her'. Some said he was inspired by god; others said he had survived the Latur earthquake; others suggested he was deranged.

Shiva's dance of destruction, as the earthquake popularly became known, brought with it noises and shaking, and led some to think that the world was coming to an end. Helplessness came to prevail on the margins of chaos: helplessness to stop the world ending; helplessness to prevent a stranger dying in the rubble; helplessness to do nothing other than pray. A few months later, and hundreds of miles away, Suresh Mehta, the industries minister, would announce to a small audience a series of tax concessions for industry locating in Kutch which would have the most dramatic effect, greater than the earthquake, on the region. Naranbhai would learn to walk again, although slower than before and with a dull ache in each foot that would not leave him. Umashankar would discover that the old woman who rented a room in his house was dead. As he had listened to his rubble, her head had been just inches beneath his feet, an arrangement of life, death and corporeality that would not leave him alone. Umashankar and his family placed themselves permanently in the custody of the saints who came to help them in open ground. We will return to him later.

Scavengers work through the rubble in search of electric waste, 2002, Bhachau.

3

AFTERMATH EPISTEMOLOGY

In the east of Gujarat, where the centres of power and politics lie, the state government rapidly formed the Gujarat State Disaster Management Authority (GSDMA). It took the Asian Development Bank (ADB) and the World Bank, representatives of USAID and the government of the Netherlands just two weeks to prepare and publish a joint assessment of the damage.[1] They put the cost of rehabilitation and reconstruction at $2.3 billion. As is often the case with death tolls, reconstruction borrowing also seems to encourage people to think in round numbers.[2] Although this figure was clearly rather arbitrary, and probably exaggerated by shock, it was the one against which loans and policies were measured and designed.[3]

Various affected sectors were divided between the intervening agencies. Bilateral donors were to focus on health awareness and the provision of medical services, 'emergency preparedness', and on improving the skills of the population to develop themselves (what in the development industry is called 'capacity building'). The World Bank was to focus on agriculture, education and transport, alongside the reform and restructuring of urban governance in Gujarat state. The ADB was to lend around a quarter of the total estimated cost, with emphasis on housing in rural areas, urban and rural infrastructure, the improvement of electricity provision, livelihood rehabilitation and 'multi-hazard disaster mitigation' and preparedness. The provision of urban housing was later passed to the World Bank because it offered lower loan fees and a longer repayment period than the ADB.

The division of life and things, the priorities and classificatory practices, as well as the general world-view of those who wrote the initial damage assessment report, reverberated into the future in ways that remain quite unknown to many who survived the earthquake. Their classificatory practices were determined by the report template provided by the development banks, that is to say a form. The restoration and development of property and infrastructure was to be the primary objective of reconstruction, urban and rural areas were to be treated distinctly, and gender equality and livelihood generation were to be key development interventions. Policy was to be designed in such a way that the structures of government and society could be fundamentally altered through reconstruction: beleaguered Gujarat was to be restructured (the neologism 'restructuration' seems apt).

In the countryside, a public–private partnership would allow houses to be rapidly rebuilt in consultation with what the documentation calls 'communities'. Newly built houses were to be provided with access roads, electricity, water and 'community buildings'. An ABD report qualifies this last item with the following words: 'thereby restoring community life'.[4] New houses were to be jointly registered in the names of both husband and wife, a policy designed to ensure 'gender equality'. Payment of housing assistance was to be made directly to the beneficiary's bank account to ensure financial transparency. More than half a million new bank accounts were eventually created for this purpose, bringing many for the first time into contact with the regulated financial system. A staggered payment system was adopted to ensure that the houses adhered to 'seismic norms' before the release of subsequent instalments. A mandatory insurance policy was to cover new houses against natural disasters for a decade. The loan agreement facilitated the penetration of private insurance companies into rural markets. Insurers, as profit seekers, did well from this. Later, a World Bank report observed that this policy 'improved the customer base of the insurance industry'.[5]

The community participation programme was implemented most intensely and obviously in rural areas. The programme was designed to encourage earthquake-affected communities to take part in planning so that they could obtain their due share of benefits, including housing assistance and access to public services. Information was to be shared. Educational activities, as well as the formation of village-level sub-centres and the encouragement of self-help groups, would monitor the reconstruction programme and be responsible for disaster preparedness in the future. Village-level government mechanisms were to be strengthened to undertake 'social audits' and to ensure 'procedural transparency'. There were to be 'gender sensitisation workshops' for all functionaries. A community-based disaster preparedness programme identified risks, vulnerable areas and people. Large volumes of printed materials were produced, and training courses, workshops, meetings and demonstrations held. In addition, there was an extensive state-wide awareness programme focusing on the hazards and the risks the people of Gujarat faced as they went about their daily lives.

As elsewhere in the world, the strategic objective of the development banks in India is to promote 'economic efficiency'. They work on the assumption that higher rates of economic growth improve employment opportunities and reduce general levels of poverty, and the benefits of this model outweigh all attendant costs. This is what has become known as the 'neo-liberal paradigm' because these aims are achieved through the reform of the public sector and the integration of this sector into the market economy.[6] This means that banks make loans for projects which work towards the deregulation of state control, to free markets, and to introduce incentives for the private sector to take over activities previously undertaken by the state. Gujarat was the first state in India to be 'chosen' (a word used by the ABD) for comprehensive economic and structural reforms, and these were well underway in advance of the earthquake.[7] It should be stressed that little of the grand policy framework used in Gujarat is new: it is at least thirty years old. Those charged with reconstruction following the earthquake in Peru in 1970 (referred to in the Introduction) used a comparable, although less costly, framework to similar effect.

In correspondence with the World Bank, the government of Gujarat put strong emphasis on the strain placed on the region by the earthquake.[8] The greater part of the state had suffered little or no damage, but specific and localised problems were generalised in the correspondence, which gave the government's loan applications an emotive and urgent pull. The earthquake also became an opportunity to speed up its reform and restructuring of its own institutions: to strengthen urban services and governance, to introduce incentives for 'service providers', and to reform local tax and planning systems to work in line with market principles. It could, of course, also be that the government had to do these things in order to become eligible for 'soft loans'.

The earthquake was a boon for those who wrote proposals for international funding because reforms to mechanisms for the provision of infrastructure, urban governance, land regulation, municipal taxation systems and urban planning regimes were at the top of the development banks' list of interests. The earthquake exposed the eccentricities and weakness of these very processes, perhaps in a way that no other disaster could. Infrastructure was found wanting, and the reconstruction effort would clearly engage with issues of urban governance and town planning. In addition, the obvious and compelling need to reconstruct the region and to make better what was broken seemed a perfect opportunity for creating new institutions and reforming how things were done.

The state government wrote to the World Bank, 'Gujarat now faces constraint in continuing this financial support owing to fiscal imbalances and the financial impact of the earthquake'.[9] In this way, the earthquake became tied to the general reform of the financial sector and, in particular, the ways in which local governments could access funds for infrastructure development, namely by being granted access to domestic capital markets and commercial banks. Alongside these new mechanisms, a whole slew of other reforms to the financial dealings of local authorities were implemented. The need to reconstruct urban areas was also seen as an opportunity to introduce new systems of land management. Likewise, rethinking towns and villages alongside the redesign of legislation allowed for the removal of protectionist measures and other forms of regulation which were seen as working against market forces (measures originally implemented, of course, to counter market forces).[10] According to the neo-liberal logic, to enable markets to work more smoothly it was also necessary to support measures such as improved land registration and titling procedures, the revision of building rules and regulations, and the simplification and acceleration of procedures for tenure regularisation and reclassification.

The state's strategy to overcome the perceived shortcomings in urban sector governance was to increase the capacity to implement 'bankable projects' (those which would secure credit with the development banks). In order to do this, and in addition to the GSDMA, the Gujarat Urban Development Company (GUDC) was formed as a state organisation operating along private-sector lines. These two bodies, along with others formed for water and sanitation provision, became the principal mechanisms (the 'implementing agencies') through which bank funds were managed. In essence, the structures of post-earthquake governance were made 'bankable' from the outset, as the disaster gave birth to new and additional offices and bureaucratic procedures.

Through the cultivation of the 'implementing agencies', power was devolved from a central authority to local agencies, which were supposed to be more efficient. GUDC was given the task of overseeing the recreation and improvement of infrastructure in fourteen towns in Gujarat (most of these were only superficially affected by the earthquake). Area Development Authorities were formed across the state for implementing infrastructure development and planning in urban areas. The aim was to develop 'holistically planned' and modern towns. The four badly damaged towns in Kutch were to be redesigned with two decades of projected growth in mind. Private planning consultancies competed for this work, establishing temporary offices in Kutch to investigate existing records, conduct surveys, hold public consultations, and to get a feel for the lie of the land. In numbers, the fourteen urban areas were to have 350 km of new roads, 702 km of water mains and 352 km of sewerage lines.

Above ground, the regulations for the design and location of buildings were amended to incorporate Indian Standard Codes for seismic and cyclone safety. The towns of Bhuj, Bhachau, Anjar and Rapar were to be provided with upgraded water supplies, modified internal road systems, bypasses, street lighting, public buildings and systems for waste-water management. Urban planning schemes and development plans were prepared to avoid haphazard and dangerous construction in the future. The maximum height of new buildings was restricted to two floors, to counter the tendency to build upwards. Congestion and overcrowding were to be eased by constructing new housing areas: 'proper layouts with wider roads'.[11] Revised regulated development zoning was to address 'urban aesthetics' and 'reduce future vulnerability' by enabling more rapid emergency response. A number of fire stations were planned, ambulances procured, and the GSDMA purchased some sophisticated medical equipment, including a cardioscope pulse oxymetre, a ventilator and a defibrillator (for a population of over 50 million). It was a bonanza. Sometimes, it seemed a struggle to spend the money.

In 2008, an ADB project report summarised the work undertaken as follows: 'the project is rated "effective" in achieving its outcome' (as if it could have been much else).[12] The same report notes that, 'Significant economic growth has been realized in the reconstructed towns subsequent to the Project, and is a testimony to the Project's successful implementation'.[13] The World Bank also considers its projects to have been successful, for they exceeded all targets. Their report also points to the results of a survey which 'reveal[s] that quality of life has exceeded pre-earthquake levels. (The baseline of 1 pre-earthquake dropped to 0.36 immediately after the earthquake and is now at 1.178)'.[14]

Policy drafted in offices in Manila, Geneva and New York rippled invisibly into provincial Gujarat. Despite the fundamental importance of the banks' aims and loan conditions, they remained little understood or acknowledged on the ground. In the process, rural and urban folk were recreated as distinct types of citizen, subject to different kinds of policy and institution. As the policies arrived in Kutch, they were translated in the same way that a game of Chinese whispers might distort an original utterance ('send reinforcements, we're going to advance' might become 'send three-and-four-pence, we're going to a dance'). The slight shifts of meaning and under-standing contributed to some bizarre moments.

In the countryside, as part of the 'gender awareness' and 'micro credit' initiatives, as well as conforming to the general ethos of 'information-sharing', many hundreds of volunteers and charity workers were sent forth into the countryside to form 'groups'. 'Groups' (the English word was used) were intended to allow village people to 'come together' to help themselves by sharing views, experiences and knowledge with one another in village settings.[15] 'Groups' were intended to make the world better. Although there have been a number of very successful cooperative agricultural experiments in Gujarat, the imposition of a 'group' structure in the name of post-earthquake reconstruction met with mixed success. Of course, 'groups' had been around before the disaster, but post-earthquake cash rendered the group-forming syndrome endemic.

I attended a number of 'group' meetings to do with the management of common lands and village governance. I heard the English word 'groups' become a verb ('I am doing groups') and 'groups' became an utterly farcical pastime and source of enter-tainment and politics. In one village in the north of Kutch, I met a group of women I knew from a previous visit waiting for a bus. I asked them where they were going because it was unusual to see women waiting for buses in this remote part of the region. 'Oh! We are going to do groups', they said. It was clearly an amusement, a new experience, which took them away from the village and into exotic settings (other villages and NGO offices). Perhaps, too, in some cases they anticipated finan-cial reward.

The idea of a 'group', in which voices are cherished and all opinion is equally val-ued, entered a realm in which people are not equal and all voices are not similarly respected. The hierarchical power of caste, the differentiating potential of religion, as well as other forms of discrimination, simply entered the 'group'. The post-earthquake 'group' tended to be formed regardless of how villagers actually organised themselves, which contributed to a sense of surreal befuddlement: the earthquake came, then strangers arrived and asked us to start behaving as if we had not known how to know those who lived amongst us. Needless to say, the typical post-earthquake 'group' itself did not bring about a neo-conservative revolution in the countryside—it is much harder to judge what the effects of travel, public speaking and mixed caste assemblies will be in the longer term. At the time, however, project workers often found them-selves chairing 'groups' which seemed to be run through with relations formed by ideas quite contrary to those they had learned about at college.

In urban areas, the shape of the government was transformed overnight with new offices and bureaucrats. Put simply, and as we shall see in Section 4, the population generally did not understand, nor were they told clearly, about the new tiers of bureaucracy, and they continued to act as if the state lived on in its pre-earthquake form. The resulting confusion preoccupied and frustrated some people for many years. In the towns of the region, it was the conflict between the people and the state they no longer recognised that became the central story of the aftermath.

While one might be tempted to tut at the wily imperialism of the banks or shrink from the implications of the conditions accompanying their lending, the banks are utterly correct in their appraisal of the reconstruction programme as having made people prosperous, happy and proud of the way reconstruction has transformed them. I think, however, and as the rest of this book seeks to explain, there is more involved in this successful outcome than the banks' concluding reports are able to acknowledge. I have also genuinely wondered if the good people of Kutch might have been happier than the World Bank's reckoning of '1.178' if the $2.3 billion had simply been dropped from a great height onto the affected region and left to flutter into the lives of the beleaguered with the breeze—but that, of course, might not have been the point.

At a broader level, by focusing on property reconstruction and linking housing reconstruction programmes to private insurance provision, the reconstruction initiative has attempted to ensure that the cost of rehabilitation in case of future calamities will be taken care of by market forces, with the state playing a facilitating role. In other words, the regulation and management of risk was to be transferred from a benevolent state to a profiteering private sector. In India, this represents a dramatic shift in the relationship between the state and citizenry at times of catastrophe. In this sense, the earthquake became an opportunity to ensure that the state could not be held responsible for clearing up after disasters in the future. That was at least the theory built into the plan.

Smoke stacks of new industry, 2005, eastern Kutch.

4

HYPERBOLIC CAPITALISM

Before the earthquake, I would often spend Saturday evenings with a friend on a beach on the southern shores of Kutch. We would chat, drink, look at the stars, and appreciate the peaceful nature of the place. In 2011, we decided to go again for old time's sake. Then, the night sky to the east was bleached yellow by light pollution and there were no stars to be seen. The towers and chimneys of Mundra's new power stations dominated the horizon. Instead of the waves breaking gently on the shore, the overriding sensation was a deep and, eventually, sickening hum caused by the workings of distant industrial machinery.

In the mid-nineteenth century, the political economist John Stuart Mill asked why countries recover so rapidly from states of devastation.[1] For him, the destruction of war or natural disaster brought about nothing other than the accelerated consumption of what had been previously produced and which would have been consumed anyway. Therefore, in some senses, and to push the argument further, disaster is a moment of hyper-consumption which necessarily, given certain general conditions, acts as a powerful economic stimulus.[2]

Later on, we will look at the wealth brought to the personal lives of those who survived the earthquake. For now, I wish to examine the much bigger picture of expansion in the industrial sector. As the loan agreements began to reform and confuse Gujarat, the new industrial tax concessions were beginning to have consequences. Alongside the partial restructuring of the state, the greatest general intervention in the aftermath of the earthquake has been the imposition of industry on the region. Frustratingly little is publicly known of this in facts and figures, but there is plenty to see, hear and smell. These interventions have been facilitated by the state, which brokered the accompanying great land giveaway in the name of reconstruction. The onslaught of private industry altered the countryside beyond recognition—more an imposition or a graft than a revolution at the grassroots.

Before the earthquake, industry had begun to creep into Kutch, notably around the port at Kandla. The Adani Group, one of India's largest enterprises, had already begun work on a jetty at Mundra with a view to building a private port. The scene was set for growth. The new post-earthquake tax concessions were intended to make 'the economic environment of Kutch district live' by encouraging investment.[3] The scheme offered excise and sales tax concessions for five years for new industries.[4] The minister responsible told me that he had taken the idea from China, where a similar scheme had been implemented after an earthquake. Once the takeover of the countryside by industry was established, the process developed a momentum of its own, and the degree to which Kutch has been industrialised has surprised everyone.

Policies encouraging industrial development by tax adjustment work slowly at first, and then their effects become visible in something of a rush. Land and services have to be made available, factories planned and constructed, distribution and storage mechanisms put in place, and a labour force recruited, trained and managed. Thus years can pass before even the first signs of tax-incentive growth become visible. Before the earthquake, the road between Bhuj and Bhachau, for example, passed through a vast landscape of acacia, broken by the occasional village and agricultural oasis. The road served hinterland villages and was a seasonal corridor for nomadic pastoralists. In 2003, the silence on the road continued to be broken only by the occasional vehicle and the rustles, burps and farts of flocks of passing woolly animals. In 2004, three years after the earthquake, a ceramics firm started to construct a manufacturing plant at the Bhachau end of the highway. By the end of 2005, there were around twenty-five medium- to large-scale units dotted along the length of the road. Subsequently, the rate of growth along the highway has been phenomenal.

Today, the road passes through a mildly surreal landscape, lined with generous slabs of factory, belching chimneys and splashes of urban-style colour of the post-modernist architecture of office blocks and reception halls. Uniformed security guards saunter around entrance gates. Periodically, there is a flurry of activity as one shift comes to an end and another starts. Company busses spill from within walled compounds, returning the labour force to Bhuj or to a nearby village. Many of the factories are unmarked, showing no logo. A solid plume of smoke is often the only sign that something is being assembled, cooked or processed within. Much of the land on both sides of the highway has been enclosed, suggesting more factories are to come or that the land has been reserved. Along some sections of the road the rows of electricity poles are ten deep, reflecting the haste and lack of planning in this development. Levels of traffic have risen dramatically and plans are in place to expand the road to four lanes.

Here, as elsewhere, the incentive scheme has been rip-roaring in its successes, having attracted hundreds of acres of factories into Kutch. The financial benefits, as well as effluent, are leaking, if not exactly trickling down, into the countryside and contributing to the new wealth of the region. Unsurprisingly, the policy pays lip-service to pollution control and corporate social responsibility, but these are not reflected precisely in the sights and sounds of the new industrial landscape.

More remarkable in many ways, however, was that the policy was not geared towards the creation of new local industry; rather, it was an open invitation for existing industries from elsewhere to open new plants.[5] The new development which litters Kutch did not emerge from the grassroots or from repositories of capital maintained by extended family structures or from artisans investing in production lines. Instead, it was grafted on to the landscape by outsiders who have been allowed to use Kutch as a large and cut-price industrial estate.

Clause 8e of the initiative scheme demands: 'As per the employment policy of the Government of Gujarat, the unit availing of the incentives, will have to recruit local persons for a minimum of 85% of the total posts and for a minimum of 60% of the managerial and supervisory posts'. Members of Group 2001, a citizen's group based in Anjar, conducted surveys when the first factories began to open in 2003. Even then, they found that most industries employed high percentages of 'outside' (that is to say non-Kutchi) labour.

As we will see in following sections, the area most affected by the earthquake had a strong regional identity, in which it took some pride. Those flocking to Kutch to stoke the furnaces of new industry spoke other languages, ate different kinds of food and were devoted to exotic religious and political ideals. These people have consequently not generally been integrated into local society. As migrants were attracted from other parts of India, shanties and poverty became visible, suggesting transience, and contributing to the erosion of a distinctive provincial ambience. In the process, the earthquake-affected region has been firmly integrated into the nation. Group 2001 also estimated that the population of Anjar had increased by one-fifth in the two years after the disaster. And, as might reasonably be expected, this had already created new tensions, resentments and a hyperbolic increase in the fear of crime and violence. Since 2003, both the numbers of industries and the population of Anjar alike have grown far more.[6] While there might not be anything intrinsically wrong with industrial development, the conditions under which this sometimes desperate cosmopolitanism has been produced formed part of the stunning shock of the aftermath for those who had lived through the earthquake.

Following the routes of new highways and the tax concessions came manufacturers of tiles, pipes, trucks and turbines. Acres of concrete have been laid over coastal mangroves. Low-grade coal is shipped from Australia, and elsewhere, to be dumped into the burners of two new power stations to provide electricity for all this activity. These burners were built on an extraordinary and rare piece of coastline. Special Economic Zones ('special' due to scaled-back tax and labour laws, the absence of environmental clearance certificates, and a public enquiry which opened five years after construction began) have been established to encourage competitive exports.[7] Four-lane highways and additional railways now connect Kutch with the major cities in the east of Gujarat and the markets of northern India. Amid the frantic scramble for profit, parts of Kutch have become desperate, as a frontier mentality has grown along the new edges of capitalism.

The rate at which rural land has been turned into an industrial landscape has been astounding to watch. Officially, the policy was to breathe new life into the economy of a region devastated by an earthquake. However, the tangible benefits have been secondary in nature because most of the new industry sends its profit to people and stock markets elsewhere. A few times during this research, I have made the trip to Gandhinagar, the administrative capital of Gujarat, to seek ministerial views on reconstruction. On one such occasion, a minister once associated with industrial development told me that the best he could expect from the incentive scheme was for Kutch to host the industries and for its people to provide ancillary support in the form of haulage, cups of sweet tea for the industrial workforce and the like. 'They have no culture of work', he said.

It is currently popular, the world over, to talk of India's recent prosperity. Much of the country's new wealth is generated in areas like Kutch, far away from the major centres of population and homes of critical journalists. Close up, there is nothing pleasant about the manufacture of India's new riches. At the centre of the boom in this region is the coastal town of Mundra, itself largely unaffected by the earthquake, but thoroughly done over in its name in the aftermath. Fifteen years ago, Mundra was a peaceful and friendly market town serving the hinterland. Today, the town is full of strangers and the atmosphere is hard and untrusting. The town's walls have started to fall, an apt metaphor for the pressures the town is facing. Prostitutes openly work the main bazaar, a fact mentioned not to be prudish but because I cannot think of anything more antithetical to the public morality and reputation of the town before the earthquake. On the outskirts, the grimy ancillary services of industry sprawl along the highways, lines of trucks roar and growl past rows of hastily built hotels, mechanical workshops and tyre and tea shops. Here, at least, it is as if Kutch has become another country.

As John Stuart Mill noted, 'natural' disasters often lead to economic booms, following the hyper-rapid consumption of goods, buildings and services. A disaster is accelerated entropy. What was there before has to be put back in some form, and this stimulates growth. Builders build, tradesmen craft and contractors contract. However, as we have seen, the shock of the earthquake is often also an opportunity to change the order of things, by privatising common lands, cheapening the terms of trade and forgoing state revenues to the enrichment of private enterprise.

Following the 1755 earthquake in Lisbon, trade flourished despite the huge losses incurred as a result of the disaster. There, the government took the opportunity to reform and nationalise the economy, reducing its semi-dependency on Britain.[8] In Gujarat, investment by the state and other concerned bodies stimulated growth. The generosity spun from both guilt and fascination among the witnesses added to the bonanza. The disaster also had a global media audience from which it could demand attention. The media, what was then called 'cyberspace', and a large and wealthy diaspora, played parts in encouraging the injection of cash.[9] In Gujarat, too, we can see that moment of disaster as an accelerated moment of consumption, the velocity and nature of which became part of a hyperbolic boom, which reverberated and amplified in the aftermath. We can also see that the earthquake served to legitimate an industrial policy designed in favour of big business, and brokered by the state, in which those affected by the earthquake were intended to become workers and servants, or *chai wallah*s.

In India, a *wallah* is someone who performs a particular task or role. The *taxi wallah* drives or arranges taxis; the *chai wallah* makes or brings tea (*chai*). On train journeys, the shout of '*chai, chai*' is as familiar in India as anything can be. Elsewhere, tea is made in small shops or cabins at the side of roads. The tea is brewed on gas burners in open pots. The benches surrounding the cabin might allow communities of regulars to form, a place where newspapers are read and gossip exchanged. As the gas burner roars and hisses, so the hands of the *chai wallah* perform their magic. The *chai wallah* is not wealthy or wise, but he takes pride in what he does. If he has ambition or worries, we probably do not know. The *chai wallah* is subservient and makes tea.

Exercise time at the Anglo-Kutchi English Medium School, 2006, Mandvi.

5

THE CARPETBAGGER

Carpet-bagger (*derog.*, chiefly *US*) a person seeking to achieve political success or private gain in a place with which he is unconnected (orig. *spec.* a northerner in the southern US after the Civil War).

New Shorter Oxford English Dictionary, 1993.

Once the broad parameters on which reconstruction would take place had been established, a great many people arrived from elsewhere, mostly from the east of Gujarat, but also from other parts of the country and abroad. Most of these people came as part of organisations sustained by particular ideologies and ideas. They came as the 'private' of the public–private partnerships, while borrowing from development banks formed the bulk of the 'public' contribution. Some of those to arrive were from development organisations, relief services and charities aiming to better the lot of the poor. Others were from religious and cultural organisations, who said they were motivated by pity and a moral sense of duty to aid. Their interventions were generally presented as 'help', 'aid', 'development' or as *seva* (a word common to many Indian languages and generally translated as 'service'). There was much humanitarian will in the mix, but a great many interventions required that those affected by the disaster modify their behaviours in some way in exchange for the assistance given.

One of those to intervene was the British educationalist Derek Slade, whose motivations and actions typify, in extreme form, the dynamics of intervention and opportunism. Slade arrived in Gujarat after the earthquake to construct a school for children orphaned by the disaster. As far as I know, he came alone and with no local knowledge, other than some introductions from Gujarati Muslims he knew in Leicester. By chance, one of my friends from before the earthquake, Awab, became Slade's man on the ground: secretary, translator and errand boy. In time, Awab told me that Mr Slade beat the pupils, claiming it was good for them: the well-known 'Oxford method' of education. Awab was concerned.

Slade was great company, a funny and engaging conversationalist, who talked passionately about the power of education. By 2004, his achievements were already significant: he had purchased land, secured necessary permissions and services, negotiated with contractors and constructed a two-storey building with classrooms, dormitories and his own quarters. The school was built on the outskirts of the coastal town of Mandvi, some sixty kilometres to the south of Bhuj, as an initiative of the International British Education Projects (IBEP). The project was also partially funded by the Leicester Gujarat Earthquake Relief Fund, to whom Slade himself had proposed the scheme. Slade told me that IBEP also ran schools in East Africa and South India, financed, he said, by the profit from a novel called *Invasion*.[1] The book is a counter-factual history in which Germany is victorious in the Second World War. In the final chapter, King Edward shoots Hitler before being shot dead himself: his last words are, 'Tell mother, I have done my duty'.

Awab encouraged me to take an interest in the project, pointing to the worth of educating Muslim children in Gujarat from under-privileged backgrounds. Despite my efforts, Slade expressed no interest in meeting local philanthropists or educationalists who I thought could advise him. As far as I know, his only other local contacts were an ex-patriot couple who happened to live nearby, a modern dancer and a non-linear artist.

Given Slade's supposed lack of interest in local society, his choice of front man was fortuitous. Awab was from a family of hereditary saints, but he had grown restless and disenchanted with the life of public piety. He flirted with rebellion and girls. He had not moved so far away from his family, however, that he was unable to draw on their reputation. Slade, I think, saw Awab's frustrations and the duplicity required for him to live in a provincial town as a non-saintly saint.

After a few attempts at attracting fee-paying pupils, Slade and Awab hit upon the idea of bringing children from the remotest parts of northern Kutch, following flooding in the area in 2003. The parents of these boys were followers of Awab's extended family. His reputation served as a guarantee for the education on offer. The school soon had around forty boys in its care. Their origins were humble: their fathers eked a living from livestock, wood-cutting and petty smuggling. They had little contact with the state or civil society, and were the sort of people for whom no one would come looking if they were to disappear.

The arrival of these children at the school meant that the project no longer had any connection to the nearby village that the Leicester funds were initially intended to help. Furthermore, the children now housed in the school were neither orphans nor earthquake affected—but this did not alter the way the school was represented in England as a post-earthquake initiative for orphaned children.

When the boys first arrived, many of them were in poor health. At least one was pot-bellied; others had lice, scabies and malaria. Between them, they had a remarkable number of lazy eyes (or 'terrace eyes' as they are known in Gujarati, as the wayward eye looks upwards towards the terrace). Realising that it would be easier to raise money in England than from the rural poor in Gujarat, Slade quickly gave up the idea of a fee-paying school. Instead, he offered free boarding, uniforms, food, health care and a rather old-fashioned, British-style education.

Slade talked about how the boys had recreated their village life in the school, importing older friendships and animosities. He spoke with marvel about how they acted out stories and danced around a fire at night, their silhouettes flickering over the walls of the school. By the way he described these performances, he thought he was watching a vestige of something elemental and primitive, something truly amazing.

The school was quite a success for a while. The boys appeared happy and content. Now fed three times daily, they also looked healthier. The advances in their exercise books were impressive—and there was talk of the brighter boys going to university. Slade took the boys on trips to the beach and museums. The modern dancer who lived nearby was keen to help out, running an excellent school magazine and holding classes in gymnastics.

Awab took to making visits to England during Ramadan to raise money from diasporic Muslims from Kutch, for whom donations to charities working with orphans are particularly meritorious. Slade gradually passed on to Awab further responsibilities and privileges as their mutual dependence grew. In time, as Awab travelled, he also became more wealthy, largely from collecting funds from followers of his family while he was on Slade's business. His complicity in Slade's violent educational regime came at a price, however. As a tangible sign of his anxiety, he lost hair and weight before employing a ritual specialist to bury a length of golden thread around the perimeter of the school. Awab told Slade that the thread was to keep badness away. Awab told me that he hoped the magical thread would help Slade with his 'illnesses'.

Then, quite unexpectedly, something unknown happened, and the enterprise collapsed into a confused mess. At some point in 2008 or 2009, Slade left India for England, seemingly in a hurry. Awab later told me that one of Slade's friends had turned up in Gujarat and had burned the possessions Slade had left behind. Among these were hand-drawn cartoons of sexual acts with children, records of beatings written in a strange language, and compact discs containing thousands of photographs of boys. In July 2010, a small article appeared in a free London newspaper announcing the start of the trial of the 'suspected paedophile', Derek Slade. He had been arrested in January and charged with fifty counts of assault against children in his care in England in the 1970s and 1980s. Despite reporting restrictions, the items recovered from Slade's house in the Midlands of England were listed as including cartoons of sexual acts with children, records of beatings written in Greek, and compact discs containing photographs of boys, many thousands of which were classified by the police as indecent. The court sentenced Slade to twenty-one years imprisonment.

In documents relating to the school in Kutch, Slade was sometimes also called Dr Edward Marsh. As Marsh, he had a PhD in educational psychology with a thesis entitled *Aspects of negative reinforcement in child socialization*. As Slade, he had a degree in classics. As both Marsh and Slade, he said he was an Oxford man (although Marsh's CV states that the doctorate was awarded by the University of Madras). As

Slade, he had studied alongside Bill Clinton when he was a Rhodes Scholar at Oxford. Edward Marsh, it turned out, had died in 1955 aged eight, and was buried in Derby. His identity was assumed by Slade following a previous conviction (which was overturned on appeal) for the harm of children in his care in Sussex in 1986.

In 2011, I visited the school in Gujarat again. Slade's rooms had been taken over by a glum-looking religious teacher. I thought back to older tensions over the role of religion in the school. Slade had argued for a secular education, but had no objection to the boys learning the Koran at the weekend. The Muslims from Leicester who had become involved in financing the school were generally more religiously minded than their brothers and cousins in Gujarat. They were keen that the boys should have a rigorous religious education—not least because it would make it easier to raise money in England. In an unforgettable conversation between Awab and some of his Leicester friends, they discussed how to 'Islamify' the reputation of the school. One man suggested, without irony, that it should be possible to stick cardboard minarets to the building to make it look more like a mosque in photographs. They, too, used the distance between Gujarat and Leicester to misrepresent local realities in pursuit of their causes. The proposed farce struck me at the time as both hilarious and peculiarly creative. As it was, at least in part, the school had been a façade for the pursuit of quite different worldly interests.

The shock of the earthquake had made it seem perfectly reasonable for someone to want to build a school for children who had suddenly lost their parents. Given the mess in and around Bhuj, it did not seem odd that the school should have been constructed in the calm of a region largely unaffected by disaster. Given the politicised plight of Muslims in the state at the time, it hardly seemed important that the pupils were neither orphans nor earthquake affected. Slade, I think, managed to see quite early on how the prevailing conditions could work to his advantage, and he planned his intervention accordingly. It was not that he found vulnerable children wandering alone in the ruins of Kutch; rather, he found a vulnerable society, which assumed, for a while at least, that the interveners had come to do no harm. Furthermore, he had identified a section of that society which was marginal and quite disconnected from the mainstream.

The public–private partnership schemes, which intensified strong local traditions of philanthropy, made it increasingly difficult for people to judge who was authentic and who had legitimacy. Slade chose his local interlocutors carefully, and harnessed their strengths and weaknesses. In the rush of all else that was going on, Slade was able to operate with less critical scrutiny than he might have done otherwise. He clearly also knew how to compel others through fiction.

Like contagion and lawlessness, the paedophile making his way through the ruins towards children sounds like one of the myths that disasters commonly throw up. But Slade was real, the intervener in extreme and exaggerated form. He exploited the shock, the fact of death, the availability of vulnerability, and the suddenly uncertain nature of authority and legitimacy in order to create around him a small and isolated community of dependent children. He was in search of something which was, in the normal run of things, forbidden to him. I have no doubt that there was sociological reasoning in his actions which allowed him to exploit diasporic networks and the emotive figure of the orphan in Muslim society. Indeed, shortly after the tsunami of 2004, he frantically tried to gather support for an orphanage in South India. In this instance, nothing came of the idea. The swiftness of his response suggested to me later that he had been waiting for another disaster, seeing them as moments responsive to his interests.

In Gujarat, Slade had worked tirelessly for a number of years in order to create an isolated community of boys of which he was head and master. At the same time, he also had to create a community of trust, albeit one inflected with violence, for without trust none of this would have worked. He improved the physical health of the boys and gave them a visible confidence in themselves. He had taught many of them to read and write, and provided them with the space and time to play. He taught them about Shakespeare, trains and the myths of continents. He had taken them to places they might not otherwise have seen. When he departed, many boys chose not to go back to their ancestral homelands—not because they were traumatised and would not know how to explain themselves to their families, but because they wanted new things for themselves. Instead, they rented a house in the local town, taking what work they could get to pay the rent and buy provisions. Last time I heard, some of them were doing rather well.

Signboards advertising the 'good work' of humanitarian organisations, 2002, Bhuj.

6

NOTES ON 'AFTERMATH'

Naomi Klein's compelling book *The shock doctrine* suggests that interventions after disasters and invasions are strategic and generic extensions of free market capitalism, as understood by the 'Chicago School' led by Milton Freidman in the 1950s.[1] In Klein's view, American capitalism uses public disorientation to control and profiteer. The invasion of Iraq, the effect of the 2004 tsunami on Sri Lanka and other examples are shown to have allowed capitalist opportunism.

States of emergency, exception and thrall allow for the authorisation of novel arrangements. The wake of a disaster is a period of possibility and potential, most obviously for those looking in at the ruins. My previous reference to Lisbon distancing itself from British economic influence after an earthquake in the eighteenth century suggests that there is more to opportunism and accumulation after a disaster than the influence of twentieth-century economists from the Windy City. However, Klein's model, ahistoricity excepted, remains bold, provocative and good to think with. The spirit of unbridled opportunism she outlines also runs through the evidence from Gujarat. The metaphors of shock and doctrine sting with accuracy. However, shock and doctrine can mean many things, operate at different levels and change over time. The shock doctrine requires subdivision. Together, the interaction of the different levels and scales of both shock and doctrine, in part and sum, makes a contemporary aftermath.

In combination, temporary insanity and familial abandonment is a different shock to having your ankles and shins splintered by a falling house and then lying with people you know as they die. These shocks make you needy and wary in distinct ways. 'Earthquake' is a bland label for a wide range of experiences. The shock of a collapsed hospital is quite different to the behaviour of shocked government personnel as they try to gather their senses. Shock sets off in many directions and at varying speeds and amplitudes in a disaster. Doctrine comes in the wake, and also takes many forms. The doctrine of the carpetbagger is dissimilar to that of a domestic tax concession to industry, which is different again to the design of restructuring loans from international development banks.

Such disaggregation is necessary and important to make sense of the ways in which individuals, collectives and institutions experience and carry expectations into aftermaths. However, the longer I watched and listened, the more it was obvious that it was not the disaster itself but the doctrines of the interveners that were truly shocking: shock-doctrine-SHOCK. Let us explore this sequence more carefully.

In urgent and confused circumstances, the gaze of those on the ground is distracted from normal things by spectacle. Rules may be suspended. At first, a sense of intensified community or humanity may blossom, as people help and talk to those they normally ignore. This period is generally short-lived. Following the aforementioned earthquake in Peru, the spirit of 'brotherhood' lasted two or three days.[2] Similar reports were provided by those I asked in Gujarat. At first, people helped one another. After a few days, some said as many as fifteen, older patterns were restored.

Experts in the sociology of natural disaster commonly use the expression *crise révélatrice* (revealing crisis), which refers to the bare bones of a society stripped of its cultural niceties. As Anthony Oliver-Smith, the leading anthropologist of disasters puts it, 'the fundamental features of society and culture are laid bare in stark relief by the reduction of priorities to basic social, cultural and material necessities'. He writes elsewhere with Susanna Hoffman, 'The basic social organizational forms and behavioural tenets of a society are exhibited and tested under conditions of stress', and 'disasters often reveal the deeper social grammar of a people that lies behind their day-to-day behaviour'.[3] This is not my approach. In my view, research conducted on other disasters suggests abnormality and confusion. People are nice to one another, undifferentiated, as victims of a common calamity. But this is a short-lived and exceptional moment, marked by the failure of everyday grammar, rather than its refinement or condensation. It is instead the aftermath that may reveal what is dear.

It is also popular to think about disasters leading to a tabula rasa, or 'blank slate'. The term refers to a society akin to the unformed and featureless mind found in the philosophy of John Locke.[4] Destruction wipes things clean so that they can be remade anew. Klein finds obvious fault with this idea and employs a metaphor of her own. She describes the experiments of psychologists who thought that if the personality of a patient could be erased, then it could be built back again without fault or disorder.[5] To this end, patients were deprived of all routine and structure, and subject to irregular and disorienting sensory stimulation. Despite initial successes, the psychologists were often frustrated by the return of elements of the patient's original personality. So too, in Gujarat, the interveners did not find the featureless mind they might have hoped for.

Aftermath refers to the second growth or crop in the same season, the new flush of grass after mowing, which is often quite different in its qualities to the first crop, but it is still grass. The second crop may grow unevenly as it races for the light, it may pale before establishing itself. Aftermath is a measure of a quality of time and growth. As I have suggested, in Gujarat, 'aftermath time' was marked most strongly by the struggle of the affected with those who intervened, the doctrine-SHOCK era. In this sense, aftermath time has both psychological and moral connotations, as new arrangements and ideas battled to find a new peace with pre-existing ones. Those bewildered by the earthquake often called the aftermath 'the second earthquake', suggesting it too was terrible.[6]

The time after the earthquake in Gujarat was dreadful indeed—perhaps worse, in absolute terms, than the earthquake itself—but I have chosen to call it the 'aftermath', rather than the 'second earthquake', because the two events were distinct—with different masters, heroes and villains; the second was not a straight copy of the first.

As we have seen, the conditions placed on loans by the development banks created the most generalised framework for reconstruction. The industrialisation of the region is the most visible consequence of the state's home-grown reconstruction policies. In these shadows there were other technocratic, linguistic and bureaucratic aspects to the post-earthquake interventions. The awe of technology contributed to the pacification of the affected, as the new district hospital was mounted on springs. The swift instrument of town planning cut through old societies, taught people how to read maps and to adopt nationalist and suburban mentalities. Signs of reconstruction appeared in Hindi, the national but previously invisible language in the region. Others brought religious and cultural ideas in their relief trucks.

In short, and in advance of what is to come, the bewildered lived among varying superimposed spheres, as different ideological forms were traced one over the other. Some new formulations of meaning took root and displaced others, and some failed. And so, in the aftermath, those who intervened with new ideas and technologies created deep anxiety over whether change and modernisation had been a cause of the disaster or were predestined to be the primary consequence.

There was a clash of cultures running through the aftermath. As we shall see in Chapter 8, the population of Gujarat is far from homogeneous, and the different cultures of eastern and western parts of the state came firmly into contact through reconstruction. Most doctrine was brought from the east, where the big cities and centres of government are to be found. The 'truths' and 'realities' with which doctrines and policies were supposed to engage were generally not the 'truths' or 'realities' of local people themselves. At various times, the state and other doctrinaires began to see the people as ungrateful when they protested about what they were being offered. Often it was said that the people of Kutch in the west, where the earthquake had had most effect, did not have enough culture or education to see the benefits in the new reconstructed scheme of things. Those who came from the east to reconstruct the west brought with them the authority of state power and a greater sense of a 'Gujarati culture'. They also came with the knowledge that those in the west were victims, and this contributed to their sense of self-confidence.

In an epic study of the consequences of the 'four monsters'—war, revolution, famine and pestilence—the now-unfashionable sociologist Pitirim Sorokin (1889–1968) concluded that calamities mould societies in their own image.[7] His argument is provocative because it grants power to nature to give society a shape. A strong counter-argument might be that pre-existing cultural understandings offer interpretative frameworks through which disasters can be understood. In this second view, a society would create a calamity in its own image, not vice versa, using its own terms of reference and history to understand the ravage. In Gujarat, we see both an 'earthquake society' formed by disaster as well as an earthquake in discursive form which gradually comes to resemble the society it affected. This is a strong dialectic. However, we also see something more: we see how those who intervened in the aftermath brought with them various understandings of tragedy and right and wrong, in addition to some well-formed ideas (however misplaced) about the kind of people they had come to help. Conversely, those affected by the disaster struggled to differentiate between those who had come to intervene.

Until recently, the decayed frames of colonial famine and flood relief measures influenced contemporary post-disaster interventions in India.[8] Private trusts and charities had also developed parallel structures to channel compassion and cash to the affected. From a laissez faire approach to disaster relief in the late nineteenth century, the twentieth century has seen the emergence of increasing state intervention and control in the aftermath of natural disasters.[9] The earthquake in Gujarat was but one of the shocks which found the existing state of affairs wanting, and prompted the state to reform old policies and design national codes for future bad happenings.[10] Consequently, doctrine came in many layers, from diverse sources, often with contradictory aims and tensions. Banks, national and state governments, local administrative units, private sector and humanitarian organisations all contributed their own favourite ingredients to the mix.

When viewed as a whole, there were a number of serious contradictory pulls in the competing policy frameworks. For example, professionals in post-disaster reconstruction are often frustrated by the inability of their industry to learn from past calamities. Such amnesia has been routinised by the 'disaster paradigm'—that is, the set of pre-existing knowledge and expectation that disasters engage. Emphasis is placed on the uniqueness of the circumstances of each disaster. Concern lies with the cultural conditions of the affected region or, similarly, the specificity of patterns of risk or vulnerability. In essence, risk or vulnerability is 'memory bumped forward' or 'the taming of chance', which, given that local conditions are always unique, necessarily means each disaster must be different.[11] Therefore, all societies are affected by disaster, but this or that society has not been affected by this or that disaster before. The disaster industry thus operates under the tense conditions of its own making: on the one hand, all disasters are unique, while on the other, the standard codes and forms discussed in Chapter 3 have been produced in an attempt to give those working in the industry a memory and a frame in which to work.

In the years after the SHOCK of intervention, the aftermath has displayed something of a self-purging quality. I have already mentioned the hundreds of arrests made for the corruption of earthquake funds. The threat of arrest has clearly become a political tool, but these now calmer times allow for the clean-up of some earlier excesses. In the early years after the earthquake, we could see a government dining out on the efficiency and effectiveness of its post-earthquake policies. By 2010, it was possible to see the same government boasting across the table about its own integrity for arresting those whose actions suggest the reconstruction of Gujarat was not quite what had been claimed earlier. The numbers of arrests speak for themselves.

Aftermaths often appear to have similar structures, characterised by the interaction of generalised shock with new intentions and plans. They cannot, however, be seen as a generic sociological condition, for the shocks, doctrines and SHOCKS vary. An aftermath is a product of the longer history of a locality. The world does not implode into the moment of disaster to emerge afresh or ready to be remade in any old way. As subsequent chapters show, older ideas will not disappear. For now, I wish to give an illustrative example. Old Bhuj was thrown into disarray by the earthquake, yet the national flag was still raised to mark Republic Day. Umashankar found his way home, despite the absence of streets and buildings. Visually, the separate structures of the town became undifferentiated. For many practical purposes, the town ceased to exist. However, in addition to the rituals of nationalism, pre-existing intentions and purposes, and in the cognition of its inhabitants, the town was also preserved in good condition in the maps and property and tax records of the state. These older records became the basis for thinking about the future, despite the fact that the town itself was no longer there. Bhuj was reconstructed from archival sources. There was no clean slate.

Within ten years, the earthquake has become part of local history. It has been domesticated and its exceptional ferocity has been tamed: it has become part of the normal run of things. In the process, a purge has gradually taken place. Those, like the carpetbagger, have been sent packing.

SECTION 2

EARTHQUAKE POLITICS

Going back in time now to shortly after the earthquake, a peaceful coup saw the leader of Gujarat replaced with another in the name of post-earthquake ineptitude. The new leader picked up on a politics in which Muslims were demonised and so introduced a sense of religious antagonism to the aftermath. The decades of effort that had gone into constructing a culturally unified state were undone by the earthquake. In time, the state used the disaster to strengthen and extend its reach. The border with Pakistan proved a fertile symbol through which the new politics could be ground into a reconstructed society. A new hero was publicised to replace the fading image of Mahatma Gandhi. Many things were named after this new hero. His name was glorified.

Ruins of the colonial-period Jubilee Hospital. When Bill Clinton held a press conference here in 2001, protesters used the structure to display signs of dissatisfaction. Michael Palin also used the location in 2008 for his television series about going around the world in 80 days, again. 2003, Bhuj.

7

REGIME CHANGE

In the aftermath, the mood in Bhuj was glum. People looked to the state to compensate and rehabilitate them. The state felt their angry stare, but had been caught without an effective post-disaster plan. Within a month there were protestors in the rubble. State-led uncertainty translated into the abandonment of self-help. Sensibly, no one wanted to repair their house if it might be demolished later—or if they were to be left living alone when Bhuj was rebuilt anew elsewhere. I know that experts were brought from around the world in those early months to advise the government on the best course of action. Knowledge of these efforts did not make it as far as Bhuj, from where it seemed, quite simply, as if the government was doing nothing.

Together, rumour, speculation and stumbling official pronouncements began to suggest that the policies of the state were to be oriented towards victims. Those who could prove that their bodies, property or interests had been damaged were to be compensated. The state was, it appeared, to become the underwriter of loss (and as we now know this was done in a way that ensured it would not be responsible for future loss). With this news, and in order to demonstrate loss, many people shifted from partially damaged homes to resettlement camps: rows of single-roomed buildings made of plastic or corrugated iron with dark and menacing communal bathrooms. The blossoming culture of expectation encouraged people to become 'victims' in anticipation of government policies. Had different conditions prevailed, then these people might just have paid for the repairs necessary to their property themselves, and then got on with things, much as they had done before.

As Bhuj waited to hear of its future, the old town remained a mess, strewn with rubble, its jagged skyline formed horridly by collapsed and damaged structures. There was severe disruption, but shops opened, many children went to school, buses ran. Not all sat by waiting to see what was going to be given to them. Mohammed, for example, whose house was badly damaged, began to find conditions in the old town intolerable. Before the earthquake, he had purchased a building plot of land some distance to the north of Bhuj. At the time, the projected housing society seemed a long way from the central attractions of the town; it was a long-term investment. Prior to the earthquake, Bhuj had been expanding. There was a discernible tendency to move away from the older core towards suburban housing colonies, of which Mohammed's investment was symptomatic. Suddenly, the small plot of land seemed like a golden opportunity to provide safe housing for his family, away from the rubble, intermittent water and general uncertainties of life in the old town. Without fuss, he built a house, and his family moved there. A few other families did the same and, by the end of 2001, a small new suburb was beginning to flourish.

In February 2002, a fire on the Sarbamati Express train outside Godhra station in eastern Gujarat killed fifty-eight people. Many of the dead were Vishwa Hindu Parishad (VHP) activists returning from the city of Ayodhya in the north of India, where attempts were being made to construct a temple on the site where a famous mosque had once stood. The death of those on the train was followed by widespread violence across Gujarat throughout March. This violence was often gratuitous and occasionally appeared premeditated. Over 1,000 people, mostly Muslims, lost their lives, and tens of thousands were forced into temporary camps.[1] Public culture in the state took on a distinctly anti-Muslim hue. At the time, it was commonly believed that the fire on the train was started by a 'mob' of Muslims.[2] Some months after the carnage, the government of Gujarat released a multi-media presentation putting forward its own version of events.[3] In the opening scenes, newspaper headlines flash on the screen accusing those who attacked the train 'in the most ghastly manner since Partition' as being 'rioters without conscience' and 'men without souls'. The headlines were made up and intended to be mistaken for those of respected English-language newspapers. The narrative does not say as much, but most of those who took time to watch the film must have already thought that the men without souls were Muslims.

The initial success of the Bharatiya Janata Party (BJP) in Gujarat in the 1980s came from opposing the Congress Party's coalition of low-status groups dubbed KHAM (Kshatriya, Harijan, Adavasi and Muslim).[4] Resistance to this pact came primarily from high castes, namely urban and semi-urban Brahmins, Jains and other Hindu mercantile castes, and the conglomeration of rural agricultural castes known generically as Patidars or Patels. The BJP capitalised on their resentment through a series of agitations against reserved quotas for the employment of low castes in government sectors. This was followed by a shift in the BJP's electioneering strategies, as they turned to mobilise subaltern castes for electoral gain by playing an anti-Muslim card.[5]

By the early 1990s, the BJP (as a political party) was a credible force in Gujarat, and the contenders for leadership presented the party with an either/or choice between Rashtriya Swayamsevak Sangh (RSS) or non-RSS candidates. The BJP won the elections of 1995 and 1998. During his reign as chief minister of Gujarat, Keshubhai Patel expanded the cabinet to win favour and to isolate his critics. He also reformed advisory committees, including those responsible for police and social justice, and packed them with those sympathetic with Hindu nationalist politics.[6] Through these and other measures, by the end of the 1990s the BJP had changed complexion. The non-RSS faction was now sidelined and the choice of leader was between RSS candidates, each with a support base rooted in particular caste interests.

At this time, RSS membership was forbidden to government employees in Gujarat following its involvement in the violence of the 'anti-reservation riots'.[7] A year before the earthquake, Patel removed the ban and paved the way for the government to integrate the concerns of the nationalist RSS into its fold. Within the year, national union home minister L.K. Advani, who stood for the BJP in the constituency of Gandhinagar (the capital of Gujarat), had been photographed sitting with the chief minister at a gathering of RSS cadres. In the photograph, Patel is dressed in the trademark khaki shorts of the organisation.

Then, in January 2001, the earthquake struck. The first wave of political after-shocks lasted nine months, first destabilising and then toppling Patel's government. In Bhuj, some of those protesting against the lack of state action claimed his scalp. They said that their demonstrations had drawn critical attention to the ineptitude of the chief minister and forced him out of office. At the time, the cabinet was also embroiled in corruption allegations and, perhaps more significantly, the party had lost a local election within the boundaries of Advani's constituency in Gandhinagar. The loss suggested that perhaps the good times were over for the BJP in Gujarat, unless something else could be done to galvanise the electorate in their favour. So it was that in October 2001, Narendra Modi, never having faced an election, replaced Patel as chief minister. He became the first RSS *pracharak* (volunteer to the cause) to hold such a post in India.[8] Only a few months after Modi took charge, the Sarbamati Express came to a halt outside Godhra railway station, a sleeper carriage caught fire, and we already know what happened next.

The Election Committee suspended the Gujarat parliament in July 2002. In September of the same year, Modi had launched the BJP's election campaign with a series of mass rallies. By then it was clear that the apparatus of the state had been somewhere between supine and complicit in the bloodshed. In the same month, Muslim gunmen entered a well-known Hindu temple in Gandhinagar and killed more than thirty people in its precincts. There has been much speculation as to who these gunmen were and why they attacked this temple in such a seemingly ill-prepared manner. Their actions have generally been represented as an attack on Hinduism and on the BJP's politics. The most noticeable consequence of their actions, however, was to consolidate a culture of fear, and thus the BJP's share of the vote. Amid these disturbed conditions, the Election Committee scheduled new state-level elections for December 2002.

The BJP–VHP–RSS combination presented the election as a referendum on the BJP government's post-Godhra stance on violence against Muslims. They again attempted to mobilise the electorate along religious lines. The choice they presented was a simple one: Hinduism/the BJP/Gujarat/prosperity versus Muslims/Congress/Pakistan/stagnation. Leading members of the RSS and VHP played roles in the BJP's campaign. Pravin Togadia, then International Secretary of the VHP, made around sixty speeches, some of which he delivered in Kutch, stressing that votes should be placed on the basis of religion so that the 'offspring of Musharraf' (then the president of Pakistan), would not come to power. He lambasted liberals for 'barking' about the violence of March 2002, and condemned Muslims, secularists and rival political parties as the evils facing Gujarat.[9] We return to this speech in Chapter 13.

In the election, the BJP gained a two-thirds majority, gaining most in areas affected by the violence. Modi was again sworn in as chief minister. Speaking at the ceremony, the president of the national party, M. Venkaiah Naidu, stressed that: 'the victory was a mandate for the ideology … [I]n Gujarat we have … proved … collective work is the key to success … Gujarat was not a mere political victory; it was a mandate for the ideology'.[10]

Several general theories have been put forward to explain the violence, the complicity of the Gujarat state, and the rise of a politics invested in religious differentiation.[11] One possibility is that religious polarisation has been intensified by the strong class and caste divisions created by the recruitment patterns of the post-Independence Nehruvian government and perpetuated by the unequal distribution of benefits from economic liberalisation. These conditions retarded the development of an alternative radical polity in Gujarat to the point that, throughout the 1970s and early 1980s, party politics stagnated around the concerns of the middle class, bolstered by the vote of the lower classes.[12]

Others have seen the violence in Gujarat as reflecting a broader crisis in the Indian political system brought about by the varied forces of globalisation, governmental authoritarianism and communalism. Globalisation has opened up new economic avenues, but it has exacerbated other iniquities and inequalities, and created a fragmented and casualised poor who live alongside an increasingly affluent middle class.[13] The anthropologist Jan Breman has suggested that the conditions for violence emerged from the promotion of a political economy which seeks to keep the working classes fragmented and in a state of dependency in order to reduce the price of their labour to the lowest possible level. Therefore, it is the working class who end up throwing stones and gas canisters at one another under the spell of manufactured hatred.[14]

Other seasoned commentators on Gujarat, notably Achyut Yagnik and Suchitra Sheth, emphasise the significance of the burgeoning and socially disenfranchised middle class. These scholars suggest that the loss of traditional markers of status consequent on the processes of urbanisation and industrialisation have led to a quest for identity which has somehow come to rest upon Hindu nationalist politics. In their view, it has been politicians who have encouraged the subalterns to throw stones and gas canisters at one another.[15] Arguably complementing these positions, the political scientist Ashutosh Varshney has suggested that politicised Hinduism is essentially a new phenomenon in Gujarat, rising in parallel to the waning of the principles of harmony and tolerance instilled by Gandhi and others and the collapse of social networks (the networks of 'civil society') that kept the communal juggernaut at bay. As we will see, he is probably correct to draw attention to the declining influence of Gandhi's associationalism—but incorrect in some of his other claims.[16]

60

The prevailing view is that the new inequalities of globalisation (however so defined) have been mirrored by a local crisis because the political system has not been able to respond equitably to changing economic conditions, and this has led to increasing authoritarianism on the part of the government. This has been described as the 'use of state apparatus to distort the existing social structure' for its own gain.[17] Or, more boldly, as the state parading as it wishes in a condition of political anarchy behind a façade of order.[18] Others see the Sangh Parivar as attempting to capture the nation-state and entrench the ideologies of nationalism by operating in the vacuum created by the decline of the political left, to consider but one possibility.[19] In the Gujarat of the earthquake, it is clear that alienation and division have been manipulated for political gain through systematic and planned penetration of society by the Sangh Parivar and other organisations with similar agendas.[20]

As we have seen, the earthquake coincided with general reforms to the administration in Gujarat. At the time, and against the backdrop of the rise of the majoritarian polity, we can see various ways in which Hindu organisations sought to re-imagine the relationship between the governors and the governed. They sought to reform the spaces in which votes are garnered, networks formed and phantasmagorical images of frightening 'others' incubated. The loan conditions imposed by the development banks on the post-earthquake reconstruction funds created an environment fecund with possibility. The privatisation of some forms of state authority and the outsourcing of state functions allowed power to flow with abundance into both civil and corporate society.

In Bhuj, in 2002, stories of Hanuman temples being desecrated by strange, mad or unknown Muslim men were commonly told in an attempt to make trouble. A curfew was imposed briefly, but little or no blood was shed. Kutch was not, however, fully immune to the contagion of fear and hostility that infected life in the east of the state. Civic and social life took on an enhanced sense of communal differentiation, and this cloud hung over even the most mundane of reconstruction activities. We know that life in a small new suburb to the north of Bhuj was beginning to flourish in late 2001, as Muslim families took the decision to move there from the chaos and disruption of the old town. In the months after the violence of 2002, the suburb was gradually deserted as its Muslim inhabitants returned to the rubble of the old town fearing for their lives in a relatively isolated and easily identifiable suburban location.

Mohammed moved his family back into his damaged house, gradually patching it up around them. He knew the house had been weakened by the earthquake, and probably would not survive another shock. Conditions were dismal. Dust made them cough. Still, they were surrounded by other Muslims, within walking distance of the mosque, and close to their caste's traditional community hall, and these things reassured them.

Mohammed became a victim of the earthquake more than a year after the event, through no fault of his own. With the move back to the old town, the uncertainties of life there and the struggle for compensation consumed the next two years of his life. For the most part, Muslims, even when they had sufficient resources to do otherwise, eventually elected to stay in the old town—not because they are a secretive minority who cluster together with sinister intentions, as Hindu discourse in the region might often suggest, but because they were encouraged to do so by the prevailing political atmosphere at the time.

Before retirement, Mohammed was an accountant. He used his professional acumen to calculate that a life lived in permanent fear, and with the ever-present threat of violence, was a potentially greater loss than living with the possibility of another earthquake in denuded circumstances. The stories of long knives and the rape and dismemberment of Muslim women in the east of Gujarat left an impression on all those who heard, read or watched them. Those deaths were dishonourable and ghastly. In contrast, death in a future earthquake, or to the slow march of a bronchial disease, was anodyne and routine: it was a death without shame. Such were the conditions at the time that this was a choice Mohammed had to make.

1883 map showing Kutch (Cutch) as an island and Saurashtra (Kattywar) as a peninsula. Modern cartographic practice places less emphasis on the uninhabitable and watery spaces between the bodies of land. The result is that modern Gujarat appears to have more territorial cohesion than in maps such as this one. Source *Letts's Popular Atlas*, statistical & general map of India, Sheet 5, London.

8

VIEW FROM THE EAST

Gujarat came into existence in 1960 following a campaign for the division of the older Bombay State into Gujarat and Maharashtra. There had been political entities known as 'Gujarat' in the past, but the modern state is not coterminous with these. Today's Gujarat is an invented tradition, formed from fragments of other kinds of polity by the will of visionary leaders. Their idea of Gujarat was thrown like a picnic blanket over rough terrain. Since inception, the eastern half of modern Gujarat has wielded most clout. This fact, and others, has meant that distinctions between the different territories from which the state was formed have remained. These have been called upon relatively often, notably when the western parts of the state perceive that their interests are not being represented by those in the east. The earthquake of 2001 once again highlighted some of these fault lines, and to understand the politics of intervention in the aftermath one needs to understand how and why these lines were there and just what was shaken by the earthquake.

The campaign for a separate Gujarat gathered momentum in the 1940s and 1950s. It was then that partisan scholarship adopted the category 'Gujarat' as the frame of reference we understand today. Included in this vision was the 'mainland', or commonly just 'Gujarat', and the 'peninsular' regions of Saurashtra and Kutch. The 'mainland' referred to the eastern portions of the state, the location of the three principal cities: Ahmedabad, Baroda and Surat. After the formation of the state, this region was also chosen for a new purpose-built administrative capital, Gandhinagar. Before Independence in 1947, the mainland was already the centre of power as it was seat of the rulers of the important state of Baroda, while other parts of the 'mainland' were directly under the colonial government which, in different ways, brought those areas closer to the principal sources of authority. The situation in both Kutch and Saurashtra was different. In Saurashtra, there was a patchwork of over two hundred semi-independent states of various sizes. Kutch was different again, and was, for the most part, a single kingdom and tributary to the colonial state, which retained its own courts, currency and traditions.

At Independence, the rulers of Kutch ceded their sovereignty. For a while, Kutch remained a distinct political entity within the new setup, under direct rule from Delhi (and known as a 'Part C state'). This situation remained until 1956, when the large Bombay State was formed out of all the territory lying between Kutch and the city of Bombay. As we shall see later, this loss of autonomy was precipitated by a destructive earthquake which occurred earlier in the same year.

In 1936, a group of lawyers and intellectuals founded the Gujarat Research Society. The society was to gather material on Gujarat, and foster the cultural unity of Gujarati speakers. Initially, the Society's journal defined the term 'Greater Gujarat' (*Maha Gujarat*), as the area 'bonded by ties of common language and culture'.[1] When the anthropologist D.N. Majumdar presented the findings of a 'survey of racial elements' a year later, he used the term 'cultural Gujarat' to refer to the entire area between Kutch and Bombay.[2] In 1947, the journal of the Society provided the following definition: 'Gujarat' consisted of four British districts administered by the Gujarat States Agency in today's Central Gujarat. What the Society called 'Greater Gujarat' included 'Gujarat', Kathiawad and Kutch. '*Brihat* Gujarat', a wonderful term referring to all areas outside Greater Gujarat where Gujaratis lived, which, by then, was just about everywhere in the world.[3]

The Society's aim was to research Gujarat into existence, to create a region through their research. The Society primarily worked towards the definition of Greater Gujarat given in 1947. To this end, surveys were conducted on geography, society and economy, and language.[4] In various ways, the Society appropriated and transformed the technologies of classification and entextualisation which had been used in previous decades by the colonial government.[5] Research was used to shift discursive realities to further the regional cause. However, the journal did not present the three regions of *Maha Gujarat* ('Gujarat', Kathiawad and Kutch) with an even hand. Of the four hundred or so papers carried by the journal during its heyday between 1939 and 1970, only five focus exclusively on Kutch. Of these, three reflect on ecological vulnerability, the others on prehistory and the educational achievements of one of Kutch's rulers. The majority of papers on Saurashtra wonder at its antiquities, customs and prehistory.

In contrast, the Society's characterisation of its own 'mainland' was quite different. The journal contained articles about the problems of housing, labour and education faced by the folk of Ahmedabad and Baroda. The urban sophisticates of the east presented themselves as having no culture worthy of investigation. They were modern and equipped for researching others, having long abandoned their quaint marriage songs, garrulous folktales and inscriptions on boulders. The easterners faced problems of development, and these 'problems' were of quite a different order from the environmental hazards faced by those in the 'backward' (a term commonly used in India) areas such as Kutch. The easterners were alone with civilisation, rather than nature. Saurashtra was presented as an antique land, and Kutch as a zone of environmental vulnerability. These images, of course, served the interests of certain developmental and political paradigms, but they also introduced a distinct form of cultural hierarchy among the constituent parts of *Maha Gujarat*, at least when looking from the east. The easterners enabled themselves to curate the primitive people of the peninsula.

Throughout the 1960s and 1970s, there were rumblings of discontent in Saurashtra against the formation of Gujarat and the monopoly the mainland, or the centre, had on power and political representation. Similar sentiments were to be found in Kutch after the earthquake, as we will see. The core/periphery division was not only a matter of power congealing at the centre because it also reflected quite clear differences in the culture of caste, political style and the history of governance between the sub-regions.[6]

Less explicitly, the representation of Gujarat in the journal, with the values of the eastern urban centre representing the whole, implied a normative Gujarati person, an ideal representative of *Maha Gujarat*: eastern, Gujarati-speaking, and Hindu or Jain (very occasionally Parsi). As we have seen, the paragons against which difference or deviance could be measured and evaluated were the urban professional elites who emerged in the industrial centres during the colonial era. Those who spoke different languages, who saw themselves as part of alternative social or imaginative networks, or who had different ideas about sovereignty, territory or diet, also became peripheral, if not deviant, to the core model of Gujarat.

The work of the Gujarat Research Society was funnelled directly into the political representations of the Maha Gujarat Parisad, an organisation founded in 1952 to further the cause of a separate state. The zenith of such representation came in 1954 in the shape of a memorandum submitted to the States Reorganisation Commission; it was confidently titled: 'Formation of Maha Gujarat'.

The memorandum drew heavily on the research of the society to argue that Gujarat was a 'physiographic' unit, in which geography, language and culture coincided.[7] The authors argued that since ancient times Gujarat was a natural unit of administration in India. This unit had been gradually dismembered from the time Bombay passed to the Portuguese in the sixteenth century. The cohesive nature of the region was further fragmented by the Mughals ('Muslims'), Marathas ('Maharashtrian') and then the British. The British, in particular, created new forms of division within the territory, tearing up Gujarat piece by piece, notably through the new forms of autonomy granted to a large number of princes, especially in Saurashtra and Kutch. These princes generally came to be seen as sycophants to the colonial British. The formation of new Gujarat was thus conceived as a moment of restoration. A former glory was reclaimed from a history of progressive loss.

The sentiments articulated by the society in the mid-twentieth century continued to live in both policy design and the popular imagination after the formation of the state of Gujarat in 1960. These were also very much the ideas the state government brought with them in the name of post-earthquake reconstruction. At one level, Kutch was seen as a peripheral district where life was dominated by hazards and vulnerabilities. At the same time, there was also a clear awareness that Kutchis were not quite like the normative Gujarati implicit in the easterner's vision of the state.

For one thing, they spoke a language that was not Gujarati, but they were also enmeshed in a variety of transnational networks and notions of identity and sovereignty which meant they remained hostile to the very idea of Gujarat.

Looking out on to the Rann of Kutch. Colonial maps labelled the area 'morass'. Part tidal, prone to inundation with the onset of rain, it is thought that the Rann was once part of a river delta. Now, the Rann forms the Indian side of the militarised border with Pakistan, 2008, northern Kutch.

9

BORDERLANDS

Mainland Gujarat looked towards Kutch and saw a remote and backward region. In turn, Kutch saw the east as a source of unwanted political authority and cultural hegemony. As mainland Gujarat looked towards Kutch, it also saw the international border with Pakistan and was reminded of Partition, the division of the sub-continent and the formation of two countries in 1947. In contrast to other regions, particularly Punjab, the partition of Kutch from Sindh was a relatively peaceful event. Culturally, linguistically and ethnographically, there were many connections between the two regions. Kutch probably had more in common with Sindh than with the other regions of modern Gujarat. The geography of that part of the world, however, continued to enforce a degree of separation between Kutch and Sindh through its deserts and water bodies. At the time of Partition, Hindus from Sindh resettled in Kutch and elsewhere. Muslims from Kutch went to Sindh, mostly to Karachi. A great many families were, however, divided by the new border.

The symbolic, imaginary and territorial margins are to the state as the exception is to the rule. States of exception—the patterns of inclusion and exclusion at the behest of the state—are laid bare at the margins and, therefore, margins are a good place to start asking questions if you want to understand what is happening at the centre.[1] The savagery, 'otherness' and wilderness invoked by the concept of 'margin' not only lies outside the safety of the state, but also threatens it from within. Those on the periphery can be used by those at the centre, and thus the marginal and peripheral become fundamental instruments in the design of the project at the centre.

As we have seen, Kutch has been historically marginal within the state of Gujarat. Today's militarised and politicised border with Pakistan has given this marginality extra potency and symbolism. In the imagination of the nation, the border is the fault between Hindu and Muslim lands. Because Partition did not divide the population as cleanly as it did the territory, this fault is rather more discursive and rhetorical than actual. Kutch has a high percentage of Muslims, perhaps 25 per cent, compared to the national average of around 12 per cent.

The Muslims of Kutch, especially those in the northern border regions, have become a precious resource for the Hindu nationalists at the centre. In the early years of the twenty-first century, strengthened by the rhetoric of local politicians and the international language of the so-called 'war on terror', Muslims in Gujarat were widely thought to be disloyal to the country and actively fostering allegiances with Pakistan and Saudi Arabia. They were seen as isolationist and backward because they clustered together in exclusively Muslim residential areas. Such myths were inter-woven with the future of divided Kashmir, the controversial constitutional status of Muslim personal law, ongoing rivalry between Pakistan and India, and disturbing memories of Partition. In addition, there were also the matters of daily life such as differences between Hindu and Muslim diets, religious economies, ritual cycles and the rivalry inherent to the gang cultures of young men, whether it revolved around criminality, competitive kite flying or cricket.

Soon after Narendra Modi came to power in Gujarat in 2001, the sensitivity to religious difference became pathological. All conversations with non-Muslims seemed only to head in one direction: the Muslim problem. I heard Muslims blamed for all manner of social ill, for which sensibly they could not be held responsible. Gaps that were already there widened to the point that many Hindus did not have the kinds of relations with Muslims to disabuse them of the notion that they were bootlegging, beef-eating and incapable of controlling their lustful natures. Quite apart from the daily grind of such convenient stereotypes, the decades after Partition had also given birth to a greater and phantasmagorical spectre of the Muslim who made his home in the borderlands. He brought guns, terrorism and trouble across the border in his gunny bag. He became the marginal Muslim on which the milch government on the Indian side of the border fattened.

This Muslim inhabits the uninhabitable Great Rann of Kutch, a vast area of mud and salt flats between India and Pakistan. From the Indian side, the Rann is only readily accessible by a single road, known, mirthfully, as the 'Ayub Khan Highway': it was built after the Pakistani field marshal's attack was repelled in 1965. The Rann has long been a subject of dispute between the two countries, centred on the tremen-dous legal question of whether it is a land-locked sea, a dead sea, a boundary lake or a unique geographical phenomenon. Each form has different consequences in law for the proper location of a boundary. The Rann is a place of mirages, spectacles and hallucinations, where extreme conditions permeate the senses.[2] There has clearly been a long history of population exchange across the Rann. Today, however, most people believe all that remains is criminalised traffic that places the region in both political and popular imagination on the margins of the nation and morality.[3] It is here, in the badlands of the border, that the otherworldly Muslim haunts. Before the earthquake, he was already infamous, making frequent newspaper headlines across Gujarat. He performed superhuman feats of endurance and defiance, but when captured his power usually absconded to leave only the weathered form of a fisherman or a hum-ble herder in his stead.

None of this is to say that mischief does not occur in the Rann, but to point to the grip that the idea of infiltration has for the imagination. Often it seemed to me as if the whole of Gujarat was taken by the thrill of the chase. In 1999, two years before the earthquake, signs of three 'infiltrators' from Pakistan were detected by footprint experts from the security forces in the Rann. The trackers swooned in the heat and lost their quarry. A reward was announced, and the trio was sighted all along the border. Rumours escalated that the men were criminals with long records, members of the militant organisation Lashkar-e-Toiba, and that they were wanted by the Americans. As the search continued, villagers from the border regions were placed in police custody without trial. On the twenty-fifth day of the pursuit, the now heavily armed militants were spotted re-entering the Rann. The police followed them, but they were forced to return for water. A few days later, those providing me with daily updates reported that the men had returned 'unnoticed' to Pakistan.

Such stories clearly become much larger than the truth at their root. They are touched by magic, such that camels can outrun jeeps and policemen need water but infiltrators can survive without. Although the border is officially closed, it is not hermetically sealed. As the anthropologist Farhana Ibrahim has described, cross-border traffic continues, often for routine family matters.[4] The chimera of anti-national infiltration exaggerates and renders threatening and frightening the figure of the transgressive and marginal non-citizen. These stories are then encouraged in the realm of popular consumption by police officers, journalists and others sympathetic to the cause of constructing an Indian nation in opposition to a Muslim identity.

Following the earthquake in 2001 and flooding in 2003, it became clear that some Hindu nationalist organisations planned to strengthen their support base in the remote border areas in the north of Kutch. Thus, largely driven by rumours they themselves had created, the Sangh Parivar commenced a march northwards along the Ayub Khan Highway. The area was predominantly populated by Harijans and Muslims and, although rather impressionistic, there appears to have been support (in the form of land) for the Harijans to move away from the border regions after the earthquake. Simultaneously, there were attempts to 'de-communitise' Muslims. New roads were built in the area to allow the government access, while public transport services were cut, which restricted the movement of the remaining population. In this scenario, Derek Slade, for example, found Muslims receptive to the offer of a respite from the endlessly and increasingly difficult conditions.

The public–private partnership scheme, which I address in detail in Section 3, allowed religious and cultural organisations to reconstruct villages. The VHP adopted the village at the 'epicentre' of the earthquake and a Hindu religious organisation called the Bochasanwasi Shri Akshar Purushottam Swaminarayan Sanstha, or BAPS for short, took responsibility for a reconstruction programme in Khavda, the largest settlement in the region.[5] Rebuilding in these places was accompanied by the provision of educational services, training classes for rural temple priests and, in the case of Khavda, a new temple dedicated to the deities of the sect. More significantly, these partnerships brought the VHP and a religious organisation as non-governmental agencies into the villages and allowed them to appear as if they had the power to govern, choosing subjects and determining the design, layout and cost of villages.

The settlement at Khavda was built around a new temple. The compound was walled and gated to include those who now aligned themselves with the temple movement and to exclude those who did not. At the inauguration of the settlement, the only Muslim present stood awkwardly on the stage, and spoke in stilted Gujarati about how wonderful the work of the sect had been in the village. At the end of his speech he brought his hands together in front of his chest, bowed his head slightly, and said '*Jai Swaminarayan*', as initiates of the sect routinely and respectfully greet each other. Whatever the man on the stage thought he was doing, the man sitting next to me in the audience tittered at the marvel of a Muslim uttering such words in public, which were closely associated with an exclusive form of Hinduism.

As the crowds dispersed, such was the atmosphere of nationalistic fervour and vigilance that I had stones thrown at me because I was clearly foreign. Bruised and a bit bloodied, on the way back to Bhuj my travelling companion said: 'That Muslim must have been paid. They even got him to praise their god on a public platform. These people have no shame. They will not let him live in that new settlement. Do you know?'

The summit of the Kala Dungar (the black or protective hills) affords an impressive view over the Rann towards Pakistan. Since the 1990s, nearby hamlets have been labelled by the Sangh Parivar as harbouring infiltrators from across the border. In April 2001, Sudarshan, the RSS leader, came to inaugurate a number of post-earthquake developments with the BJP member of parliament for the constituency. The pair stopped in a number of villages to make speeches urging Hindu unity and vigilance against 'foreign powers'. Some months later, the parliamentarian told me, in a rather straightforward tone, that their mission had been to instil a sense of nationalism among the villagers.

A Border People's Welfare Society was formed by the RSS and other interested parties. Subsequently, they pressed for the construction of a public road to the summit of the hill. The ancient temple was demolished and a new larger structure was erected. Signs of syncretic religious practices were removed. Publicity materials now describe the temple as 'The Guardian of the Western Border'. The public face of the deity has been 'Hinduised', as the promoters of the temple have attempted to develop a reputation for divine national protection. Over the last few years, they have also given momentum to an annual pilgrimage to the temple from Bhuj. Hundreds of 'pilgrims' are bussed in to enliven the area with nationalist sentiment, and to celebrate the ritual protection of the highly symbolic border from Muslim predation.

In Gujarat, and within India more generally, Kutch in its entirety is regarded as a border region: a vulnerable zone at the edge of the nation. Therefore, and given the political climate at the time, the prevailing ethos of much of the intervention after the earthquake was to strengthen the border area against Pakistan—not by rolling out more barbed wire, but by attempting to create new citizens of various kinds, with loyalties that lead them to look affectionately to the east: towards Gujarat and the Indian nation.

Although the preoccupation with Muslims died off somewhat towards the end of the noughties, at the time of writing, as then, it is the phantasmagorical mirage of the Muslim in the Rann that must be hunted, but surely never to the point of extinction, for his death might bring an end to the sovereign's power.

Statues of Bhanumati and Shyamji Krishnavarma in conversation before the recreation of 'India House' (Highgate, London) built in scrubby-land on the southern shore of Kutch, 2011, Mandvi.

10

(RE)BIRTH OF AN ICON

In 2003, posters appeared on the fractured walls of Bhuj showing the stern face of a man named Shyamji Krishnavarma. The poster announced the arrival of the mortal remains of a forgotten hero, a scholar, philanthropist, and nationalist freedom fighter. His ashes had been reclaimed from Geneva, where they had lain since his death in 1930. From the moment the remains entered Gujarat, they were joined by a cavalcade of politicians and musicians.

After twelve days in the media spotlight, Krishnavarma re-entered the house into which he was born in 1857 in the coastal town of Mandvi. He was welcomed by the chief minister of Gujarat, Narendra Modi, and L.K. Advani, then deputy leader of the national BJP. Advani lauded the affair, saying that bringing back the revolutionary's ashes would infuse much-needed 'vitamin P' ('p' for patriotism) in today's youth. Outside the house, Congress Party workers and elderly Gandhians observed a silent protest at the return of Krishnavarma.

The promotion of Krishnavarma by the BJP was conceived to challenge and supplant the values of tolerance and non-violence with which Gujarat and the Gandhian legacy of their main political rivals, the Congress, were synonymous. He was intended to become a new hero for the new political landscape of a prosperous and assertive land. In the early years of the twentieth century, Krishnavarma promoted strategic aggression and 'disassociation' (carefully differentiated from Gandhi's 'non-cooperation') as fitting responses to the colonial presence in India. He was outspoken, and made no concession to those he opposed, including Gandhi. Breathing new life into these values was intended to dislodge the obstinate Gandhian political legacy—which for the BJP was both restrictive and difficult to control—with new kinds of malleable political imagery of their own making. In the aftermath of the earthquake, Krishnavarma's name was cultivated amid the ruins.

The Indian National Congress (INC or commonly the Congress) is one of the major political parties in India. It was formed in the late nineteenth century by

77

members of the Theosophist Society, and sits at the centre-left of the country's contemporary political scene. One of its original aims was to ensure greater electoral representation for Indians in the colonial government. Gradually, the party developed a more explicit anti-colonial stance. Mahatma Gandhi was associated with the Congress in various capacities for much of his life. Many of his ideas became synonymous with what the party stood for: non-violence, economic self-sufficiency and cottage industries; it was anti-communal and pro-poor. After the assassination of Gandhi in 1948, Congress held uninterrupted power at the national level until 1977. Under Nehru and later leaders, India embraced other ideas aside from those put forth by Gandhi, but his face remained an icon for the party.

Gandhi's famous image continues to represent personal conviction of the highest order, sacrifice and national freedom. It is impossible to simply discredit many of the qualities and associations for which Gandhi is known because they are so fundamental to the modern history of India. Speaking against Gandhi is still often seen as speaking against the nation, however unfashionable some of his ideas have become. Rival political parties have had to treat his legacy cautiously, generally choosing to remain silent rather than shouting abuse.

Krishnavarma has been raised as an alternative to Gandhi by the BJP in Gujarat. His face has been promoted on tens of thousands of posters: a new visual icon for a different politics. He has been heralded as a fitting hero for a new Gujarat, whose revolutionary ideas on freedom for India were spawned by the classical language and literature of Hindu civilisation. Krishnavarma's political creed, it is claimed, although radical, was fundamentally rooted in Indian traditions and religious understandings.

In the second half of the nineteenth century, Krishnavarma's father left Kutch to seek fortune in the colonial city of Bombay. Atypically, the father's failure to make good was noted.[1] As if to compensate, another merchant, also from Kutch, developed a great interest in the boy's intellect, and sponsored him to study at the English-language university in Bombay and at a Sanskrit-language college. Perhaps, like the boy himself, from that moment Krishnavarma's biographers lose sight of the life, and death, of his father. Having proved himself as a Sanskrit scholar and efficient networker in Bombay, Krishnavarma then went on to study law and to assist a professor of classical Indian languages at the University of Oxford. Later, he enrolled as an advocate in Bombay and went on to hold an administrative position in the state of Rutlam.

Krishnavarma, like others of his era, also saw opportunity in the industry and technology of cotton. He invested in processing factories around Ajmer in the late 1880s. He was successful in this venture, and could live without further work for the rest of his life.[2] In his earlier years in Bombay, Krishnavarma associated with the social and religious reformers.[3] Now in Ajmer, he took over the management of their printing presses. Relations quickly turned sour, however, and the reformers dissolved his powers. Next, he went to serve as the chief minister in Udaipur in 1893, before moving to Junagadh in 1894.

Politics on the slopes of Junagadh's Mount Girnar were cut-throat, and Krishnavarma was soon embroiled in rumours of corruption and, finally, it seems, in a conspiracy which circled around the use of state resources for the benefit of a British acquaintance from his Oxford days. The friend seemingly betrayed him, and Junagadh and the local British administration plotted against him. Krishnavarma was dismissed, losing his salary, his friend, probably his pride, and almost certainly his trust in the British.

In 1897, however, Krishnavarma left India for good, settling in Highgate in north London. In 1905, he formed the Society for Home Rule in India, opened a hostel for Indian students called India House, and started a monthly journal (an 'organ of freedom') called the *Indian Sociologist*. The journal was circulated in Europe and India, and largely carried Krishnavarma's own opinions on the colonial occupation of India. He wrote boldly and with tenacity in favour of political assassinations and armed struggle in the name of independence. He considered the ethics of dynamite, and the revolutionary potential of noiseless guns.[4]

Unsparingly, he denounced others involved in movements for a free India, especially those he saw as cooperating with the colonial government. Gradually, he both distanced and alienated himself from many of those involved in the freedom movement. To give one example, in 1908 he accused Annie Besant, a former ally in the freedom struggle, of blowing 'hot and cold', and denounced her as 'one of the most subtle and inveterate enemies of real political freedom in India'.[5] Besant did not forget the insult, and in 1910 described Krishnavarma as a 'wretched man' and a 'coward', who pushed boys to martyrdom from the safety of Europe.

Unsurprisingly, Krishnavarma's activities brought him to the attention of the British government. His journal was labelled a 'seditious rag' which 'openly glorified murder', and the hostel in Highgate became 'notorious as a centre of sedition'.[6] His case was discussed in parliament and, fearing arrest, Krishnavarma decamped for Paris. In France, amid death threats, the harassment of 'Indian Government detectives abroad' and other political intrigues, Krishnavarma continued his anti-colonial mission. He moved to Geneva with the onset of the First World War, and died there in 1930.[7] Krishnavarma was not entirely forgotten in death, as some of his supporters tended the places he had rested in life. It took the jolt of the earthquake in Gujarat in 2001 to rekindle memories of him in India.

Amid the reconstruction of Kutch, the rebuilt airport and new university were named after Krishnavarma.[8] A few years after the earthquake, at the inauguration of the new civic hospital (the flagship project mounted on springs to the awe of the local population), the then prime minister, Atal Bihari Vajpayee, took the opportunity to announce the republication of a celebratory biography of Krishnavarma.[9] In subsequent years, Narendra Modi has given speeches at Krishnavarma's birthplace in Mandvi, and has championed new statues and a memorial park in Krishnavarma's name.

On the surface, Krishnavarma was an ideal discovery for the BJP, for his life and work seemed the perfect counter to everything the party held to have gone wrong with India in the twentieth century. Krishnavarma funded the early studies in London of Vinayak Damodar Savarkar, one of the most outspoken Hindu nationalist voices of the freedom struggle (Savarkar was later also implicated in the assassination of Gandhi). Krishnavarma opposed the Congress because it was dominated by what he called the 'Anglo-Indian autocracy', in whose interests it was to let the British remain in India.[10] Furthermore, the scholarships he offered students came with the condition that the Indian graduate holding a fellowship under this scheme should not accept any post, office, emoluments or service under the British government after his return to India. At the time, this too must have seemed to undermine the Congress, which put great store in its representatives holding top jobs. Yet, in 2003, it was Congress politicians who led the protests against the false 'saffronisation' of the image of Krishnavarma when his ashes were returned 'home'.

It was repeated loudly and often in 2003 that Krishnavarma opposed Gandhi's politics. In the pages of the London editions of his journal, the *Indian Sociologist*, Krishnavarma wrote against Gandhi twice. In 1908, he criticised Gandhi for siding with the British in the Boer War. But, as the trade unionist and scholar Indulal Yajnik dryly notes in his biography of Krishnavarma, the justice of the Boers' cause must have been much clearer from the drawing rooms of the capital of the Empire than amid the confusion of Southern Africa.[11] At the time, Krishnavarma wrote:

Mr Gandhi is such an estimable person that one does not like to quarrel with him. His gentility and suavity of manners endear him to all … Our personal regard for him does not, however, debar us from exposing him for the mischief he is doing by his public acts and utterances in the cause of political freedom.[12]

He went on to suggest Gandhi was 'misguided' and 'weak-minded', for the Boers' defeat 'served them right' because they had trusted the British in the first place. In this instance, Krishnavarma was criticising Gandhi for his cooperation with the British; non-cooperation was, of course, something Gandhi himself would later use to great effect. Later, when Gandhi was arrested for demonstrating against the lack of rights for Indians in South Africa, Krishnavarma opined that the misery of imprisonment might be curative, and would remind Gandhi he was a voteless helot in colonial South Africa.[13]

Krishnavarma's second criticism of Gandhi was his response to an editorial published in the newspaper *Indian Opinion* on 26 July 1914. In the piece, Gandhi quoted T.H. Huxley to the following effect: 'The law of survival of the fittest is the law of the brute, but the law of self-sacrifice is the law of evolution for the man'. Huxley was a biologist and palaeontologist, and also known as 'Darwin's Bulldog' for his public promotion of evolutionary ideas. In the quote, Gandhi contrasted the brute survival of Huxley with the Christian creeds of turning the other cheek in the face of aggression and loving thy neighbour unconditionally. Krishnavarma thought the piece 'mischievous' and 'deluded' and asked: 'How can there be social self-preservation, while internal and external enemies are continuously at work to destroy it, unless an effort is made individually and collectively to check or restrain them using force defensively against force used aggressively?' Krishnavarma failed to see the logic in offering additional cheeks for an enemy to smite while calculating to thwart the same enemy.

Unlike the practical divergence of political philosophy suggested by the difference between the terms 'non-cooperation' and 'disassociation', this second criticism of Gandhi reveals a more fundamental divergence in thought on the nature of the self and the relationship between self and society. In Krishnavarma's view, the sociologist Herbert Spencer was the intellectual champion of the era. Spencer was a conservative sociologist and political theorist, influenced by social evolution and the idea of universal law. Krishnavarma, however, read Spencer as an anti-imperialist, having courageously pleaded the case of India.

Krishnavarma attributed to Spencer a condemnation of the use of native soldiers to extend native subjection, the salt monopoly and the merciless taxation of the peasantry. Spencer had shown the British Empire to operate on the basis of self-interest, calling the English a 'sociophagous', or a society-eating nation. Furthermore, Spencer seemed to support the idea that Indians should throw off the foreign yoke because the country would be in a better position without the British—and Britain in a better position without India.[14]

Krishnavarma seems to have had an almost obsessive relationship with Spencer's ideas.[15] He spoke at Spencer's graveside and established a memorial lectureship in Oxford.[16] The title banner of his journal always carried a brace of quotes from Spencer. The first was from his *Principles of ethics*: 'Every man is free to do that which he wills, provided he infringes not the equal freedom of any other man'.[17] According to Krishnavarma, this was the first principle of the fundamental truth of social science. The promotion of Spencer's libertarian mandate succinctly expresses what the pages of the journal reveal at length: Krishnavarma was not fighting for the poor or downtrodden, but for freedom and for the right to self-determination under a sovereign. This is probably why he had no time for other critical thinkers of the age, such as Karl Marx.

The second quote from Spencer carried by the journal was from *The study of sociology*: 'Resistance to aggression is not simply justifiable but imperative. Non-resistance hurts both altruism and egoism'.[18] Krishnavarma was quiet on what he took from this quote for many years, choosing to explain it only in 1914 as part of his criticism of Gandhi's editorial in *Indian Opinion*. He led the assault with the following from Spencer:

The absurdity of unqualified altruism becomes, indeed, glaring on remembering that it can be extensively practised only if in the same society there coexist one moiety altruistic and one moiety egoistic. Only those who are intensely selfish will allow their fellows habitually to behave to them with extreme unselfishness. If all are duly regardful of others, there are none to accept the sacrifices which others are ready to make. If a high degree of sympathy characterises all, no one can be so unsympathetic as to let another receive positive or negative injury that he may benefit. So that pure altruism in a society implies a nature which makes pure altruism impossible, from the absence of those towards whom it may be exercised![19]

Underpinning differences in opinion on the utility of violence and the efficacy of relations with colonials were differing ideas about the nature of both ideal and practical selves.[20] Gandhi advocated giving in order to take the nation. Krishnavarma, in contrast, with his own version of Spencer's ideas, thought this nonsense. For Krishnavarma, this was akin to aiding the colonial oppressor; instead, he pressed home the importance of individual radicalism.

Historians have traced Gandhi's selective use of his Saurashtrian heritage and values in his political methodology, and these values also resonated with certain sections of society in Ahmedabad when Gandhi returned to India from South Africa in 1915.[21] Others have spelled out the effect on Gandhi of meeting educated and cosmopolitan Indians and India-sympathisers in London at the turn of the twentieth century. Encounters with the theosophists and others, Krishnavarma included, led Gandhi to develop a distinctly Indian political philosophy which took Hinduism seriously and countered the revolutionary emphasis on Western rationality. In contrast, in his journal, Krishnavarma largely eschewed religious and cultural idioms of political expression. As a self-fashioned Indian sociologist, he wrote of 'Indian' rather than 'Hindu' nationalism.

Krishnavarma's biographers have generally read his early career as one of rags to riches. With only the slightest shift of emphasis we could see him as an opportunist, who perhaps engaged in corruption, rather than merely being an innocent victim of it. We could also see Krishnavarma as a troubled man, whose difficult childhood led to a frustrated and angry adulthood. He carried with him no obvious friendships, and remained childless. His high-handed, almost autocratic, way of dealing with those around him frequently led to controversy. When trouble came, Krishnavarma invariably turned his back and decamped for pastures new. While this might be thought of as cowardly, or as revealing a limit of Krishnavarma's political or interpersonal skills, he himself wrote something to the effect that 'it is better not to put your foot in the mud at all than to put it in and wash it'.[22]

Along with Krishnavarma's mortal remains came some rather eclectic ideas about the self and the nature of individual freedom. In the heyday of his political career, he was influenced as much by Victorian sociology as he was Indian nationalism. He advocated a political self, which sits uneasily alongside many of the greater ideals of the political Hinduism he has been called upon by the BJP to support. It might also be the case that his vitriolic modes of expression were simply born of personal eccentricity as much as they signified his sacrifice to the nation—as is frequently suggested in Gujarat today.

His principal biographer, Indulal Yajnik, was probably correct in asserting Krishnavarma's politics were only possible at the time because he spoke from genteel London. Likewise, his reincarnation in Gujarat is only possible today because much of him has been left behind in Europe. Regardless of the evidence about his personality and ideas that it is possible to glean from reading what he actually wrote, the claims made today on his individual radicalism in Gujarat suggest an active and instrumental will within the dominant political classes. They have aimed to transform the way people relate to one another, pursue their aims, and deal with those who oppose them. Social Darwinism has once again become popular.

Krishnavarma's name has been associated with a selection of ideas which have been imposed on a beleaguered population in the hope that they will stick. In this instance, the initiative has the weight of the Gujarat state and the party political machinery of the BJP behind it. In 2010, Narendra Modi inaugurated a remarkable memorial to Krishnavarma amid coastal scrub to the east of Mandvi. The complex is architecturally bold and graceful, including a gallery depicting the campaign to return Krishnavarma's ashes, and scenes from his life.

My driver initially thought the building was a memorial to the work Modi had done in Gujarat because there are so many images of him on display. Uniformed security guards then asked my driver whether I had come to cause trouble, given that Krishnavarma had been so hostile to foreigners. I had lived in Mandvi, a cosmopolitan Indian Ocean trading town, for nearly two years in the late 1990s, and was jarred by how readily the new ideas of hostility and xenophobia had taken root.

The centrepiece of the complex is a concrete recreation of India House, the three-storey Victorian property in north London which Krishnavarma ran as a hostel for students. From a distance, the very familiar (to me) architectural proportions rise wonderfully from the marshy scrubland. Inside the house are further galleries displaying the portraits of other select heroes of the nation, with whom Krishnavarma was either associated in life or with whom the curators of the exhibition wanted to associate his image.

When I last visited the site in 2011, hoards of school children had been brought by bus to visit the complex at the expense of the local state. I talked to children who were not old enough to remember the earthquake. Neither would they ever know, nor be able to imagine, a time when the name, face and creed of Krishnavarma were not synonymous with Gujarat.

SECTION 3

VILLAGES

Going back in time again to shortly after the earthquake, the neo-liberal agreement allowed private organisations to adopt villages. Many saw this as an opportunity to create what they thought would be the best of all possible worlds. Some laid out their vision with language. Others used concrete and architecture to get their message across. There was disagreement over where the epicentre of the earthquake had been. Along with the keys to new houses, devotional Hinduism, metropolitan nationalism and integral humanism were among the ideas presented to villagers.

Many new structures provoked questions about the appropriateness of the design for the local culture. In the foreground is a tradiitional form of shelter, preferred, in this instance, to the new concrete house, which was used to keep animals, 2004, Indraprashta.

11

VILLAGE 'ADOPTION'

The first reconstruction package announced by the government was for rural areas. It permitted 'suitably qualified' organisations to reconstruct destroyed villages in new locations.[1] On the whole, villagers did not want to move and they demonstrated angrily. The distant new sites, they reasoned, would put them far from agricultural land, temples and graveyards—things villagers held dear but which could not be readily moved. Perhaps underlying these pragmatic concerns was a more general fear of the loss of the symbiosis between people and their place. There was endless talk about how the United Nations did not support relocation in the aftermath of tragedy because it added a new layer of distress to the lives of those already injured. In the face of criticism, the reconstruction policy was revised so that, where possible, the new village would be on the same or similar site. This public–private partnership scheme colloquially became known as the 'village adoption scheme'. The private partner was to reconstruct the village, with up to half of the basic cost provided by the state.

The reconstruction of rural Kutch is a tangle of fascinating stories, incorporating the extremes of aftermath cynicism and humanitarian excellence. The scheme opened the way for a range of interest groups to reconstruct villages, largely as they saw fit. A vast number of Indian and overseas aid organisations, religious groups, political parties, state governments, social campaign movements, construction contractors and captains of industry stepped into the mêlée. Tens of thousands of houses were to be built anew in hundreds of separate locations.[2] Basic infrastructural and building regulations were specified by the government, but in practice, and in the end, these were often unevenly applied.

The scramble for the rights to give, distribute and receive aid allowed for the expression of historical animosities as well as new forms of political aspiration. The violence of 2002 and the upsurge of communal politics led to the hardening of the lines between religious communities. As we will see, in some instances, Muslims were excluded from new settlements due to the discriminatory ideas promoted by private organisations. These instances are significant and should not be forgotten, even though Islamic relief and development organisations often compensated for such neglect. I also think that discrimination against Muslims was convenient and well publicised, for not only was it broadly acceptable to mainstream Hindu society at the time, it also distracted attention from other kinds of social engineering and injustice.

The discussions of the aftermath enlivened the otherwise invisible connections between the villages of Kutch, other parts of India and the world. The earthquake revealed how, although some villages were well catered for in terms of housing and infrastructure, for most of the year they were largely uninhabited because the 'villagers' lived and worked elsewhere. The earthquake unmasked two of the largest settlements in eastern Kutch as suburbs or satellites of Mumbai, with little or no connection to the rest of modern Gujarat. These 'villages', along with a number of others, were reconstructed by the government of Maharashtra. The earthquake also revealed the global nature of society in Kutch, as signboards advertising good works charted a myriad of diasporic connections. The history of a diaspora, to East Africa, Europe and the United States, appeared as a series of signs in the hedgerows and along the byways of the region.

Those villages which elected to reconstruct their own houses (the so-called 'owner-driven approach') according to their own preferences generally seem to have produced more sensible results than those built by contractors and other outside agencies. This method also encouraged the refinement of building skills and improved the awareness of housing design and safety as people discussed these issues in public and, in the process, were forced to think about them. The model also clearly benefited the local economy, providing work to labourers and artisans, and profit to those dealing in building materials. In this scheme, people were also often permitted to construct a building they wanted. It is unclear to me whether this, on the whole, gave new life to vernacular housing styles or quickened their disappearance. Many houses were rebuilt using the owner-driven model, often facilitated by a private organisation.[3] In this scheme, cash payments were released by the government in stages, pegged to surveys of the building: 40 per cent at the preparatory stage, and when the walls were in place, the remaining amount was paid on completion.

In other villages, on which I primarily focus, construction was led by contractors and other agencies. In the process, varieties of new social, political and religious ideologies were inscribed on rural Kutch. Such interventions were frequently associated with religious expansion and political opportunism. At the time, and not only to me, these efforts seemed pernicious—exploitative of the vulnerability of the stunned, dispossessed and the vertiginous. The aftermath seemed to spell the end to village life as it had been practised in the past. Flying into Bhuj in 2003, the extent of the reconfiguration of the countryside was already clearly visible. Many villages were of two parts, the old section clustered around temples and water tanks, and divided by meandering roads, and the new part some distance away with houses laid out in neat grids.

As those working in the field struggled to find solutions for collapsed villages, they realised that there could not be just a single policy to fit all approaches because the village as a single sociological or geographical entity was a chimera. The difficulties of humanitarians were greatest when they insisted that there was such a thing as a village—rather than a range of interest groups with often quite different geographic loyalties. The village existed because you could see it, name it and drive into it; it did not exist when you tried to engage it in conversation. As I have mentioned, some villages were, in part, owned by those living in Mumbai, London and New Jersey. The views of such people as to what should be done were often very different from those of the villagers who remained at home. There was also a range of more parochial divisions within villages, which further complicated the process of deciding what the future should hold.

Consequently, the adoption scheme polarised interest groups in many villages. In some cases, settlements divided on the basis of caste. In others, wealthier sections of the population spurned offers of reconstruction, viewing offers as paltry, and the style, size and quality of the houses as inadequate. When this happened, some opted for financial compensation rather than the reconstruction package. In yet other cases, some groups within villages chose self-funded reconstruction programmes, unfettered by budget restrictions and bothersome government surveyors.

The adoption scheme produced competition between private interest groups for particular villages and between villages for the attention of particular sponsoring organisations. Organisations with affinities to the politics of the ruling government were able to adopt high-profile villages, such as those at the epicentre and along the main highway, forming something of a saffron strip between Bhuj and Bhachau. Villages with certain social, caste and religious configurations were more appealing to some private agencies. Conversely, villagers quickly learned that if they supported an initial expression of interest from a private organisation, they were not bound to their commitment. If they could see that a neighbouring village was benefiting from a greater endowment than their own, they could approach that generous organisation and request them to reconstruct their village, and a kind of philanthropic gazumping game started. Both kinds of competition ultimately relied on the approval of the state, and this has had clear consequences.

There were discussions about the radical transformation of housing design to deny the ravage of future earthquakes: fibre glass domes and lunar exploration technologies. In the end, concrete and steel predominated. Even so, a wide range of different house styles appeared across the district. Inevitably, many of these new structures provoked questions about the appropriateness of the design for the local culture. There were technical issues: houses stored heat, utilised poor-quality materials and incorporated shoddy construction methods. There were practical issues: inadequate elevation led to monsoon inundations, and contractors vanished with advance payments, leaving works incomplete. Other houses were perceived to be inappropriate for rural or agricultural lifestyles, lacking suitable storage spaces for livestock, fodder, grain, tools and so forth. I have seen villages in which the 'beneficiaries' have preferred to let their animals live in the new house while they camp outside in the open air—much, perhaps, as they would have done before the earthquake and before they had a bank account and a house.

There were discussions of other 'cultural' problems relating to the provision of rural houses. Such discussions succinctly illustrate some of the profound contradictions and thus the intractable problems that were intertwined with the rebuilding of rural areas. As a condition of their loans, the development banks required bank accounts to be opened in joint names to promote equal gender access to property. This measure was accompanied by a mass initiative to sensitise rural populations to gender issues. At a lower level of intervention, many organisations attempted to understand and thus work with local ideas of culture and gender. The tension between these two quite different aims forced intervening agencies to informally determine 'good' and 'bad' local gender practices—along with all the attendant problems that such misplaced value judgments entail. Then, of course, many intervening organisations had their own ideas about gender politics and what sensitisation should mean.

Was it a problem if the design of a house did not allow established gender roles to be enacted? Open-fronted houses, for example, offered inadequate levels of privacy or seclusion for women when considered in local terms. Some houses were constructed with kitchen blocks at the front, when ideally they would have been open at the back to hide the woman and protect the purity of the hearth. Should intervening agencies be perpetuating the seclusion of women through their housing design? Should or could they interfere with gender relations within families? I will leave these questions open.

In many villages built by contractors, the traditional village form—a nucleus with clusters of houses reflecting caste, religious and material distinctions—has largely (especially along the main highway) been replaced by uniform rows of houses built on a grid pattern. Some villages have been renamed to reflect the values of the adopting organisation. New colonies and sub-settlements in older villages have also been given new names and separate entrance gates to distinguish them from the settlement of which they were previously a part. Sharp divisions along the lines of religion and caste have been inscribed into numerous villages; this is after all how villagers choose to live. If you are going to ask a villager to participate in the decision as to whether a kitchen is built to the front or rear of a house, then it seems only right to ask them who they would want as a neighbour, however opposed, in principle, a development organisation might be to the hierarchy of caste or the discriminatory potential of religion. In this sense, the participation of villagers in reconstruction (at least when 'participation' meant to solicit opinion) opened up a Pandora's box of social division, which, otherwise, was latent and casually conceived. Residential distinctions between castes and sects might have been vague before the earthquake, but the approach to participatory reconstruction in rural areas enlivened such distinctions and encouraged them in the planning of new villages.

In a number of villages built by a Catholic organisation, ceramic plaques were set in the walls of each house displaying the logo of the sponsoring organisation and either the words 'lab' and 'sub' or the number '786'. This initiative started as an attempt at being 'sensitive' to local customs. Hindus often place stickers or designs each side of their doorways, and Muslims may decorate their house with the number, which is a numerological representation of the first verse of the Koran and thought to attract god's grace. In this case, the rather sinister effect, given the political climate described in previous sections, was to corporatise the design, and to mark for all to see the religion of the occupants of every house in the village.

Rural reconstruction was run through with what development specialists variously call 'elite capture', 'selection bias' and 'interest group capture', whereby some sections of the village benefit more than others because their needs are reflected more than the others in the goods or services provided.[4] Some villagers brokering public–private partnerships have built handsome residences for themselves from the spoils. In contrast, in a village adopted by Kutchi Jains living in Mumbai, Mahavir, the central deity of Jainism has been installed in a new temple above the head of the village deity, establishing a hierarchy of gods, mirroring the worldly hierarchy of patrons and clients.

Together, these examples illustrate how various forms of division and inequality have been incorporated into the aftermath by the interaction of the affected and the intervener. Fundamentally, interventions were based on the restoration of a schematised model of what had been lost, rather than on the basis of need or for the promotion of greater social equality. Compensation levels were based on pre-existing property relations: landless labourers being restored with less than marginal farmers, who were restored with less than small farmers and artisans, who were, in turn, restored with less than those owning more than four hectares of land. Similar forms of compensation also translated into some, but not all, of the villages in which housing was built by NGOs. In these instances, the size of landholding did not always correspond to the caste position of the beneficiaries, and this too led to endless wrangling. It was not possible, for one example out of many permutations, to allocate a row of houses to members of the same caste, but then to build different sized houses within that row because members of the caste owned varying amounts of land. The resolution of such disputes led to many differentiated solutions, which often took the reconstruction programme far away from the specifications of the underlying policy.

In addition to the logistical and moral problems associated with the provision of rural housing, there is also another story to be explored here. The scheme for rural reconstruction allowed organisations to adopt entire villages, of which houses were but a part. To focus only on the design of the house is to miss entirely the ambition some organisations had for the design of a village as a whole. Let me give one brute example in order to pave the way towards the more elaborate examples of the following three chapters.

A temple association run by people of Gujarati origin in the United States constructed a village of huts with thatched roofs for the population of its adopted village. The huts were shoddy exhibition pieces, badly built to appear authentic, but without traditional construction methods. The design of the village and the message of the information signs scattered around it incorporated a confusion of Gandhian notions of self-sufficiency and conceptions about the innocence of rural life. In addition, the villagers themselves were supposed to live almost as if exhibits. The village was conceived of as a 'drive-in' for tourists in search of handicrafts and traditional rural life—much as many returning diasporic Gujaratis like to experience village life. In essence, they built the kind of village that a motorised, wealthy, Gujarati-American would like to visit when on tour back home.

The need to imagine a future for stricken villages prompted bold thoughts. How can we remake the best of all possible worlds in rural Gujarat? In a sense, and as I will show, various understandings of the ideal nation offered a straightforward (from the perspective of its proponents) paradigm for some planners, social workers and charitable institutions. Using the values of the ideal nation it became possible to build villages with particular kinds of schools and social services, just as it became possible to determine who would populate the settlement and how different kinds of people would be distributed throughout its carefully designed streets. Layers of brokers and managers entered rural life to negotiate resources and settle disputes. Often such people were dressed in the robes of religion or the cloth of party politics. As we will see, the partnership scheme allowed many private organisations to take on functions resembling those previously administered by the state. In the process, the state was re-imagined at the grassroots.

Sign directing attention to the village and sponsors of Narayan Nagar, 2003.

12

SERVICE

There are many strong traditions of philanthropy and charitable work in India.[1] Many of these are at the core of the daily routines of individuals leading a good life. There is no single explanation for the logic of giving because different religious and philosophical traditions have their own terms. In the same way, there are differences in the ways caste and class groups understand and organise charity. At the broadest level, however, the *dana* (giving, of which there are different types) of Hinduism is a central part of *dharma* (or religious duty). Giving may include *seva*, which is often translated as 'service'. Such service is ideally non-reciprocal and non-self-interested (*nishkam seva*, selfless service). From the point of view of those who hold such ideas, service is a form of righteousness, which, when done with a correct understanding of god, strengthens the soul, burns away the sins of previous lives, and can lead to an individual's detachment from the mundane world. Service is nothing less than the path to liberation.

Through service, the practitioner accrues merit, which, in turn, relates to *karma*. The theory of *karma* is that every action has a consequence, so a person's condition is determined by good or bad deeds in this and previous lives. In turn, *karma* is inseparable from *dharma* as a moral code through which good and bad actions are evaluated. It usually follows that unfortunate and premature deaths (murders and accidents for example) are understood as the fruit of bad deeds.

Traditional forms of giving or service include donations of time or resources to priests, temples and the poor. Devotional religious movements now also see merit in working in social development: education, health, water conservation and, indeed, relief at the time of disasters. The idea of service has also long been a form of community building and social reform. Some organisations have enjoined the ideals of *seva* with the broader aim of strengthening the nation or some other cause.

In the aftermath of the earthquake, many intervening organisations arrived with extremely refined senses of the ways in which social service is a part of spiritual existence. They had websites, books and pamphlets explaining the ideals of their activities. Thus, for example, giving a blanket, constructing a temple, or sharing the teaching of a guru with the non-initiated was not simply 'aid' or socially meritorious; these actions, if performed selflessly, were perfect spiritual acts—they were, in short, god's work.

There is also a strong tradition of hospitality in Gujarat, in which the guest is idealised as a deity. This idiom is widespread and not confined to particular religious traditions. A visitor may bring gifts, but it is up to the host to water, feed and listen earnestly to what the visitor has to say. There is largesse at stake: 'while you are in my place I will provide everything for you'; but these are also the things one does as a part of living well and, also, as one aspect of the tradition of service outlined above. In the aftermath, these forms of accommodation ran into difficulty, especially in rural areas where the relationship between villagers and guests was institutionalised by public–private partnerships. Villagers remained keen to show that they were well mannered and lived good lives. Their own offers of hospitality were not, however, always understood or even seen. Visitors competed to provide things and fought to prove their resourcefulness. Hosts became recipients. Such topsy-turvy arrangements did not lead to crisis, but contributed quite directly to the atmosphere of absurdity, confusion and plenty.

I have already suggested that those affected by the disaster were more aware of the cultural battles waged in the aftermath than those who came to intervene. Differences were apparent to them because they could feel and see that those who intervened wanted them to start doing certain things differently. In some instances, those who arrived would not let villagers act as hosts. The interveners came with their own ideas as to what should be done, and how (if they did not have such ideas, then presumably they would never have made it as far as Kutch).

Some interventions in Gujarat were brutal and strategic. Others were said to be saturated in the love of humanity and god in all forms. In all instances, intervention, whether straightforwardly cynical or conducted in the name of service, had consequences which were, one might hope, incidental and secondary to the purposes of the adopting organisation.

During the winter of 2003, I visited the village of Jiyapar regularly with my friend Dilip. We both conducted a series of interviews with some of the men who lived there, including Visanji, who sold building materials, and Vishram, who had retired; others contributed to the conversation as they passed by. The village is on the western periphery of the zone severely affected by the earthquake. There were no fatalities reported to us and the damage to property was moderate when compared to other locations. The visible ruination of the village was caused as much by abandonment as it was by the quaking of the earth. The village had been adopted for reconstruction by Bochasanwasi Shri Akshar Purushottam Swaminarayan Sanstha (BAPS). This organisation is one of the branches of Hinduism in western India to follow the teaching of Lord Swaminarayan. The movement has become popular among the Gujarati diaspora. Consequently, BAPS has hundreds of temples throughout the world, including a major one in London and a huge complex in New Delhi. The ethos of the movement is best introduced with its own words:

[BAPS] is a socio-spiritual Hindu organization with its roots in the Vedas. It was revealed by Bhagwan Swaminarayan (1781–1830) in the late 18th century and established in 1907 by Shastriji Maharaj (1865–1951). Founded on the pillars of practical spirituality, the BAPS reaches out far and wide to address the spiritual, moral and social challenges and issues we face in our world. Its strength lies in the purity of its nature and purpose. BAPS strives to care for the world by caring for societies, families and individuals. This is done by mass motivation and individual attention, through elevating projects for all, irrespective of class, creed, colour or country … Today, a million or more Swaminarayan followers begin their day with puja and meditation, lead upright, honest lives and donate regular hours in serving others. No Alcohol, No Addictions, No Adultery, No Meat, No Impurity of body and mind are their five lifetime vows. Such pure morality and spirituality forms the foundation of the humanitarian services performed by BAPS.[2]

In Gujarat, BAPS is a high-profile organisation. Its most well-known temple is in Gandhinagar, close to the seat of state power. BAPS runs campaigns throughout the state aimed at the mass transformation of society. In the immediate aftermath of the earthquake, the tiered and widespread organisational structure of the movement meant that it was at the forefront of relief efforts. Through public–private partnerships, BAPS was involved in the construction of nine villages and a number of other reconstruction projects, often relying on funds raised overseas. Many of the other big agencies working in the region adopted clusters of villages, or concentrated their efforts in particular localities in order to maximise efficiency. In contrast, BAPS adopted villages spaced throughout the entire earthquake-affected region. In most cases, the 'adopted' site was close to a well-serviced highway. In all cases, BAPS also constructed a temple at the centre of the village.

BAPS's intervention in Jiyapar was socially divisive. What happened in this village highlights many issues relating to property and other rights raised by the village adoption scheme more generally. BAPS built a new village, with fine houses and an excellent infrastructure, which it called Narayan Nagar, after the founding deity in the movement's local pantheon. The new settlement was some distance away from the damaged village, although within its original administrative and revenue boundary, and was not therefore technically a 'relocation'. Those Dilip and I interviewed had not wanted to move to the new village. They had not wanted to leave their undamaged or moderately damaged homes; nor did they understand why they should do so for the convenience of an 'outside' religious organisation.[3]

In our conversations, Vishram and Visanji often seemed to be thinking aloud about what was happening to relations between themselves and those who had moved to the new village, what it meant for the village to have split, and what consequences there might be in the future. For much of the time, we were seated on rope beds in the shade of a large tree near to what had been the centre of the village. On other occasions, we wandered around visiting sites of particular interest or dispute. This was a story that the men wanted to tell. It was clear from the outset that they had honed their case in previous conversations with journalists, administrators and politicians.

In what follows, I have reproduced sections of one of our conversations. The anxieties, confusions and ambiguities evident in the edited transcript were widespread and not confined to them or their village. According to Vishram, no one in Jiyapar followed BAPS before the earthquake. He said that some of the people who had moved to 'NN' (Narayan Nagar) had recently started to attend the new temple because the saints had said 'adopt this religion, for only then will you get a house'. According to him, in the first village meeting after the earthquake in March 2001, it was decided that no one would leave the old village.

Vishram: Then we decided that the poor, those who could not dream of owning their own houses, should be allowed to take up the offer of a new house. We then passed a resolution saying that those who wished to move could do so ... However, the process was hijacked by vested interests and the letter that was actually sent to the government stated that we all wished to move and that we wished for BAPS to adopt our village. We did not all wish to move, and very few people then knew what BAPS was.

We appealed. Here is the letter [he took the letter to show me from a bulging file of paperwork he had collected since the earthquake—others must have had other files archiving and tracing different stories]. We complained to the Collector [the chief administrator of Kutch], arguing that we had not opted for Package 1 [the relocation of the village] but for Package 2 [the reconstruction of the village in situ].[4] The village council misrepresented what we had agreed. Package 2 granted us household compensation, and allowed us to stay where we were to rebuild our own houses. We took an 85–year-old man to the Collector's office in Bhuj to say that he did not want to move from the place where he had spent his entire life. We filed petition after petition, but no one seemed to give us a fair hearing. We thought the rule was that if 70 per cent of houses had been damaged only then was a village to be relocated. In Jiyapar, only 49 per cent of the houses suffered damage, and much of this was slight. The rules did not seem to apply to our village. We felt hopeless. There were other problems too.

Let me explain these clearly, and then you will understand the situation. Mr Lakhamsinh's house was classified as a 'G1 house', meaning it was not badly damaged by the earthquake.[5] However, he decided to move to the BAPS village. There, the financial aid equivalent to Rs 96,000 was paid [as per Vishram's understanding of the rules of compensation] but, according to his G1 classification, he was only entitled to compensation of Rs 3,000. In this way, the government incurred a huge loss on payments towards a house to which Mr Lakhamsinh is not entitled. Even we do not understand the whole situation. Then there are also the cases of G2 and G3 houses, many of these people have moved to NN and the government has paid for their houses.

Under the reconstruction legislation, the government is to give 50 per cent towards building a new house and the *sanstha* [sect] is to provide the rest. This means that for each family that has moved to NN, the government has paid Rs 48,000. In our village, there were 329 buildings, including temples. After the earthquake, 76 were classified as G4 and 11 as G5. The effect is that many people in NN have been given new houses when they were not entitled to anything at all. 129 families decided to remain in Jiyapar. Do you see? There are also some 80 houses in the new village which cannot be accounted for.

We eventually got the financial aid we were entitled to under Package 2, but we had to fight for it. What I am trying to say is that the government has been duped. I got my Rs 3,000 compensation for my G1 house. Others in Jiyapar who opted for Package 2 got G1: Rs 3,000, G2: Rs 7,000, G3: Rs 15,000 and G4: Rs 30,000. The G4 and G5 families who moved to NN have not received any cash. The G5 families who stayed in Jiyapar received compensation of Rs 90,000 paid in three instalments. God knows where the money for NN really came from.

Dilip: So have the people who moved to NN become devotees of Lord Swaminarayan?

Visanji: Not all of them have converted, but BAPS is trying.

Vishram: Let me tell you one more thing. Seventy houses over there have been given to families who live in Bombay, while at the same time they have huge empty bungalows over here in Jiyapar.

Dilip: Is BAPS spreading its religion?

Visanji: Oh yes, 100 per cent. That was one of the conditions before they began to build NN. And the village council secretly agreed to it. What I want to ask you is whether people would have agreed to this new village if they had known they would also have to convert to their sect as a condition? I am telling you that it was only four or five of the village councillors who passed the resolution without informing the village of this condition. Now they have built a new temple in NN and are making every attempt they can to convert the people who live there.

Vishram: Even after endlessly deceiving us, hardly 10 per cent of people over there are going to the temple. But BAPS is still trying to buy the villagers by giving them various things.

I had gone to the sadhu [a man initiated to the sect] myself and told him that we have 200 plots over here in the village. BAPS could build houses on these plots and we would donate the land. But the sadhu said that they will build houses the way they want to. Some of them who have gone to NN say that the land they had in Jiyapar continues to belong to them. The government rules say that those who have opted for Package 1 have to forfeit their land. The village council has records of the land, but I worry that now even the head of the village has gone to live in NN, the true situation of who owns land here will be forgotten …

Dilip: What has happened to the Muslims who lived in this village?

Vishram: There were twenty to twenty-five families; some of them have gone to NN. This was their choice. Muslims will not convert because they are such staunch believers in their own faith …

Visanji: We told the Swami [a respectful way of addressing those initiated to the sect] not to harass us. He said that no one would help us. He said we should all come and live in NN. I responded to this remark by saying that god is our caretaker and we are capable of taking care of ourselves. We are not cripples. Swamiji tried to block the financial aid that we were supposed to get.

At this point, and without visible forewarning, Visanji started to cry. An old man shuffles into the conversation, curious to see what is happening.

Vishram [turning to the old man]: This man had gone to live in Narayan Nagar but now he has come back.

Old Man: I did not like it there. Water started to come into the house. It is okay over here. We had our own house here and have moved back.

Dilip: What conditions did the Swamiji attempt to impose on your compensation?

Visanji: He said we had to move to NN. For a year he managed to block our compensation.

Dilip: But how can he stop compensation being paid to you?

Visanji [now chuckling]: He can block our compensation. He would do this to put pressure on us so that we would choose Package 1 and move to NN.

Dilip: Is there a Swami in the temple in NN?

Old Man: The Swami comes every Tuesday.

Vishram: These are his customers [alluding to the old man and chuckling].

Old Man: The Swami organises *sanstha* [a congregational meeting for religious and moral lessons] for about an hour and goes away again in a car. They have employed a few servants to clean the temple. Families like us are asked to pay a fine of Rs 100 if we fail to go to the temple.

Dilip: Is the temple priest from this village?

Old Man: Yes, he is a Patel.

Dilip: Was he the temple priest before?

Old Man: No, before someone from our village used to look after the temples.

Dilip: What happened to the old temple priest?

Visanji: What about the house that you left behind in NN? Who does it belong to?

Old Man: It belongs to me. The electricity meter is registered in my name. I have not deserted it. I just do not like living there. As I already said, I would prefer to live here in Jiyapar…

It is not at all difficult to see how those accused of various kinds of misdemeanour in this conversation might have different perspectives, challenge the numbers, and see different points of importance in what happened. The new village may well have been constructed with the intention of making the best of all possible worlds with the approval of the majority. The members of the village council who brokered the adoption might have thought they were acting in the best interests of the entire village. Perhaps they were used to Vishram and his friends disrupting the consensus. Perhaps they also considered their new affiliation with the sect to be a sign of their distinction and self-improvement. For those who remained in the old site, however, the new village raised a series of significant practical, legal and moral problems—not least of which were the 200 privately-owned undeveloped building plots that BAPS had not wanted to use. An NGO had arrived with the sanction of the state to manage the village, and even seemed to tax those who did not engage with the new institutions at the centre of the settlement. These men could also see that forces more powerful than themselves had made decisions to which they had not been privy.

Invisible decisions divided the village and introduced a sense of restlessness. There was a superabundance of resources after the earthquake, and these men, as we shall see, felt as if they had been discriminated against, or at least had lost out. There was a sense, almost panic, that others had benefited more than they had from the disaster. Between Vishram's words lurk the corruption and suggestibility of individuals and groups in decision-making and financial affairs. Why had so many more houses been built than had been damaged?[6] What was to happen to the old undamaged property of those who had moved to the new village? Ambiguity and uncertainties such as these were introduced into village governance. Village adoption rendered social divisions clear and introduced bitterness and frustration. Those designing the new village did little or nothing to develop relationships between their creation and what was there before.

The legal position on conversion and proselytism in India is complex and controversial. From the late nineteenth century, and in tandem with the emergence of the nationalist idea that the Indian was Hindu, Hindus developed vocabulary to describe 'conversion' activities: 'reclamation', 're-conversion', 'turning back' and 'purification'.[7] Common to these labels is an insistence that people are being returned to their 'natural' (that is, Hindu) state. Therefore, this is not 'conversion' but a corrective measure. According to Raymond Williams, an authority on BAPS: 'In spite of an emphasis on religious tolerance, concerted efforts are made to attract new members in Gujarat'.[8] The confluence of these reasons explains, in part, why Hindu organisations, and BAPS notably, were able to build temples as part of each village reconstruction programme without fear of sanction. The political atmosphere in Gujarat at the time is another reason. The seal of approval granted to BAPS by the chief minister of Gujarat at the inauguration of the Jiyapar project is another. Had Islamic or Christian organisations attempted similar statements with new architecture, then there would have been an awful brouhaha.

A resident of Bhuj who had his finger firmly on the pulse of reconstruction saw something else in the activities of BAPS. Sandeep Virmani writes of 'religious sects', including BAPS:

[They] have used the disaster and the money raised thereafter to further their religious ideologies. Not necessarily through direct conversion, as that would have attracted censure, but by promoting their organizational identities as 'do-gooders'. More often than not they changed the names of the villages and put large sign boards proclaiming the name of the village after their religious saints, most of whom the villagers have barely heard of.

BAPS even used the donation money to give special benefits to their followers, like whole new villages like Ukharmora and Gunatitpur. These were home to rich Patels from Nakatrana, Mundra and Mandvi who owned farmland in Bhuj *taluka* [sub-district]. Ukharmora and Gunitatpur were built by BAPS near their farms even though they had homes in Nakatrana and could easily afford to make their own farm houses if they chose to do so.[9]

101

While this analysis may well be correct, there also seem to be further layers of consequence in the Jiyapar case. The village was home to many absentee landlords, but it was also commonly associated with heterodox religion, as we shall see presently in Visanji's tears.

In an interview in November 2003, the then temple priest of the village of Ukhadmora, now renamed by BAPS as Yogi Nagar, described what had happened there:

The Swami usually comes here in a white jeep on Saturdays. There is a public gathering in the temple from 8.00 to 10.00 pm. Everyone gathers in the temple for *satsang* [congregation]. The Swami will give lessons on Lord Swaminarayan and then we sing devotional songs. The Ahir caste that lives in this village used to worship Lord Krishna, but since they moved to this new place everyone has slowly become a devotee of Swaminarayan. The Swami told us that there are different names and forms of god but ultimately there is only one god.

The discord between the account of Sandeep Virmani and the temple priest might suggest that the intervention was supposed to be more persuasive than prescriptive. In the case of the village of Nani Mau, now renamed by BAPS as Shriji Nagar, at least according to those to whom I spoke in the village, one family regularly visited the temple in Bhuj and, after the earthquake, petitioned the sect for assistance. Here too, despite objections from other villagers, BAPS rebuilt the village around a temple and strongly encouraged attendance.

The inhabitants of Nani Mau lived from the land, and, along with many other landholders and pastoralists, they worshiped Lord Ram and local goddesses. These deities are hot and fierce in quality, and associated with power, hierarchy and sacrifice. Scholars have often noted a fundamental division and struggle in Gujarat between two tendencies in Hindu religious society: crudely hot and cold. There is much to be said on this subject, but in brief, and without making a lengthy detour into ethnology, the provincial, martial, traditional ruling castes are seen as sturdy, hot blooded, consumers of meat and alcohol, prone to violence, and aligned with the cults of divine kingship I describe in Chapters 16 and 22. In contrast, the urban trading estate, with which BAPS is associated (albeit often in rural areas), is seen as cool blooded, controlled, disciplined, vegetarian, and in endless search of purity.

In parallel to this division, religious practices, forms of polity, geography and the morals of everyday life are seen as differing between the two estates.[10] The former group cluster around the hierarchy, power and sacrifice of mother goddess cults; the latter are more egalitarian under a hierarchy of gurus within the structure of an organised religion. The latter tend to regard the former as superstitious, associated with magic and past times. In politics, the former are generally seen as combative, the latter discursive. Geographically, the former are associated with the west, the latter with the east of the state, and the relationship between them is the key to the antagonistic history of state-building that I describe in Chapter 8, with the east endlessly trying to consume the west. The former might crudely be thought to represent the traditional polity, while the latter represents a perennial state of reform, which, although present in many guises through the centuries, takes a particularly strong shape in the form of the followers of the teaching of Lord Swaminarayan.

In a sense which is more than heuristic, BAPS represents the cold, and the pre-earthquake society of Nani Mau the hot. The people of this village would greet strangers affectionately with names of their gods, '*Ram Ram*' or '*Jai Mataji*' (life to the goddess), raising an open palm towards the person they were hailing as they did so. With the gift of their new houses, they were instructed to stop these practices and to greet each other by raising both hands, pressing their palms together in front of their chest, pointing their fingers upwards and bowing their heads while saying the words '*Jai Swaminarayan*'.

In 2002, many proselytes in Nani Mau were not proficient at this new performance. Some, especially older men, were uncomfortable, clumsy and hesitant with the imposition of a new bodily movement and the invocation of a new god. To me, they looked as if their bodies were being forced to do something which had no resonance with anything present in their hearts or minds. Yet I repeatedly saw how careful they were to greet any stranger who came to the village in this fashion—they feared reprimand, they said. Of course, their 'conversion' to the movement in exchange for a house does not automatically or necessarily signal any radical break with their previous cosmological convictions. The transformation of fundamental lifelong gestures and bodily habits seems a lot to ask, however, given their vulnerable and denuded circumstances.

Back in Narayan Nagar, caste division was cemented both into the splitting of the settlement and the layout of the new village. Houses of three types were constructed in two clusters on each side of a road.[11] The larger ones, to the west of the road around the temple, were mostly given to upper and dominant castes, and the smaller ones, east of the road, to other Hindu castes, Harijans and Muslims. Here, as in many other locations, and despite the lack of caste restriction within BAPS, the encounter between village and civil society redistributed state compensation into a graded hierarchy based on caste and religion—but, as I discussed in the previous chapter, the intersection of caste, progressive rates of compensation relating to the size of landholdings, parameters for housing design laid out by the state, and the complexities of village life meant it was simply impossible for anyone to follow all of the rules and to accommodate the interests of all villagers amicably. It might also have been that, for some traders, compensation based on the size of prior landholdings might have meant new and uncommonly poor neighbours in Narayan Nagar; or, in the case of other traders, that they would have to forsake their previous investments in landholdings already designated for lucrative non-agricultural use.

At the entrance to Narayan Nagar, impressive gates give details of those who made the building project possible: inspired by the spiritual leader of BAPS, Pramukh Swami, sponsored by Gujaratis living in New York, Ohio and Michigan, and inaugurated by Narendra Modi, chief minister of Gujarat.[12] Such gates, which are a prominent feature of many reconstructed villages, previously marked the edge of the village and the boundary between ideally pure, domestic and civil space on the one side, and impure, savage wilderness on the other. These gates continue to attest to such a division, only now they also record the names of new spiritual and political patrons and their direct association.

Narayan Nagar has been equipped with a community hall (a feature practically unknown before the earthquake), office, primary health centre and buildings for farmers' cooperatives. Water, sanitation, roads, electricity, street lights and an extensive garden area have also been provided. There is a 'Socio-Spiritual Cultural Centre'. A planned library was to contain 10,000 books (I am not sure that it ever did), and according to BAPS's promotional literature was intended to be the 'beacon of spreading good reading habits'.[13] The temple (the 'Cultural Centre') is the largest building in the village, far bigger than the primary school. The fact sheet BAPS produced on its achievements in Nayan Nagar does not mention the temple, but instead describes how the 'complex will be used for festivals, celebrations and annual rituals'.

Before the earthquake, the population of Jiyapar consisted of a number of different caste groups. Patels dominated (185 families out of 285). They were divided in their loyalties by two different religious affiliations: Laxmi Narayan and Sat Panthi. The former is another branch of the Swaminarayan movement—rivals, one might say, to BAPS for the affections of Gujarat. The latter is widely regarded as heterodox and commonly associated by Hindus with 'Islam'. Sat Panthis (sometimes called *pirana pith*) do not worship idols, and their prayers are private and congregational. In fact, a curious friend from Bhuj who first introduced me to the village repeatedly asked followers of the sect if they were Muslims, and if fakirs rather than Brahmins performed their rituals. They became angry; my friend had clearly touched a nerve. They dismissed his questions as vulgar and uninformed. Such rumours and ideas had been spread about them by other Hindus, who were seeking to create a unified population and thus a convenient vote bank, they said. Being Sat Panthis, to them, was to be part of a long and successful line of religious practice in the region.

The actions of BAPS in the village both isolated some of the followers of Sat Panthi and attracted followers from a rival Swaminarayan sect to its own new temple. The Sat Panthis were, on the whole, among the wealthiest inhabitants, which meant they were less seducible by the offer of a new house, and were keen not to forfeit what they already had. They elected to stay in Jiyapar close to their own congregational hall and property. Conversion was not an issue because they were staunch believers in their own faith. Their new isolation made them conspicuous and, therefore, potentially vulnerable, and liable to tears when they reflect upon how they fared in the aftermath.

In the language of service, intervening agencies made attempts to alter pre-existing gods, gestures and organisations of village life. Many of those who came to intervene saw the objects of their service as victims in a double sense: victims of tragedy and victims of impoverished cultural and religious regimes. The public–private partnership allowed those intervening to gift new forms of understanding. State sanction allowed these interventionists to build villages imbued with particular ideologies, some possibly with longer-term collaborative goals in mind.

In 2012, Sewa International opened a centre in Jiyapar with the aim of training rural artisans. The new facility is adjacent to the BAPS temple. Sewa International is part of the Hindu Swayamsevak Sangh, an international organisation inspired by the ideas of the RSS. Narendra Modi landed on the village's new helipad to inaugurate the centre. He is reported as having paid homage to Dr Hedgewar, the founder of the RSS. He also took the opportunity of reminding people of the changes that have come about in Kutch following the earthquake.[14] In his speech he appeared to confuse the name of the village with the spiritual leader of BAPS, calling it 'Pramukh Swami Nagar'.

Keshav Nagar spruced up for the inauguration and key-handing over ceremony, 2002.

13

JIHADI, DOG AND SECULARIST

The convulsions of the earth were most probably triggered by a slippage on the south dipping North Wagad Reverse Fault in the Kutch aulacogen, or failed rift. According to the initial reporting of the Indian Meteorological Department, the earthquake measured 6.9 on the Richter scale. Teleseismic studies in Japan and the United States put it at 7.9.[1] The Indian Meteorological Department declared the epicentre to have been close to the village of Lodai, some twenty-eight kilometres to the northeast of Bhuj. The latitude and longitude they provided (23.6° N, 69.8° E) placed the epicentre some 22 kilometres further north, in the uninhabited and inaccessible Rann of Kutch, where, as we know, anything can happen. This inconvenient fact was overlooked, and Lodai, a short drive along a well-made road from the airport at Bhuj, became the rural focus of international media attention. Press reports from just after the earthquake suggested that the village had become a tourist hotspot. The site showed the deep imprints of the quake as the earth spewed black, blue and green liquids. People flocked to gaze in marvel at the ooze and to study cracks in the ground.

International scientists not only differed with the Indian meteorologists over the intensity of the earthquake, but also disagreed about the location of the seismic activity, placing its epicentre elsewhere. The Jan Sangharsh Manch, an NGO based in Ahmedabad, filed a Public Interest Litigation suit, sensibly arguing that it was important to know the true location of the epicentre to allow for subsequent risk zoning of reconstruction and rehabilitation programmes.[2] They made their point, and the Indian scientists admitted their initial pronouncements had been made on the basis of insufficient data. Subsequently, the Indian government issued the revised coordinates (23.4° N, 70.28° E). These put the epicentre some sixty-five kilometres east-north-east of Bhuj, near the village of Bandhadi on the edge of the Rann of Kutch, some forty kilometres or approximately ten villages to the east of Lodai.

If you ask people in Bhuj today where the epicentre of the earthquake was, most will point in the direction of Lodai. In Lodai, too, many villagers I met on the tenth anniversary of the earthquake still claimed this inglorious accolade as their own. The pronouncements of the judges in the distant courts of Ahmedabad have done little to dislodge the early wisdom of the scientists and the enthusiasm of journalists. The initial stories of where the earthquake occurred have had a much longer half-life than later corrections, revisions and displays of legalistic proof. For many people, an epicentre in the Rann was convenient, out of sight, and far less troubling than having an epicentre in an inhabited place. An epicentre out of sight also sat comfortably with dominant forms of political myth-making and strategising about the border-lands with Pakistan—aspects of which we have already encountered. Some people quickly saw the emotive and marvellous potential of Lodai as a site of suffering.

On a hot October day in 2002, some twenty months after the earthquake, Pravin Togadia, then the international secretary of the Vishwa Hindu Parishad (VHP), addressed an audience of a few thousand people at the inauguration ceremony of a newly constructed settlement, called New Keshavnagar Township, a short distance from Lodai. Only days before Togadia was due to stand on stage, the township was a dismal and fly-blown collection of half-finished concrete structures grafted onto a bare hillside. The organisers had worked around the clock to make the site appear ready for the visiting dignitaries and newspaper reporters. A tarmac road running into the village was hastily laid over the sandy soil. The bare concrete of half-finished houses was spruced up with a lick of paint. The aim was to give the village an air of order and completion. As it was, within the week, the road had crumbled and it was upwards of a year later before most of the houses were ready for occupation.

Constructed in the name of the VHP, the funds came from a caste organisation, a number of temple committees run by Gujaratis in the United States, and from government borrowing from development banks. The new village was promoted as a particularly symbolic site: it was the epicentre of the earthquake (which we know it was not) and offered a commanding view onto the vast salt flats that lead to the border with Pakistan (which we know was politically charged). Huge tents had been erected to shade the audience from the sun. Togadia shared the stage with a number of prominent ministers from the state government, who at times looked uncomfortable, but they too took the opportunity to launch their campaigns for the election which was due to take place that December. But it was as a VHP man that Togadia was speaking to his large audience and, as was then the trend in Gujarat, he used religious issues as political platforms, and a political platform to discuss religious issues.

Other than a brief passing mention to those fortunate enough to have received new houses from the VHP, he used the opportunity to make a hard-hitting election-eering speech. The events of the last two years in Gujarat, and India more generally, gave him much material: the heightened tensions along the border with Pakistan, the burning of a train in Godhra and the death of its Hindu passengers returning from Ayodhya, the religious violence in cities in the east of the state, the ensuing dissolution of the government, and the attack on the BAPS's Akshardham temple in Gandhinagar. Togadia expressed his concern that 'browbeating in Gujarat' would delay forthcoming elections and encourage divisions along caste lines, as each community jostled to position their own candidate. He urged the assembled to vote on the basis of religion and not caste, so that the 'offspring of Musharraf', the then president of Pakistan, would not come to power.

Referring to the reaction to the violence in Gujarat earlier in the year he said: 'First, the puppies of Gujarat made noises and started barking. When it was felt that this noise would not do, dogs from all over the country started coming here … Then we heard that a dog from Italy also made the rounds here'.[3] The final insulting reference was to Sonia Gandhi, leader of Congress, who had recently toured the area.

Togadia's speech was angry, passionate and calculated. He upped the political ante by referring to the 'Italian dog', seamlessly combining political aspiration and earthquake reconstruction. His comments, received with cries glorifying Lord Ram and Mother India, ensured that he and his organisation had a great deal of press coverage.

He identified three evils threatening the assembled: Muslims, secularists and rival political parties. Each one of the evils he termed as a form of 'Ghazni', alluding to Mohammed of Ghazni, one of the first so-called 'Turkish' conquerors of western India, who is reputed to have destroyed the famous Hindu temple at Somnath in the eleventh century. This temple demolition lives on as a striking reminder of Hindu–Muslim antipathy in India because politicians (not only spokesmen of the VHP) have repeatedly characterised its reconstruction as the first stage in a campaign to reinstate the ancient symbols of unity and amity in India—the liberation of Ram's birth place in Ayodhya was to be the second. Thus the name of Ghazni has become synonymous with foreign invasion and the destruction and erosion of Hindu culture.

On that day, Pravin Togadia was haunted by three modern 'Ghaznis': '*jihadi* Ghaznis', 'secular Ghaznis' and 'political Ghaznis'. His triad was a reiteration, albeit in his own style, of a set of beliefs long held among sections of the Hindu population in India, and commonly seen in the writing of M.S. Golwalkar, the second leader of the RSS. Togadia's *jihadi* Ghaznis' are Muslims, converts from Hinduism, Pakistan, Osama bin Laden, and those who are said to have destroyed the temple at Somnath.

The boundary between Togadia's 'political Ghazni' and his secular ones is unclear. The Congress is his political opposition, and its supporters are often described as being 'secular'. Secularism in India has a history very different from that of both Europe and America. It grew out of the freedom movement, from the opposition to British rule. Pre-Independence secularism was a stance, a political option; it was not the 'poor things platform' for minority protection, a policy of appeasement that the Bharatiya Janata Party (BJP) now routinely describes. The nationalist vision underlying Togadia's claims explicitly rejects the 'composite culture' idea that grew out of the freedom struggle, the protection of minority rights and the desire for a government working with secular protectionist principles.

Togadia's 'political Ghaznis' are the BJP's rivals for power, those for whom the concepts Hindu and nation are distinct and should be kept separate: the Congress and its retrograde policies. The leader of the Congress is an Italian, a foreigner and representative of the ideas that Togadia feels have retarded the Hindu nation. He argued, though it must be said not utterly coherently: 'Our sister Sonia is imported from abroad. But Muslims of India are not imported. Indian Muslims are converted Muslims. Therefore, Sonia is a foreigner to us but Muslims are not'. He then suggested that Indian Muslims should go for blood tests to prove that it was not the blood of the Prophet Mohammad that sustained them but the blood of Lord Ram and Lord Krishna. Looking out beyond the crowd, towards Pakistan, his remedies for the ills of the country were that the *jihadis* were to be hanged, the secular Hindus were to be ostracised, and the political Ghaznis were to be unseated.

Before the earthquake, the village of Lodai had a mixed population of Hindu pastoralists, a small numbers of other castes, and a significant number of Harijans and Muslims. Keshavnagar, built on the top of a hill overlooking the old village, was constructed exclusively for caste Hindus (Ahirs, Rabaris and Barots). Harijans, Muslims and others remained in the old village at the base of the hill, and made do with the evidently inferior houses provided by a relief organisation that stepped in once it was obvious that the VHP plans ignored certain sections of the population. The design of the new village around a temple dedicated to Ram and Krishna, and its carefully selected inhabitants, in this case really did reflect Indian civilisation as Togadia envisaged it: exclusive, disciplined, strong and Hindu.

At the time, and although an extreme example, that day typified the spirit of much rural reconstruction as I saw it. Naked political opportunism and the manipulation and division of those affected by the earthquake sat alongside the brute and unpleasant fact that the village Togadia had come to inaugurate was uninhabitable and incomplete. For those unfamiliar with the Indian political scene, it is perhaps also worth pointing out that the use of words such as 'dog' to describe an opponent or 'hanged' to diagnose a solution for a perceived social problem is unusually extreme. This was indeed a speech of such extremes, but perhaps Keshavnagar had been constructed from the outset to serve as an emotive and powerful platform for the promotion of such views.

At the time, however discomforting it might be, what Togadia said is what I imagine many Hindus in the region privately fantasised. The way in which he articulated his solutions in such confrontational language was out of kilter with the local, and rather more elliptical, language of inter-personal diplomacy and politics. But he was capitalising upon a moment of strong Hindu feeling at all levels of society, pushing it deeper, but not attempting to impose something on people who thought something radically different. Hindu nationalism of this type was not an extreme position at all; rather, it was the stance of the majority and culturally mainstream. It was reasonable and logical—and, in this sense, was purely ideological in its operation and reach. What sometimes seemed from my perspective to be chauvinistic was, from the perspective of its proponents, entirely sensible. Sane urban Hindus talked openly and without fear about the threat they perceived to their nation from dirty and dangerous Muslims. You had to be there to fully understand just how naturalised these political ideas had become in Gujarat at the time.

Notwithstanding the manufacture and entrenchment of hate, the ways in which communalism became a way of understanding and seeing the world have clearly had other consequences. Some of these are entirely obvious and relate to the ways in which Muslims and Muslim issues were represented (or not) in the popular media: divided residential patterns, educational discrimination and so forth.[4] One less obvious consequence, I would like to suggest, is that the epicentre of the earthquake has not been allowed to move. As we have seen, the epicentre was quickly swallowed up by the pre-existing master narrative of infiltration, margins and borders. The epicentre near Lodai allowed the earthquake to make a particular kind of sense and to carry particular associations with general evil. This sense already had ideological (grass) roots and cultural inertia. It was, therefore, readily appropriated by those who used the epicentre to further their causes. Too many other things would have to be rearranged if the epicentre were moved from a marginal wilderness into the populated heart of the nationalists' own terrain.

Houses at the north-west of the village, Indraprastha, 2003.

14

BUILDING POLITICS

Other politicians were attracted to northern Kutch by the aftermath of the earthquake. Some distance to the east of Lodai, an organisation called Rashtriya Swabhiman (RAS, 'dignity' or 'pride' in the nation) was offered the opportunity by the Gujarat government, with which it had particular political affinity, to adopt a village known as Dudhai on the Bhuj to Bhachau highway. The village had been badly damaged in the earthquake, and tales of the corpses left to rot in damaged temples travelled widely. As with Lodai, the adopting agency found the tangle of rubble, caste interest and history in the old village too complicated to unravel, and resistant to authoritarian management. In order to circumvent the problems raised by those affected by the earthquake, the RAS established a new site nearby, which it named Indraprastha.

The RAS was registered as a society in 1998 by Sahib Singh Verma, a noted politician on the national stage. Earlier he had been worker and activist for the Rashtriya Swayamsevak Sangh. He wrote a doctoral thesis on libraries and literacy in his native North India, and served as a librarian at the Shaheed Bhagat Singh College of Delhi University. According to one of Verma's followers, the contemplation of the life and times of Bhagat Singh made a distinct impression on Verma. In the Punjab of the 1920s, Singh fought for an independent India. Significantly, he, like Shyamji Krishnavarma, was against resistance to the colonial oppressor through exclusively non-violent means. This also pitched him against Gandhi and his followers, and against the majority of those within the Indian National Congress at the time. Singh was connected with a bomb, a bomb plot and the shooting of a policeman. He was hanged in Lahore in 1931, becoming a martyr (the 'Shaheed' in the name of the college) for the nation. The ethos of strength and the strategic use of force in the face of injustice and oppression also became part of Verma's creed.

In addition to his post in the university library, Verma had a very successful political career, holding numerous prominent public positions, first as chief minister in Delhi, and later as head of the labour ministry in the national government. The name given to the new village in Gujarat, Indraprastha, is from the Mahabharata (one of the epic tales of Hindu mythology), the magnificent capital of the warring Pandavas. The name means 'city of the god Indra' and is considered by some to have been the ancient name for Delhi. In earlier years, Verma himself had led an unsuccessful campaign to rename the nation's capital, New Delhi, as Indraprashta. Where he had failed in North India, in Gujarat he had a free hand, to incongruous effect.

In this spirit, the village Verma set about creating in Gujarat was to be a model for others to emulate, inspired by his personal philosophy for the nation. In his view, successful development was to be fostered through the promotion of cultures of self-sufficiency and self-reliance. While the words might echo the sentiments for which Gandhi is famous, the means and the creed, as I hope is already clear, are quite different. Verma wanted global power for India, and this was to come through the embrace of technology, strength, education of particular kinds, and disciplined religious and cultural purity. On the surface, Indraprashta was a manifestation in concrete of his vision. The village he built amid the acacias was equipped with schools, a college, a technical education centre, a bank, community and agricultural centres, a handicraft park, an old-age home, and an orphanage. Verma imagined Indraprastha would become a centre to which neighbouring villages would turn for goods and services, and, in this regard, time has proved him to be mostly correct.

As an indicator of Verma's influence, the inauguration ceremony of his village in June 2001 was attended by the Indian prime minister and his deputy. Press coverage of the event also shows a rather pressured-looking Keshubhai Patel (who was then still chief minister of Gujarat, but who must also have known his time was limited). In the early months of the project, Verma would visit frequently to oversee construction work. Later, he installed a retired colonel to oversee proceedings and to shout at the villagers when necessary. The colonel (as everyone called him) was generous with his time and hospitality, but was always stressed—either fretting about the health and wealth of his family in distant North India, or harassed to near breaking point by the antics of the villagers.

The colonel would talk to me while seated in the village's Special Study Centre, a library of nationalist and Vedic literature mostly written in Hindi and English. Many of the villagers were barely literate. For those who could read, Gujarati was their preferred language. The library was consequently largely unused, and over the years it has fallen into a state of decline. In the Special Study Centre hung Verma's portrait, flanked by those of other national heroes, the contours and lines of their faces painted in blood donated by Verma's followers; Gandhi was conspicuous in his absence.

Human blood is a relatively common medium for images of 'freedom fighters' who lost their lives in the struggle for independence. The nationalist leader Subhas Chandra Bose famously said, 'Give me your blood, and I will give you freedom', at a rally in Burma in 1944. Bose was a political rival to Gandhi within the Congress, advocating violent means to achieve independence. Today, 'Hindu nationalist activists have, broadly speaking, been at the forefront of developing a political aesthetics of blood'. Such 'sanguinary politics' plays on widely understood ideas of contestation, memory and martyrdom.[1]

In later times, the colonel would entertain me in his own quarters. He was a kind and generous man who was interested in the world. He was also devoted in his service to Verma, and would only occasionally moan about his posting to rural Gujarat—where neither good food nor strong liquor were readily available. For his public disdain of local ways of life, as well as for other good reasons, he was not much liked in Indraprashta. I heard people describe him as the 'camp commandant', and, indeed, when Indraprashta was first constructed, the uniform grey lines of its houses also gave it something of this air.

In such a model village, it seemed only right to the colonel that the place should be kept clean and well ordered. But many villagers were not well equipped to be the kind of model citizens required. Some initially moved their animals into the new houses, choosing themselves to lodge in airy and well-ventilated tents from where they could protect their valuable livestock. Numerous campaigns were waged in an attempt to influence the behaviour of the residents. Fresh messages relating to health and hygiene were constantly appearing on walls, sometimes supported by public meetings and 'workshops'. At the time, the colonel attempted single-handedly to police the hygiene and waste-disposal practices of the villagers. In contrast to what he thought they should do, the villagers mostly liked to shit outside and to throw their rubbish onto the street outside their houses. Like other regular visitors, I began to worry about his blood pressure. To make matters worse, he was in constant dispute with a few individuals in the village, and he could often be heard shouting. There were also greater stresses for him emanating from the poor construction quality of the houses, and the more fundamental question of whose houses they actually were. The trust had obtained the land, but was supposed to hand over the legal deeds of the houses to the new occupants. The RAS took an inordinate length of time to transfer ownership rights, and while this was not the colonel's fault, it was he who became the target of quick and spiteful tongues. Here, as in many other locations in Kutch, the policy adopted for rural reconstruction created, for a while at least, villages of tenants dependent on the good will and whims of their adopter. Unsurprisingly, this caused a great deal of anxiety and sometimes anger, much of which was directed at the colonel.

The colonel showed me around the parts of the village he knew that he would not be abused in. The architecture and the scale of the planning instantly reflected how much the project must have cost, as the comforts and mores of urban life had been brought to the countryside. The village was a bold and ambitious intervention in Gujarat, which only faltered when it came into contact with the ideas of rural people. The site is adjacent to the main highway into Kutch, and its presence is marked by huge signboards, more fitting for a major city than a small village. Behind the leafy gardens of the Special Study Centre are temples dedicated to the national deities Ram and Krishna. After protracted negotiation, it was also decided to build a smaller temple for the provincial Gujarati sect of Swaminarayan in a failed attempt to entice the high-caste followers of the movement.

Unlike the New Keshavnagar Township, where the centre of the village was built around a temple and a small row of shops (but no 'Special Education Centre'), the main residential areas in Indraprastha are further away from the highway and more modest in design. If Keshavnagar was designed as a political stage aimed at winning local votes, then Indraprastha was perhaps designed with a broader aim in mind. The ten sections of the village, formed by a grid of roads, carry the names of national heroes both historic and mythological. The streets and squares carry the names of places in Delhi, the capital's Chandani Chowk, Sudar Bazar and so on.

Unlike many other villages in the region, all of the houses in Indraprashta were built to approximately the same specification. There were no big houses for high or dominant castes and smaller houses for low castes and the subservient, as there were in Narayan Nagar. Whatever Verma's original intent, the meaning was lost by the time the plan was put into effect in rural Gujarat, where it caused commotion. Horse-trading began to restore order, and high castes were quickly promised better locations in the absence of larger properties. Thus it was that the residential colonies nearer the road were handed over to the high castes, or at least the few families of Jains and Patels who left the old site. Those in the middle of the settlement were given to low caste Hindus and Harijans. The two blocks furthest to the north, those furthest from the main road, were for Muslims.

Unlike Keshavnagar, Muslims and Harijans were welcomed to Indraprastha from the outset, but the houses they were eventually granted were furthest from the improbably huge bazaar and the other facilities concentrated along the western flank of the village. Moving from the entrance towards the wilderness to the north, one passes the education complexes, temples, houses arranged on the basis of caste, and eventually the Muslim areas. A reflection of the ideology underlying the plan, the layout gives a hierarchically ordered value and priority to each area. The Muslims, although promised a mosque, were left to their own devices to construct one on a plot beyond the northern fringes of the main village, a refraction of the dominant idea that they are a problematic adjunct to national and local planning paradigms.

The admission of Harijans and Muslims into the village, the fact that the houses were uniform in shape and quality, and the fact that it was constructed by the intellectualist, Sanskritic and North Indian RAS, have meant that elite caste groups such as Jains and Patels were mostly not attracted to the new settlement. The Patels opted to stay in the old village and to rebuild their own residential enclave around a temple. This decision reflects a much more widespread tendency of the aftermath to form exclusive residential colonies and enclaves structured around community-inspired buildings of religious denomination.

On the outskirts of Indraprastha, Verma constructed a monument to those who died in the earthquake, which he called Tiger Hill. On top of a small hillock there is a plaque set into the foundations of a pole for the national flag. This memorial always struck me as one of the most idiosyncratic aftermath interventions. The hill lies between the village and the wilderness, beyond which it is easy to imagine Pakistan, just as the Tiger Hill from which the monument derives its name lies between India and Pakistan in Kashmir. I will return to this memorial in Chapter 34.

In addition to this strange complex, scattered around Indraprastha were other slogans in Hindi: 'True love alone generates the sentiment of sacrifice'; 'everything is possible with self-confidence, true labour, and strong will'. And, most confidently of all, but strangely in English, 'Purity is power'. The 'purity' of this last slogan is to be found in devotion (to Hinduism), in scholarship (of the appropriate traditions) and in discipline. Verma's rather elite brand of nationalism and sacrifice is knowledge-led, Sanskrit-based, and premised on the myth of the traditional and harmonious Indian village. The benefactor created the village as he saw India: diverse, hierarchical, Hindu at the core, with potent signs of contestation, conflict and martyrdom on the periphery.

In 2007, Sahib Singh Verma was killed in a car crash in Rajasthan. In many ways, the village he had built is a concrete manifestation of a nationalist vision, albeit a rather eclectic one and compromised by the stubborn sanitary regimes and agricultural practices of the inhabitants. We can also see that Indraprastha is a monument to a life's work: an assemblage of Verma's achievements, campaigns and interests. Despite the claim to a broader social vision, plans for the village had been drawn from his own personal and moral memory. After all, Verma liked books, libraries, Delhi, martyrs, and had been heavily involved in politicking both during and in the aftermath of the Kargil battle for Tiger Hill (see Chapter 34). In the absence of anything more obvious, these are the things he gave to the earthquake-affected people of Gujarat, along with a highly-strung colonel.

'Purity is power', 2003, Indraprastha.

15

INTEGRAL HUMANISM

Some distance to the east of Indraprastha, Pramod Mahajan, another RSS youth turned successful BJP politician, also tried his hand at building a village. At the time, he was national minister for telecommunications, and his village swiftly received instruments which allowed the inhabitants to communicate with the rest of the world. Mahajan also brought with him the clout of the national Housing and Urban Development Corporation (HUDCO). He donated his discretionary allowance as a member of parliament to undertake the work. Reconstruction was carried out in the name of a private trust which Mahajan headed, the Rambhau Mhalgi Prabodhini Trust (commonly known as the 'Mahajan Trust' in Dholavera, the adopted village).

The story of the reconstruction work in Dholavera is similar to many others. The houses were reconstructed quickly, but people complained that the contractors from North India used materials of inappropriate quality, often purchased at inflated prices. There was conflict between locals and outsiders, money leaked from the project, and some work was left incomplete. There was also the neglected promise of the development of the village as a tourist destination (it is adjacent to an important archaeological site). As elsewhere, however, in Dholavera the hidden politics of intervention, although much harder to see, are more interesting and consequential than the perceived inadequacies and corruption involving the building of houses.

In 1979, Pramod Mahajan was part of a select batch of RSS cadres co-opted into the newly formed BJP to help boost its political fortunes. He proved to be an efficient organiser and eloquent speaker, rising to play a major role in propelling the party towards federal power. His political credentials are typified by the close support he gave the then party leader L.K. Advani in the early 1990s to organise an infamous procession from Somnath to Ayodhya. The stunt was part of the campaign to build a temple to the Hindu god Lord Ram on the spot where a sixteenth-century mosque had stood. This was the site from where those burned on the train in Godhra were returning, an event which led to the widespread violence in Gujarat in 2002. The mosque was demolished in 1992, an act which was accompanied by violence between Hindus and Muslims across India. The campaign translated into votes for the BJP. The party assumed power at the national level in 1998, and remained in office for six years.

As in Indraprashta, the status and resources of a national ministerial position flowed into rural Gujarat in the name of a private trust. In this instance, the trust was established in the name of Rambhau Mhalgi, an RSS worker and BJP politician from Maharashtra who served in the national parliament on and off between 1957 up to his death in 1982. The promotional literature of the trust established in his memory outlines its objectives thus:

Governance is one of the toughest challenges of the modern world. The quality of a government depends upon the quality of the elected representatives of the people. The quality of the representatives depends, in turn, upon the quality of the citizens. In a Democracy, a citizen's life is governed in a large measure by the policy decisions and laws adopted by various houses of representatives from the national level, down to the village level.

Rambhau Mhalgi Prabodhini (RMP) … strives to mould such leaders, representatives and decision makers, by imparting specialised knowledge, analytical techniques and penetrating insight, which enables them to offer good governance, with a view to make resurgent India, a genuine world super power.[1]

In the trust's literature and popular imagination, Mhalgi is connected to the person, career and philosophy of Deendayal Upadhyaya, who was general secretary of the Bharatiya Jana Sangh (one of the earlier parties from which the BJP emerged) from 1953. He was elected president of the party in 1967, and died in mysterious circumstances on a train the following year.[2]

Upadhyaya is known for having developed a philosophy called 'integral humanism'.[3] His ideas were based on what he saw as core values of Indian civilisation, and formed a critique of both communism and capitalism. He rejected the political systems of Western countries on the basis that they were lost and directionless. The West, he thought, made a distinction between secular and religious domains which was irrelevant in the Indian context. In India, the Congress and others, who had attempted to force into being a secular post-colonial state, had damaged indigenous politico-religious philosophy through the blind adoption of alien concepts. He likened the Congress to a magic box in which a mongoose and a cobra co-inhabited.[4]

Upadhyaya wrote:

Independence is intimately related to one's own culture. If culture does not form the basis of independence, then the political movement for independence would be reduced simply to a scramble by selfish and power-seeking persons. Independence can be meaningful only if it becomes an instrument for the expression of our culture. Such expression will not only contribute to our progress, but the effort required will also give us the experience of joy. Therefore, both from the national as well as human standpoint, it has become essential that we think of the principles of Bharatiya culture.[5]

'Bharatiya [Indian] culture' was equated with 'dynamic Vedic religion'. Drawing on the ancient texts known as the Upanishads and other sources, he proposed that

120

the ultimate principle of this culture (or the 'efforts that befit a man') was the operation of *dharma*. For him, *dharma* was rooted in religious life, but it was far more than 'religion' (which he saw as a Western concept). He broadly defined *dharma* as a universal and eternal system of rules or 'innate laws'. He envisaged a political society in which the state and Hinduism existed together: sovereignty resided in *dharma*, and a state too big and powerful could stifle the creative forces of strong *dharmic* life.

In his view, all sentiment in India was bound up with *dharma*. Thus it was important to embrace rather than forsake such law. He thought that the state should be run on the basis of *dharma*. A secular state, in his opinion, should not mean a state without *dharma*. In India, the word 'religion' was a tenet. The state should not and could not belong to any particular sect, for all must be equal in the eyes of the state. Rather, for him, the ideal state should be 'non-sectarian'; however, such a state, even without being partial to a particular sect or against some other sect, could encourage ways and means of achieving both material and spiritual progress, and thus be called *Dharma Rajya*.

For Upadhyaya, the ideal state was to be constituted according to what he saw as the principles of Indian polity, where the organic groupings of people function unhindered, where the order and discipline inherent in these groupings is protected. In such a *rajya* or state, the forces of nature would also remain in their benign aspect, all is well ordered, everyone is healthy, happy and cared for. It is a non-sectarian state and not a theocracy.

These proposals, in which Hindu ideas are seen as the basis of a civilisation and political order, formed a central part of the intellectual and moral genealogy of the BJP. The ideas discussed here were also Mahajan's direct political inheritance; they became a legacy when he was shot dead by his brother in Bombay in 2006. In post-earthquake Gujarat, the sovereignty granted to *dharma* and Upadhyaya's corresponding mistrust of a powerful state was enacted through the structures and ethos of the public–private partnership scheme and the neo-corporatist ethos of the ruling party. The conditions imposed by the development banks in the wake of the earthquake, the rolling back of state functions, and the involvement of private enterprises, proved fertile ground for the implementation and promulgation of 'integral humanism'.

Revealed in post-earthquake Gujarat is a map of non-Congress Indian nationalist politics of the twentieth century, of which Verma, Mahajan and their own political hagiographies are but influential fragments. In a more general sense, the networks and connections forged by RSS childhoods and BJP adulthoods became apparent to the outsider through the more noticeable cronyism of reconstruction and inauguration. Many of those discussed in this section saw the opportunity of bumping forward a politics from the mid-twentieth century (and earlier in the case of Shyamji Krishnavarma discussed in Chapter 10), which had not been as successful in the early post-colonial decades as the policies and legacy of the Congress. They breathed new life into these older ideologies by making villages out of them.

As we have seen, names, doctrines and gestures were grafted onto a denuded and vulnerable social order. People came and insisted that the divine be approached in particular ways, in particular temples, and using a particular language. In the gestures of old men, this was awkward and uncomfortable. We have also seen how trusts motivated by various nationalist and political ideas came to inscribe these in concrete. From a sociological perspective, religiously prescribed service, hate speeches, barking colonels and new political subjectivities fit snugly into the mould of what the French sociologist Pierre Bourdieu called 'symbolic violence or domination'.[6] This phrase is not intended to conjure guns, gashing or genocide, but rather, tacit or unconscious modes of domination which commonly occur in everyday life.

For Bourdieu, symbolic violence is exercised upon someone with their complicity and confirms a place in a social hierarchy. Symbolic violence requires a dominator, but it also requires the dominated to accept their position in the exchange of social value that occurs between them. Symbolic violence maintains its effect through the misrecognition of power relations. Misrecognition means that the economic and political interests present in a set of actions are denied. Symbolic practices deflect attention from the interested character of actions, and thereby contribute to their appearance as disinterested pursuits. This misrecognition legitimises these practices, and thereby contributes to the reproduction (or formation in this instance) of the social order in which they are embedded. Activities and resources gain in symbolic power, or legitimacy, to the extent that they become separated from underlying material interests, and hence go misrecognised as representing disinterested forms of activity.

SECTION 4

THE SEVEN CROWS

The great efforts of reconstruction focused on Bhuj to the neglect of other towns. Some of Bhuj's secrets were revealed by the town's fall. Uncertainty and protest found expression in the ruins. Planners arrived to determine what was to be done with the mess. The spot people thought they were rooted in began to look less certain. Old Bhuj was cut up to fit the shape of the new plan.

Aerial view of rambling and collapsing palaces, 2004, Bhuj.

16

THE PLACE OF BHUJ

We now return to Bhuj, as well as to Kant and his analytic of the sublime. Kant suggested that the sublime is the pleasure produced by the mind as it reaches its own limits. When this happens, the mind is rescued by reason. After an earthquake, the mind reminds itself of the irreducible dignity of the human calling to live as free moral agents who make the laws of their own reason. The mind restores its own power by calling on its own superiority to nature by building walls and gardens, protesting in the name of regional identity, and buying into a new consumer society.

Kant's abstraction, at least thus tailored, fits well with the great changes that have taken place in Kutch. The earthquake was humiliating. The alienating conditions of the aftermath led to particular forms of self-contemplation, most obviously through political protests led by people we shall meet soon, such as Kundanlal Dholakia and Dr Shyam Sundar, and through which regional identity came to the fore. Town planning, technology and a consumer boom contributed to the restoration of dignity and a sense of superiority over nature.

Of all the chatter about discrimination and state-sponsored inequality in the aftermath of the earthquake, none that I am aware of has been devoted to the disproportionate amount of time and money spent on Bhuj in relation to the other damaged towns of the region. Indeed, it hardly seems just in the scale of most humanitarian measures that the disaster has often been named 'the Bhuj earthquake'.[1] There were more deaths and higher levels of destruction in Bhachau (4,713 recorded deaths and 53,281 houses destroyed), and certain parts of Anjar were severely rattled (2,676 recorded deaths and 21,889 houses destroyed). Yet these places have been neglected in comparison to Bhuj, where there were 3,089 recorded deaths and 30,866 houses destroyed.[2] In gross and general terms, I am pretty confident that the bias in spending is more significant per capita than any committed in the name of either religion or caste. People in Anjar noticed the shortfall, but their complaints were diluted by the pull of other concerns and never found their way above the parapet of very local interest. In Bhachau, as we know, there were few people left to protest.

A massive infrastructural and house-building programme was eventually put in place in Bhuj. Similar efforts in both Bhachau and Anjar were, in comparison, feeble. A large number of intervening agencies located their offices in Bhuj, regardless of where they were working.[3] In time, USAID, the body responsible for furthering America's interests overseas while improving lives in the developing world, funded various initiatives in Bhuj to examine history and heritage as forms of collective catharsis—nothing similar happened in Bhachau or Anjar. The royal palaces and other buildings in Bhuj became the focus of national campaigns to preserve the architectural heritage of western India—nothing similar happened in Bhachau or Anjar. Various organisations worked in Bhuj to resurrect musical, craft and artistic traditions. Bhuj became subject of a number of books, films and artistic projects to do with the earthquake—no similar projects were undertaken in either Bhachau or Anjar.

In rural areas, villagers had often successfully played intervening agencies off against one another to better their lot. Left-leaning media and civil society organisations readily publicised stories about the neglect of Muslims and Dalits.[4] Men in Jiyapar became visibly distressed when they thought that others might have benefited from the disaster to a greater extent than themselves. In short, there was great sensitivity to and interest in certain kinds of bias and favouritism when it came to the allocation and distribution of new resources. Why then, we might sensibly ask, was there no public discussion or protest about the bias towards post-earthquake spending on Bhuj?

Some of the reasons why the focus of reconstruction should have fallen on the town are obvious: the population was greatest, roads led there, flights arrived at its airport, the town was photogenic, and it was the administrative capital of the district. Furthermore, journalists and many of the region's most-educated and well-connected folk lived there. At first, and with consequence, Bhuj was also said to be the closest town to the epicentre (until that was silently moved closer to Bhachau). There is also a sizable military garrison there, adjacent to the India–Pakistan border. Therefore, a good new infrastructure would benefit the movement of personnel and their war machines (or, alternatively, people quipped, hasten the passage of invaders). While these facts may well explain the attraction of the town for the state, foreign journalists and outside agencies, together they do not explain the conspicuous neglect of two of the region's other principal towns.

I suggest that the care lavished on Bhuj seemed only natural and proper to its residents after a tragedy had befallen the region as a whole. It was not something worthy of critical comment, for the bias confirmed the order of things. Over the years of talking to people in Bhuj, it became evident that they saw a hierarchy of victims and legitimate need. The hierarchy was more than a reflection of self-interested preservation: 'I am more worthy of attention because I am me'. Instead, there was a more general logic, which was also understood by those below the apex of the hierarchy of significance: 'I am more worthy of attention because I am part of this place'. Events and circumstances in Bhachau were unfortunate, terrible even, but Bhuj was to come first. Conversely, in both Anjar and Bhachau, I have seen and heard the lack of surprise that Bhuj should be doing better.

In ways that are perhaps still more surprising, those who came to intervene also saw Bhuj as central to the region and their activities within it. They did not fall into the thrall of Bhuj because of calculations made in relation to earthquake damage, the distribution of vulnerability, the quantity of lives lost or even the relative suggestibility of the population to their new ideas; rather, Bhuj was enchanting because the intertwined history of politics and power in Kutch made it extremely difficult, if not impossible, for them to see the district in any other way.

In colonial times, when Kutch had its own rulers, the strength of the town was a reflection of the well-being of the kingdom in the most general sense. Bhuj lay at the apex of a hierarchy of places, which was parallel to the ranked kinship of the ruling families. Practically all roads, rituals and litigation seemed to pass through Bhuj at some point. Since the formation of the British colonial residency in the early part of the nineteenth century, written records have confirmed and enforced the town's central role in the history of the kingdom as the primary seat of its rulers, and the symbolic centre from which all lesser and provincial power emanated. The power of the Bhuj sovereign encompassed that of the headmen (who were called *bhayad*) of the lesser towns and, in turn, their dependent villages.[5] These relationships were cemented though hierarchical patterns of marriage, taxation and tribute. Places and people were not easily divisible, but rather bound together in particular ways to give the kingdom a distinct sense of itself, a sense which, to be clear, emanated largely from Bhuj.

Gradually, over the remaining sections of this book, I add flesh here and there to this argument because I think it is fundamental to understanding the cultures and conflicts of reconstruction which emerged in Bhuj and other urban areas. My intention is not to show that people in Kutch were merely subordinate vassals to the ideologies of their rulers, for it is pretty clear that they had never been so completely, and that other networks of devotion and charisma spilled out beyond the influence of the royal complex; rather, I wish to show how they actively conceptualise the relationships between landscape, humanity and place—those things which were shaken by the earthquake and then manipulated by people from outside the region in the process of reconstruction. I believe these relationships survived the postcolonial period and now form a complex quite distinct from the personalities and names of particular rulers and the institutions of a now derelict kingship. The logic of such a regional identity—that which makes Kutch Kutch and not some other place—was challenged and exposed in the aftermath by a range of different nationalist and technocratic ideologies. Again, I suggest, as in rural areas, most of those who intervened in the towns of Kutch were poor sighted in relation to local ways of understanding, either wittingly or unwittingly. The result was to add yet a further unsettling layer to post-earthquake reconstruction for the local population.

In the language and narrative structures of written history too, Bhuj had become synonymous with the kingdom of which it was the capital. In this sense, Bhuj was Kutch and vice versa, and all the other lesser towns and villages were dependent on its success. The power of this invisible model, as I explore in what follows, seduced nearly all who passed by.

Along with a new British colonial presence, a rush of literary-minded folk arrived in Bhuj in the 1820s and 1830s. As we shall see in Chapters 30 and 31, these people arrived in the aftermath of a powerful earthquake. Then, as now, it is quite plausible to think that a great rearrangement of ideas was taking place among a stunned population. At the time, vested colonial interests, as well, perhaps, as the ways in which the population was discussing itself, drew these writers to portray Bhuj as the seat of royal power, indistinguishable from the broader kingdom.

Significant among the early accounts are T. Ogilvy's genealogy of the rulers of Bhuj and a transcribed interview with the king on the origin of the kingdom and the formation of the city.[6] S.N. Raikes wrote a memoir on the state, which focused largely on the political history of Bhuj.[7] Lumsden surveyed the terrain, population and settlements, ranking them in order of importance in relation to Bhuj—as, he reasoned, was the indigenous mode.[8] Charles Walters and James Burnes sketched histories of the kingdom, structuring their accounts around the succession of rulers to have held the throne.[9] Marianne Postans stayed in Bhuj for a spell in the 1830s, and published a lively account of life amid the 'phlegmatic and slothful Cutchees'. She was concerned with political history and ethnology, and curious about infanticide, widow-burning, opium, eunuchs and negroes, but her focus, too, eventually fell firmly on the rulers of Bhuj, the rituals of the kingdom, and the associated monumental architecture of the town.[10]

In subsequent decades, colonial scholarship gathered momentum and claimed for itself a sense of orderliness. Alongside the official census and ethnological operations of the colonial state, other studies were undertaken, often driven by personal interest.[11] These sources of scholarship, in addition to the earlier ones, were incorporated within the colonial gazetteers, a publication project initiated in 1843, which finally bore fruit between 1877 and 1914. The set for the Bombay presidency amounts to some 17,800 pages, of which Kutch, along with neighbouring Palanpur and Mahi Kantha, forms the fifth volume.[12] Much of the Kutch section was written and compiled by L.C. Barton, who was the British political agent in Bhuj during the 1870s. He revised the older colonial sources and wrote of Kutch as if it had always been the martial Hindu kingdom he saw before him, replete with the newly invented Victorian traditions of royalty, which had been encouraged by the British.

The production of knowledge in colonial society was not, of course, simply an academic exercise. The details of history were also refined through investigations into a number of territorial disputes between Kutch and its neighbours, notably Sindh, Jamnagar and a particularly long-running and rancorous dispute with Morvi over an enclave of territory inside Kutch called Adhoi (which gains significance and poignancy in the story of the aftermath in Chapter 34). In the colonial period, such disputes were primarily interpreted to be about rights relating to sovereignty. Consequently, ideas about legitimate descent and primogeniture became important and were glossed further. In such cases, the history of Kutch was reduced to a procession of rulers through the chapters of time, essentially a repetition of Ogilvy's early genealogy.

Colonial interest in genealogy and legitimacy among the native princes led to the increased importance of foundation myths. In 1827, Walters opened his account of the history of Kutch with the story of the foundation of Bhuj and the commencement of the reign of Khengarji in 1549. Aside from a seemingly compulsory nod to ancient history, he did away with all that went before by recording that, 'the spot on which the city now stands had long been an asylum for plunderers and robbers of every description'.[13] No mention is made of who these desperados were, or from whom Khengarji took the land. The gazetteer of 1880 notes, in very similar terms, that Khengarji's choice of capital 'had long been a haunt of robbers and marauders, after much difficulty they were driven out and his dependents agreed to settle there'.[14]

Many decades later, the academic and political entrepreneur L.F. Rushbrook Williams published a history of Kutch, *The black hills*, in 1958. He too emphasised the foundation of Bhuj and the Jadeja lineage at Bhuj as the dawning of a modern and distinct era. Clearly copying from Walters's text, he wrote: 'The place had fallen upon evil days, and the country round about was full of brigands and freebooters. The Rao drove them away, established firm order, and largely restored the prosperity of the city and the strength of its old fort'.[15] Rushbrook Williams had changed a few words here and there, but the story was, again, essentially the same as Walters's account of 1827.

The genealogy of the story of the formation of Bhuj is indicative of how history has been generally reproduced. Primary evidence is scant and secondary sources, mostly written in the first half of the nineteenth century, become the point of departure. The story of the foundation of Bhuj also contains within it something rather odd, however, because like Adam and Eve in the prelapsarian garden, we are told there are other people around, robbers, brigands and the like, but they simply are of no account, and their land and fort are usurped on a whim. In the accounts of Walters and Burnes, those presumably the most loyal to the traditions of the rulers of Bhuj at the time, what went before appears moribund, and plays no role in the later Hindu sovereign patriarchy. Patriarchal genealogy becomes the essence of the history of Bhuj, which, as we have seen, was cast in a distinctive fashion in the early half of the nineteenth century.

I am not sure how many of those charged with reconstruction after the earthquake read the historical sources with care. There was an unquestionable increase in the circulation of these texts, and a number of them were reprinted (the resurgence of history after the earthquake is examined in Chapters 21, 22 and 23). In many ways, however, those who came to the ruins did not need to bother with dusty tomes or poor quality photocopies because the same sentiments I have traced through the colonial texts are also expressed prominently in all guides and other forms of reference material available for the region. The point is that for Bhuj there was a written history, which could be consulted and found relatively easily using library catalogues and bibliographies. What Bhuj had been, or at least how it had been represented in the colonially derived corpus, was knowable. There were descriptions of Bhuj to be read. What had fallen down in the earthquake had a history, albeit rather plagiarised and selective. Kutch appeared as a Jadeja dynasty, with a hierarchy of places, and a concentration of things worthy of interest in Bhuj. Of course, this history excluded sections of the population who had other forms of understanding and other methods of reckoning—that is, after all, the purpose of constructing a self-serving and glorifying history.

The centrality of Bhuj endlessly repeated in the literature explains by extension why it seemed only natural to the citizenry that the reconstruction of their town should take priority, to the neglect of lesser settlements. I assume here that the trends outlined in the written record probably reflect some of the core realities of power and patronage from the era when the Jadejas held the throne at the centre, and I will elaborate some of these connections in later chapters. Without doubt, the focus on Bhuj after the earthquake contributed to the relative neglect of Anjar and Bhachau. I am not aware of any historical or sociological writing on either of these places. Neither site was a great seat of power, nor were either particularly famed for their religious sites or cultural riches. Rather, Anjar and Bhachau were mercantile towns and, otherwise, without much influence. Those who arrived after the earthquake knew them to be nondescript, primarily because no one had stopped to describe them before. It was not only that Bhuj had a written history which related to a broader sense of importance and the other towns did not; rather, the written history of Bhuj insisted that those other towns were of little or no account and were most certainly subordinate to the interests of Bhuj itself. When they fell down, there was little surviving evidence to suggest to those who intervened what had been there before or why it had been important. It is also perhaps the case that most interveners came in search of humanity, which was then strikingly absent in Bhachau and certain parts of Anjar.

Cleared ground looking north from Soniwad towards the palaces. This was one of the most densely populated areas of the town. It is the location of the rituals of reconstruction described in Chapter 23 and Umashankar's old house visited in Chapter 24, 2003, Bhuj.

17

WHERE TO START?

How many things have you left half done? If you died unexpectedly, what would those left to tidy up your affairs discover? The fact of life often shields the undone from scrutiny. So it was also with the Bhuj that was to fall in the earthquake. As things collapsed, the artifices of life were revealed and many certainties were exposed as wanting.

The town had developed in fits and starts over the centuries, and had clearly put off many things for tomorrow. Its form reflected the interwoven histories of politics, caste, class, prosperity and poverty, as well as the changing fashions and technologies of construction. More than 2,000 people died in Bhuj on the morning of the earthquake, many due to past compromises made by their own fathers and grandfathers—an unfortunate inheritance. The northern section of the old walled town was most thoroughly damaged, and a number of newer low-rise apartment blocks collapsed ignobly onto themselves.

Those charged with mending Bhuj faced a monumental question: are we to act on our sympathy for the population and patch things up quickly without doing further damage? Or, are we going to make things worse now so life in the town will be better in the future?

In history, this question has always been central to putting things back together after collapse and ruination. As the celebrated Marquês de Pombal faced the ruins of Lisbon after the earthquake of 1755, he saw four possible courses of action. He could order Lisbon to be rebuilt as it had been, where it was. Or, he could move the city to a new and hopefully safer location. He could elect to build a redesigned city on the old site in accordance with a safer plan. Or, finally, the damaged sections could be rebuilt on a new plan, and the rest of the city could be left to expand on the pre-earthquake plan.[1] While the first option, replication, is a theoretical possibility, it also strikes me as a red herring. Replication is an improbable reaction to mass death and destruction: 'in response to sublime tragedy we will build our own future tomb in the image of the one that just killed our nearest and dearest'. As in Lisbon, this option did not detain the residents of Bhuj.

To consider the remaining alternatives through the institutional and governmental arrangements that existed in Gujarat in 2001 would have taken many years of surveys, committees, sub-committees, reports, consultations, injunctions, public litigation and so on and so forth. Rubble and suffering urged something exceptional. At all levels, the earthquake initially showed itself to be stronger than the state. There was no functional post-disaster policy. There were not even useful guidelines on what to do in the event of a major disaster. Consequently, no one came forward with clear notions about what should be done.

Perhaps the lack of leadership led to the upsurge of speculation amid which the destruction of Bhuj began to raise further questions. Nestling within the question of whether things should be made worse was the urgent question of whether the town should be relocated or rebuilt where it was (what Indian planners call 'in situ'). In Bhuj, this was understood as an existential question to do with what it means to belong and be, as much as it was a practical matter spawned of fear. The discussions I recorded in the first years after the earthquake were raw and untamed responses to tragedy.

At the time, some discussed the possibility of de-populating Kutch, abandoning the land to earthquakes and drought. Some people did indeed leave. A few stayed away, but after the initial knee-jerk of shock many loyally returned. Others reasoned that Bhuj was located on unstable land and that its ruins should be left as a permanent reminder of the danger of earthquakes. For them, this was an opportunity to build a new spacious city, with well-designed streets and zoned industrial and commercial areas with fabled 'earthquake proof' buildings. They could leave behind the scenes of death which they would forever associate with life in the old city. New industries could be designed as part of the social fabric: hospitals might attract health tourists from the Middle East, for example. Others argued that the mass death meant either that the old town would be haunted in the future, or that the earthquake had occurred because of the accumulated sin of the citizenry. Either way, it was probably better to start again somewhere else. Some of those who thought Bhuj should be shifted were rumoured to own land in the proposed new locations.

Within a week of the disaster there was public discussion about the damage to the town's landmarks that gave Bhuj shape and character. These included the cremation memorials for the former kings of Kutch, the royal palaces, and the town's ancient gates, walls and temples. The pathos of ruined palaces did not escape media attention. Some of the family of the former rulers moved into tents in the courtyard of their crumbling palace and invited journalists to lunch with them. Their seemingly reduced circumstances were presented to the world as an example of the levelling effects of nature (rather than as a story of five post-colonial decades in which the former rulers had gradually but inexorably slid down the hierarchy and were now unable to maintain their former lifestyles or palaces). Such contrivances notwithstanding, the collapsing palaces at the core of Bhuj became powerful and emotive symbols of the collapse of a social order.

In many ways, Bhuj had been a material representation of a socio-moral arrangement which the inhabitants understood because they had grown up with it. Certain areas were associated with particular castes or religious groups, as well as with prescribed kinds of activity. Knowing where people and things were in town was far more than simply a matter of practical knowledge: it was a form of moral reasoning which gave predictable order and pattern to daily life. The vegetarian could hope to avoid the areas associated with the pollution of meat products and meat-eaters. Those needing a padlock or a long length of golden thread would have a pretty clear idea of the area in which such things were sold.

Of course, patterns of urban life in pre-earthquake Bhuj were not unchanging and the order of castes and substances throughout the city was far from perfect. On the whole, however, the people I knew before the earthquake would often speak about the town as if they knew everything there was to know; or, rather, as if what they knew was what they needed to know. This is not to say that people were not curious, for they were, but to say that generally people I knew then were reluctant to display ignorance, especially on matters of local sociology. Knowing about other people was a form of social currency, not knowing and appearing keen to learn (as an anthropologist might) was not the generally accepted paradigm of social intercourse. It was as if by limiting what they knew and by ascribing predictable attributes to who they knew, they were able to disguise the inevitable and actual disorder of a town, which, by the time of the earthquake, had around 150,000 inhabitants (far too many for any individual to know more than a small selection). In sum, even if the town was socially chaotic, the people of Bhuj had developed social and discursive mechanisms to mask the disorderliness. They preferred the illusion of order rather than the frisson and danger of disorder, which was so efficiently brought to light by the earthquake.

The moral familiarity of the town, as well as the perception of order and the tug of both regal and everyday architecture, meant that those who wished to keep Bhuj where it was gained the upper hand. Those who had grown up with the town realised that Bhuj had, in part, made them who and what they were. It was not only that they remembered themselves being and doing in the town. There was more to it than that. Bhuj had given pattern and texture to their reasoning. Living in the town had encouraged them to make associations between particular things and people. In a sense, the town and their journeys within it had structured the ways they could think. The town informed the senses of those who lived there, affording them certain scents and lights, but not others. The town had honed their sensibilities and tastes in particular ways, but not in others. The intimate relationship between people and place suddenly became painfully obvious when much of the town collapsed and once-familiar people were scattered to the winds in panic. The chaos, in other words, was profound.

It is clear that in eighteenth-century Portugal, Pombal largely saw the decision he faced in Lisbon as a matter of practicality. While practicalities were discussed in Bhuj, it is notable that emotional and cultural arguments stood at the front of the discussion. In the midst of panic, compassion and uncertainty, this was not an easy or straightforward choice, and nor were the many variables (the ifs and buts) easy to grasp or measure. Like Pombal, those looking on the ruins of Bhuj eventually plumped for the compromised fourth option, choosing, in addition to modify what was damaged, to expand the plans for the rest of the city. As the months wore on, and despite what they had witnessed there, the old town was just too precious to abandon, although it was clear that it could not stay as it had been.

The decision to make things worse in Bhuj did not belong to a Pombal or even a committee, but to the circumstances covered in the earlier sections of this book: governmental failure, ready finance with particular strings, the fashionable nature of infrastructure projects, and the uneven history of the formation of the state of Gujarat. In the years that were to follow, Bhuj more or less stayed where it was, although its centre of gravity crept to the south. In the process, things were made worse, much worse as it turned out, in the hope of making things better for the future.

The planning and reconstruction of the town is at the heart of the story of post-earthquake Gujarat, as it is in this book. The development banks' division of reconstruction into rural and urban sections created two kinds of development culture. Reconstruction in rural areas was swift but left rural folk at the mercy of private institutions. In urban areas, reconstruction proved to be rather more protracted. The alterations required of the population were harder to discern, but no less dramatic in the end than those undertaken by their rural counterparts.

From the perspective of Bhuj's citizens, many of whom were of course from villages and had regular intercourse with villagers, it was ludicrous that rural areas should have received so much attention: 'those who had little have gained a lot, those who had a lot have lost out', they complained. While those in rural areas had long settled into their new houses, in Bhuj, Anjar and Bhachau conditions remained unpleasant: tin shelters, plastic huts and so forth. There was a widespread perception that the democratic state was doing little for Bhuj, and people became angry.

In their anger, some called for Kutch to be made a separate state, and for the reinstatement of the pre-Independence rulers. Others demanded a return to the fondly remembered days in the 1950s, after Independence, when Kutch was ruled directly from New Delhi. Others simply asked that the national government take charge of reconstruction to save them from the insensitivity and corruption of the government of Gujarat. All shared the concern that the 'outsiders' (and this also included those who had come from elsewhere in Gujarat) governing and reconstructing the land had no clue about local conditions. Through the ham-fisted efforts of 'outsiders', the sensitivities of the population were being ignored, and the nuances of a local culture were being systematically destroyed.

Group 2001 was an organisation of the respectable citizens of Anjar, headed by the indomitable Dr Shyam Sundar, one of the town's leading general medical practitioners. Members of the group burned the government's initial reconstruction policy papers, pledged to write 2001 letters in their own blood to the president of the country, and went on a series of loud and long protest marches. At about the same time, a newly formed organisation in Mumbai, Vatan (or 'Homeland'), launched an appeal for Kutch to be made a union territory—to be ruled directly from Delhi and not as part of the state of Gujarat. Vatan wrote to the prime minister, urging him to visit the region because the 'political tours' offered by the government of Gujarat misleadingly conferred the impression that the state government was in control of the situation.

The then prime minister, A.B. Vajpayee, and his deputy, L.K. Advani, visited Bhuj in June 2001. In the days leading up to their visit, Congress party activists pledged to hang black flags around the ruins to reflect the 'simmering wrath' over the clumsy and inefficient handling of the disaster by the government of Gujarat. Ratnakar Dholakia, one of the leaders of the emerging people's movement in Bhuj, also faxed the prime minister, asking him to intervene directly in the reconstruction. While the Gujarat branch of the ruling BJP had placed advertisements in local newspapers asking people to go about their business as usual, Pushpadan Gadhvi, then the BJP representative for Kutch in the national parliament, publicly backed the idea of union territory status.

The visit of the national leaders was indeed met with a strike, and black flags fluttered on the streets, which must have caused the leaders some personal unease. One of those to meet with the prime minister was Kundanlal Dholakia, an intense and articulate man who was then in his eighties. Dholakia was no stranger to politics, having served as a local municipal leader and later as speaker in the state-level parliament. He told me how he had complained to the prime minister of the 'stepmotherly attitude' of the government of Gujarat towards Kutch. He expressed what he saw as a 'deep yearning' for making Kutch a union territory.

The protests in Bhuj harked back to the moment four decades earlier, when Bombay State had been divided and Kutch became part of Gujarat (discussed in Chapter 8). The earthquake had once again brought to the fore questions of equality and representation within the political organisation of the new state. The earthquake brought to the surface lines of difference that decades of state-building had attempted to bury. A tragedy had befallen Kutch, and the state, an entity people saw as charged with their protection, was either behaving like a buffoon or lacked compassion at the core.

On the public stage during their visit to Bhuj, as well as when speaking elsewhere, both Vajpayee and his deputy, Advani, clearly and forcefully dismissed the demand for regional autonomy—in any form. While the protests did not meet their stated aims, the early disruption they caused added fuel to the fire of those who wished to oust Keshubhai Patel from office as the chief minister of Gujarat (discussed in Chapter 7). Having seen Patel deposed in the name of post-earthquake reconstruction, Narendra Modi, in the early years at least, appeared no better to the residents of Bhuj, as he seemed to continue the policy of neglect.

The protests were significant, however, for what was to happen next in Bhuj. Importantly, the protests focused people's attention on who they were and what was happening to them. They drew attention to the old idea that Kutch was not Gujarat, and thus allowed people to evaluate what was happening to them in these terms. Conversely, the protests also allowed the Gujarat state to present the people of Kutch as ungrateful and as undeserving recipients of the generosity and care it offered. The people of Kutch were thus portrayed as not knowing what was good for them, which justified the firm actions of the state. What had started as a popular appeal for compassion eventually placed the people and the state at loggerheads, and flavoured the first few years of urban aftermath.

In time, as the unwieldy machinery of post-earthquake urban governance began to find its footing, the people, the state and the invisible policies of international financial institutions came face to face in the ruins, although often they could not see one another because they did not know what it was they were looking at. There was much confusion, and the urban aftermath became horrid and alienating.

Seven crows descended on the carcass of Bhuj. The metaphor was popularly used to evoke the sense of predation experienced by the people of the town. Although the identity of each crow was not always the same, the flock included the government, development banks, planners, construction engineers, religious organisations and NGOs. In the folds of their feathers, they brought roaring bulldozers, choking dust and the supernatural ability to make decisions, which, in the pre-earthquake era, they would not have had the wherewithal to make.

The levels of disruption and anxiety inflicted upon those who had survived the earthquake were, with hindsight, quite extraordinary. Buildings were razed, ground levelled, the town redesigned and rebuilt. For a few years, life in Bhuj was indescribably noisy, unsettling, and stressful. In the midst of all this confusion, people continued to get on with their daily business, although, for many, surviving the aftermath became their daily bread.

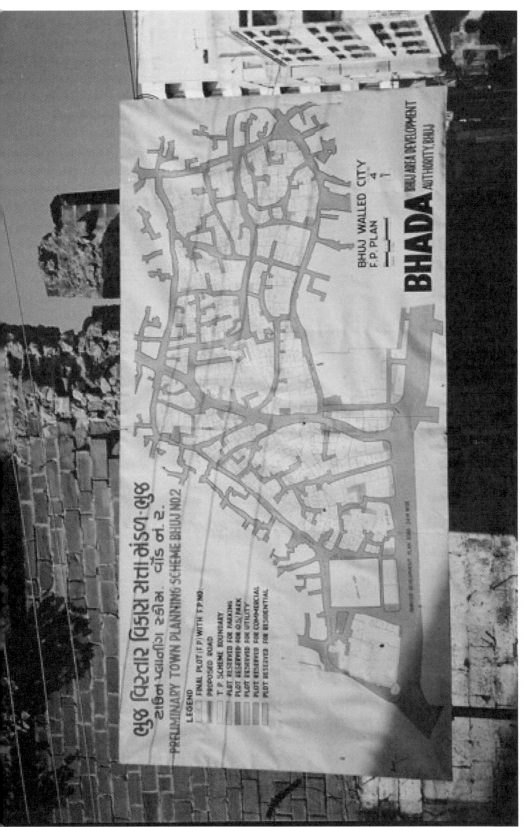

Signboard showing the new layout of the town, 2004, Bhuj.

18

PLANNERS

A few days after the earthquake, the organisation Environmental Planning Collaborative (EPC) established an office in Bhuj in a tent at a relief camp operated by the NGO Abhiyan (a shortened form of Kutch Nav Nirman Abhiyan, KNNA). With support from the USAID-FIRE(D) Project (an American initiative to commercialise the provision of urban environmental services), EPC piloted research into participatory planning in the region.[1]

USAID-FIRE(D) aided the government of Gujarat in developing an institutional framework for reconstruction and managing finances in a 'bankable' way. As discussed in Chapter 4, the Gujarat State Disaster Management Authority (GSDMA) was formed in February 2001 to oversee reconstruction and to develop disaster management plans.[2] The Gujarat Urban Development Company (GUDC) became the implementing agency for urban rebuilding. It was not, however, until May 2001 that the Area Development Authorities (ADAs) in Bhuj, Bhachau, Anjar and Rapar were created under the 1976 Gujarat Town Planning and Urban Development Act.[3] Town and infrastructure planning was outsourced to the private sector, of which EPC was a non-profit-making part. Five months after the earthquake, and based on the strength of its earlier pilot study, EPC was commissioned by GUDC to prepare a development plan for Bhuj, a contract later extended to include a plan for the walled city. Other agencies planned for the other towns, although never with the same resources or support that EPC enjoyed in Bhuj.

EPC consisted of a lively bunch of fiercely intelligent and ambitious people from all over India. Their head offices were in Ahmedabad, and they brought metropolitan ways with them. In Bhuj, they rented a large house in one of the more up-market colonies, where they worked, planned, ate and often slept—behaviour found quite remarkable by many local people. The planners, although Indian, were probably an anathema—rather like foreigners—for most of the town's inhabitants. They mostly spoke and wrote in English to each other, and seemed to behave as if they had no proper culture: they appeared unmarried, slept where they worked, and could be seen prying and measuring things outside government working hours.

The planners brought with them a work ethos and an organisational culture in which it was evident that religion, caste and gender were less significant than they were for most people living in Bhuj. This translated into their planning practices and philosophies too. For the planners to think about planning in terms of caste, for example, was unconstitutional and retrograde. For the town, though, caste was often a deeply important marker of sense and sensibility. Space, the fundamental resource of planning, was a manifestation of the caste order in the town, at least ideally. Consequently, at first, the values and intentions of the planners were broadly mistrusted.

Decisions relating to the reconstruction of Bhuj were mostly invisibly made in faraway places. Symptomatic signs of these policies would then appear in the town, often only inadequately explained. In turn, these signs became the bases of rumours, uncertainty and anxiety. While newspapers and some NGOs made valiant attempts at translating policies (into local languages and unpicking technical concepts), they were often working with only partial information, and their efforts frequently only added to the uncertainty.

The outsourcing of everyday state functions arrived unannounced at a difficult time for the inhabitants of Bhuj. This was not the first privatisation, but it was the first that most people had then encountered face to face. The municipality, once the bumbling but dependable hub of local government, lost much of its influence to the new ADAs, and the relationship between the two bureaucracies was uncertain—even to employees.

Conversely, according to one of the planners:

citizens showed little respect for a municipality that had a record of poor enforcement of whatever regulations had earlier existed, and as a result unregulated development in the months following the earthquake have proven difficult to control. Citizens showed no culture of conforming to rules that should apply to society as a whole, in a disaster situation or otherwise.[4]

In addition to the bureaucratic confusion, at different levels, the planners and those planned for brought different understandings of what was at stake to the process. Thus it was that planning became a bewildering and upsetting experience for many inhabitants. This was not primarily because the people were straightforwardly lawless and self-interested as the planner had pointedly suggested; nor was it due to the incompetence of the planners, as the people sometimes suggested, for the planners were clearly highly skilled at planning.

Mutual misunderstanding was compounded because the planners were guided by a set of rules which were invisible to the townsfolk. They did not know that what the planners had to do had already been largely laid out in the hastily drawn up agreements between Gujarat state and the development banks. The initial public version of the urban reconstruction package was announced in April 2001. At this stage, it was already determined in the broadest sense how Bhuj was going to be put back together. EPC was, in essence, to work on finer details; other agencies had similarly been contracted to refine the planned new infrastructure. Again, this delineation of responsibility was poorly understood in Bhuj, and the planners were often blamed and shouted at for things they could not influence.

Rebuilding a town the size of Bhuj was never going to be easy or pleasant for the inhabitants. The novel neo-liberal and neo-corporatist arrangements of the aftermath contributed an extra thick layer to the palimpsest of anguish. There were several unexplained delays in policy design and decision-making at the higher levels of government—some of these are now understandable given the scale of destruction, others remain incomprehensible and must be attributed, as my friends in Bhuj would do, to unknown 'politics'. The uncertainty caused by the perception of government inaction was compounded by poor communication at all levels. While far away in the east of the state, various departments of government were busy talking to experts about the best course of action, it appeared in Bhuj as if nothing was being done to address the disorganisation of the town.

The fundamental uncertainty in the planning of Bhuj lay in new structures of governance. These were simply misrecognised by the people they were supposed to assist. At the time, most people in Bhuj did not understand that EPC was the immediate face of the structural reforms undertaken as a condition of loans from the development banks; nor did they understand the relation between EPC and the local state planners. In the words of Pramod Jethi, curator at one of the palace museums, 'the government had become a monster without a face'. He was angered at not being able to find out to whom he should address simple questions about housing compensation. It was like a nightmare in which everything looked more or less the same as before, but nothing worked or responded as it was expected to.

Offices which had administered development regulations, property tax and planning applications continued to exist and had personnel, but they no longer functioned. Instead, a large, white, low-lying prefabricated building appeared, quite close to the planners' house, which became home to the Bhuj Area Development Authority, whose acronym (BHADA) was transmuted into 'badder'. The acronym distinguished it from BADA in Bhachau; the second informal designation referred to the quality of the work undertaken.

The people thought, from previous experience, that they knew how the state worked. They knew where the appropriate offices were, who the officers were and how best to approach them. In the aftermath, people drew on their pre-existing knowledge of how to approach the state, and were often frustrated with the result. Literally, they found that they did not know where the appropriate office was, who the officers were or how best to approach them. Those staffing the new offices were also often unfamiliar with local conditions, blind to hierarchy and deaf to many colloquial idioms. While such a separation from the local scene might appear desirable in terms of equity and transparency, the over-riding result was confusion. There were often slow-moving queues, shouting and anger in the BHADA building. Together, these conditions led to the emergence of a class of brokers who encouraged mass fraud on a tremendous scale, entrepreneurially aiding people through the labyrinth of new bureaucratic procedures. BHADA became the source of the town's new personal wealth, primarily through the distribution of compensation for damaged property. It is unfortunately the case that many people got carried away with being cash rich on the payment of the first instalment of compensation, and spent the money on things other than houses.

Aside from rebuilding Bhuj, the state government saw an opportunity to make the town safer, and to impose stricter regulations on what was built and how it was constructed. The initial proposals were a prescription for anxiety. They contained ominous phrases such as 'to be pulled down' and 'option for relocation'.[5] Other clauses generated more general uncertainty: 'houses, which might obstruct proper town planning and do not conform to development regulations, will be relocated'. While 'relocated' is a careless euphemism, as we know from the planner, a great many buildings in Bhuj did not meet pre-earthquake development regulations. Did this mean that the whole town was to be demolished? Then there was the then unknown extent of 'town planning'. What was this? Where was this going to take place? What form would it take? Could its direction and scope be influenced?

The language and signs of planning are relatively straightforward to comprehend, but to plan well, to anticipate consequences, is an art. In Bhuj, the art seemed to have two principal aims: to take control of the present, and to serve as a form of futurology. As a form of control, signboards were posted around Bhuj displaying the new order, making things appear as if they were fixed and certain once again. The intricacies of planning as futurology was largely lost on those angered in Bhuj, who were after a quick fix to some rather obvious problems. Three aspects of planning (as futurology) were to have particularly dramatic consequences, both for the ways in which those planned for initially understood what the planners were doing to them, and for what Bhuj became.

First, there was to be a reduction in 'development intensity' (a phrase easy to write, but with implications difficult to grasp in reality). This reduction was to be achieved by restricting both building height and the permissible 'floor space index' (FSI). In quite a specific sense, this meant that some multi-storey blocks would not meet the new development regulations and would 'lose FSI': they were to be decapitated or, if collapsed, rebuilt to a lower level. Either way, this would leave some of those who previously lived there without apartments. In a more general sense, the reduction in development intensity meant that Bhuj was to be spread out horizontally, becoming bigger, lower and less densely populated.

Although the earthquake had damaged quite a section of the old town, the majority of buildings remained upright and inhabited, a condition which presented an obstacle to allowing the town to become bigger, lower and less densely populated intentional repetition?. These buildings, in part or in whole, would have to be tampered with. The planned manoeuvres were obviously going to create radical disruption. Those living in these structures, probably still quite glad they had not been crushed to death, and taking continued life as a sign that there was not too much wrong with their house, were going to find good reason to object to their proposed relocation.

Secondly, to guide and regulate the city's reconstruction and growth, 'town planning' would be undertaken and 'development control regulations' (relating to the size and quality of particular buildings) would be revised.[6] The development control regulations were subject to several alterations, which delayed rebuilding and caused confusion. In this instance, town planning means something quite specific, to do with the redistribution of land rather than being a generic term for a profession. Town planning was the most disruptive aspect of the reduction of development intensity. I will discuss some of the specific consequences of 'town planning' in the following two chapters. In essence, the policy provides a mechanism for taking away a percentage of land from many private parties in order to make a large section of land available for public or collective use. For understandable reasons, this policy works best when the land is not built upon because it is easier to move the boundary of a field than the walls of a house.

Thirdly, the package offered 'plots' (land on which to build a house) at specific 'relocation sites' around Bhuj. These sites were intended for those whose houses were damaged beyond safety by the earthquake, and for those whose houses were going to be demolished by the new town planning schemes: 'The families relocated will be given land in the nearby areas such as areas in the northern part near police line, Rawalwadi area, Mirzapur area, etc.'.[7] At the time, this notion was insulting and upsetting to residents of the old town. The proposed relocation sites then seemed far from Bhuj (some kilometres and upwards from the town centre), almost in the untamed jungle.

It seemed as if they were being ordered to surrender their house in the centre of the town for a piece of worthless land far away with no roads, shops, schools or temples. Townsfolk, the sophisticates of Kutch, were to be displaced to the untamed wilderness, where snakes and other wild things lived. Literally, it seemed as if people were to be alienated from their property and then expected to move to nowhere where there was nothing. Furthermore, the plots of land were to be 'allotted by draw of lots', which introduced a further level of uncertainty as people imagined being separated from friends, neighbours and relatives, scattered like confetti throughout the city by the luck of the draw.

Unsurprisingly, these policies were cursed a great deal. They introduced new waves of protest and contempt for the state government. It seems beyond the banal to point out that these announcements could have been presented in a language more positive than the draconian terms of demolition and compulsory possession. Indeed, the planners might not have been so mistrusted, and the government might have been forgiven the delays, had the future been worded differently.

Site clearance and levelling at the Rawalwadi Relocation site, 2003, Bhuj.

19

G NUMBERS

EPC worked on the draft plan between May and September 2001.[1] It was published by BHADA, a response then sought from the public, and submitted to the government of Gujarat in December. The draft was approved soon after, but politics and violence in other parts of the state delayed matters. In mid-2002, government planning officers were appointed to Bhuj to implement the plan. Then the third stage, known as the 'final scheme', saw the settlement of rates of compensation and the amount known as the 'betterment charge' that citizens would have to contribute towards the cost of the new Bhuj. BHADA acquired land for roads, public works and reconstruction sites. The town planning schemes went through a first public hearing in October and the second in November. In February 2003, twenty-five months after the earthquake, the final town plans for Bhuj were published. The bulk of Bhuj was rebuilt between 2003 and 2005.

Some of the events and encounters which occurred between the official rubber stamps of progress are powerfully indicative of the way the design of the aftermath was experienced in Bhuj itself. It is to the underside of this just-so planning narrative to which I now turn.

I have a pretty good sense of direction, but was often frustrated in my aims by the old Bhuj of before the earthquake. Even if I knew the general direction of where I wanted to go, the town would often not allow it. Most streets were not very long; some seemed to run for miles. Many twisted and turned unexpectedly into dead ends, as if part of a Gordian knot. Strangers, of course, often looked lost. The progressive disorientation caused by walking in the town, as one road heading in an unanticipated direction led into another, was often quite bewildering. Most streets were too narrow for cars (not a bad thing of course). When unwitting or overly-ambitious motorists wedged their vehicles between buildings, the resulting disruption could be significant. Overhanging structures reduced the arrival of daylight, and a musty smell in some areas suggested that air did not circulate well. Trees, verandas, terraces and wayside shrines often stood as unauthorised street furniture.

Of course, people who lived in old Bhuj knew their way around, or at least around parts of their town. Much of the confusing layout of the town was not randomly chaotic because streets offered protection and privacy, and segregated particular social groups. There was also an arrangement within the layout of the streets which permitted monsoon rainwater to flow unimpeded out of the town. Before the earthquake, people who lived there derived a sense of well-being and safety from the proximate and intimate nature of life. Afterwards, towering buildings on overloaded foundations became sinister and threatening, at least for a while.

After the earthquake, the old town was to be depopulated and tidied up. In time, it became clear that it was not going to be practical or politically possible to 'relocate' all the buildings which did not conform to the new development regulations. It would simply have been too expensive, and the population was already fractious about the disruption. Bhuj was not going to be demolished wholesale. Like many other places in history, Bhuj was going to be rebuilt with compromises. The power of the new building regulations thus defeated, people began to have hope, seeing it was possible to fight and argue with the faceless monster. Compromise, obscured later by miscellaneous 'retrofitting' of older structures, left the planners with around 12,000 irregular shaped plots of land in the walled city to reorder. They had one of those grid-like picture puzzles where one square is missing and the other squares are pushed around in a frame to form an image of a face or a castle or something else—but, in this instance, the puzzle was vast.

As they started to get to grips with the town, EPC held a series of public consultations with those identified as 'opinion leaders' and 'stakeholders'. Almost inevitably, this exercise elevated a small group of men to the position of spokesmen for the interests of the town. EPC recorded a range of diverse opinions, most of which were entirely self-serving and did nothing to suggest that there might be a community consensus on the best course of action (interesting data as a consequence—but difficult to plan with!). They also found how difficult it could be to communicate planning decisions to a general population primarily interested in their own survival. In the end, EPC developed a relationship with Bhuj Development Council (BDC), a body set up by those associated with EPC for the purposes of collaboration. By the time EPC set to work on the fine details of the plan, BDC had offices in the eight wards of the walled city for interaction with the public.

Planners like to take their lead from existing plans and records rather than recreate things anew at each intervention. For planners, maps represent the history of decisions. Unfortunately, one of the things Bhuj had put off until an unspecified date in the future was the maintenance and organisation of its cartographic repositories. When EPC started to work in Bhuj, it was discovered that the last development plan dated from the 1970s, and the city had not been resurveyed since. Existing maps were, therefore, inadequate. The city had to be resurveyed before even preparatory planning work could commence. When the survey was complete, the planners found that the result did not correspond in some key respects with the government's cadastral maps. Matching the results of the new survey with the existing maps and land records involved the examination of all property records, a laborious task which took four months.

The state government carried out a separate assessment of the damage inflicted by the earthquake, and each building was classified on a scale of G0 to G5, with G5 being the most severely damaged (I do not know what the 'G' represented). The results were daubed in red paint on each house, an act which aided the surveyors, and allowed everyone to see how damaged everyone else had been and how much compensation they would be entitled to. Given the amounts of compensation at stake, the number paired with a 'G' became an important indicator of future prospects. Some used sledge hammers and others greased palms to ensure their house was sufficiently damaged. This survey identified buildings by municipal house number, while the new base map created by the planners used city survey numbers. The records in Bhuj that matched city survey numbers with municipal house numbers contained only an old scheme of numbering. At some point in the past, the town had been renumbered and no record had been kept which included both sets of numbers. The planners then had to carry out an additional survey to cross-reference the new base map with actual patterns of damage in the city. Only then could they begin the work of planning.

From the planners' point of view, it was important to identify G5s and severely damaged G4s because these were to become the empty spaces, so to speak, which would allow for new roads and the reduction of development intensity. G5s were to be razed. The policy also allowed for G4s to be demolished, but only if irreparably damaged. The G4 level of compensation was lower than that for G5s, although the results—demolition and homelessness—were to be the same for the owners of both types of property. This led many people to lobby for their G4 to be reclassified as G5 so that they could get more compensation. The policy also allowed people to make the opposite and more consequential argument: 'you have classified my house as G5 but it is damaged in the same way as my neighbour's, which you have classified as a not severely damaged G4. Therefore, I wish that you reclassify my house as G4 because then I will be able to stay where I am and you will not shift me to an unknown place in the jungle'. The anxiety and confusion caused by these poorly distinguished categories of damage delayed the movement of the pieces of the Bhuj puzzle.

The planners' remit was to improve access to the old town, in order to permit the ingress of motor and rescue vehicles, should the need arise. They thought that new roads built through old neighbourhoods might break structures of association and community. After working through a series of possible schemes, it was proposed that a specific set of new wider roads be created in the old town to minimise social fragmentation. New roads would be constructed to form loops, running from the walls into the heart of the old town and out again (today, if one enters the town on a loop road and follows it to the end one will leave the town; if one strays from the loop one is as liable to get as lost as before the earthquake). These roads, they reasoned, would give general access from outside the walls to the markets and commercial areas. The bazaars could then become pedestrian zones, which, unfortunately, they have never really become. In areas such as the town's principal bazaar, where many buildings survived the earthquake, the disruption of demolition could be avoided. In the end, though, this did not occur, for reasons beyond the influence of EPC.

In Gujarat, the 'town planning scheme' is a legislative mechanism which allows private property to be reorganised. A certain percentage of each plot in a given area is retained to make space for new developments. The town planning scheme is usually deployed to convert agricultural land to urban use. But, in the case of Bhuj, the method was tailored to reorganise and redistribute land in the old town, to create space for the loops and to reduce the intensity of development.

The responsibility placed upon the planners and the pressure they faced was extraordinary. On the Indian planning scene, this was acclaimed as an innovative and ambitious piece of work. The plan was to reduce the size of all empty plots over 30 square metres: plots of 30 to 100 square metres were deducted 10 per cent; plots of 100 to 200 square metres, 20 per cent; plots of 200 to 500 square metres, 30 per cent; and plots of more than 500 square metres, 35 per cent. In the end, the tax on wealth was not allowed to take such a progressive form, and a solution closer to the demands of the status quo was implemented.

As the intervention forced a consideration of the minute details of property boundaries in Bhuj, the planners also had an opportunity to improve the general layout of plots in relation to one another, and in relation to the planned new road network. This mechanism spread the burden of land and property loss over a greater proportion of the population than other alternatives (such as simply widening existing roads). Standing buildings were spared deduction, unless they were affected by the proposed new roads or by the realignment or widening of existing roads. On the face of it, the initial drafts of the design were quietly revolutionary as a progressive taxation on space, promoting, if not exactly greater equality then less inequality in landholding. Stepping back a bit from the detail, it is also possible to see that this proposal placed the burden of development exclusively on those whose property was either severely affected by the earthquake, or was due for demolition in order to make way for new roads: a progressive taxation on general misfortune.

As the plan was implemented, the town planning scheme and the reduction of development intensity became the focus of life in Bhuj. There were numerous channels through which complaints could be made, grievances pursued and injustices addressed. Information cells were established, leaflets circulated, and a daily television bulletin addressed issues relating to the reconstruction of the town, with one particular journalist often managing to make light of a situation which was anything but. Local newspapers ran stories about procedural anomalies and categorical errors, highlighting particular instances of suffering and insensitivity on the part of the state.

Despite the superabundance of information, public engagement with the plan and later with the complaint procedures was primarily at the level of private property, and not generally concerned with the overall layout and ethos of the town. People were motivated to action when their property or the future of their family was in question. Participation was a defensive position focused on preservation rather than being a proactive stance. The plight of religious buildings were the only instances I am aware of which produced a collective response. Threats made by the planners to temples, mosques and graveyards often met with opposition from shouting groups of men or the ominous quiet of a hunger striker.

Initially, the most prominent example of 'cutting' was in the northern part of the old town. A row of lock-up shops, which had survived the earthquake unscathed, was 'cut' to make way for a loop, 2003, Bhuj.

20

THE UNBEARABLE INTENSITY OF REDUCTION

During the implementation of the town planning scheme, a number of English-language terms became part of normal speech. I noticed the arrival of the word 'mugging' and an increase in the use of 'tension'. The adoption of foreign terms reflected the general sense of alienation and dislocation. Haresh, the manager of a bank in Bhuj, claimed that the 'tension' of life after the earthquake had eaten away at people's brains. He saw in his bank how people worried about money, where they were to live, and how they were to get what they were entitled to from the complicated machinery of the state. 'Tension', he said, 'was life threatening'. According to him, although the earthquake took thousands of lives, the aftermath had slowly killed many more. In his view, 'tension' was given by the state in the form of financial and physical insecurity, the uncertainty of policies, and the demolition of what was familiar.

I do not know anyone who was 'mugged', but the fear of crime increased, and became a normal topic of conversation. Unerringly, labourers from other parts of the country, who were in town to work on construction sites, were blamed for a spate of burglaries. In 2004, Dilip's house was smashed open, and jewellery and cash taken. In sixty-five years, he had never had anything stolen. The novelty of the idea that someone had come into his house and taken his things struck him as tremendous. His smile was incredulous as he showed me the extra steel grills and padlocks he had installed. Burglary had brought with it a cognitive leap.

No one was seen or heard robbing Dilip's house, and the stolen goods were never recovered. The thieves remained unknown, and were therefore unaccountable to the normal networks of redress and sanction that townsfolk liked to imagine existed and kept them safe. The migrant labourers were easy to blame as they too were largely unknown and nameless. It was the case, however, that they had no attachment or responsibility to the place, and had come to profit in their own small ways from the disaster. For the people of Bhuj, the shadowy tatters of the labour camps which had appeared around the town contained anti-social elements, non-humans almost, who had come to take what they could from the carcase of Bhuj.

'Tension' was the aftermath illness, post-traumatic stress disorder without a strong emphasis on the 'post'. The presence of anti-social strangers helping themselves to the treasures of intimate spaces was a symptom of a runaway world. Similarly, in every-day language, town planning became known as 'TP' and synonymous with 'cutting' and 'demolition' (also English words), rather than with improvements to the built environment. 'Cutting' involved, quite literally, cutting old Bhuj to the shape of the new plan. If a new road was to pass through the corner of your house, then that corner was cut away by the demolition teams contracted by the state. In such a case, you had the right to a plot in a relocation site on the surrender of what remained of your old plot. If you did not want to move to the relocation site, and many people did not, you could fight to remain in your now corner-less house—a structure presumably less robust than before.

Initially, the most prominent example of 'cutting' was in the northern part of the old town. A row of lock-up shops, which had survived the earthquake unscathed, was 'cut' to make way for a loop. The cut started at the rear wall of the structure and moved through the partition walls between the shops at a shallow diagonal (forming an acute scalene triangle). The result was that the first shop in the row was little more than a suggestion of space in front of what had been the rear wall, while the deepest shop at the other end of the row was perhaps two metres at most from front to back. What had been a sizable building was reduced to its rear wall and the studs of partitions.

The planner's work of tidying Bhuj up on paper led in practice to a large number of bizarrely shaped structures. Perhaps it had been assumed that 'cut' buildings would be abandoned, but in fact they were very often patched up. Should these structures survive, they will intrigue future archaeologists, who will see in them evidence of a society's improbable use of acute and oblique angles in their domestic architecture. For years, the seemingly unusable lock-up shops stood empty, open to the weather, staring unblinking onto the new road before them. Their ridiculousness was a daily reminder of the costs of TP. After about eight years, one of them became a general store, and then another became a laundry.

Bhuj was also subject to other kinds of 'cutting': buildings which were not earthquake affected but did not conform to new regulations or had been built in disregard of previous regulations wording. At the time, everyone in the town could see that this form of 'cutting' was applied selectively and unevenly. 'Cutting', in such instances, seemed to be a punishment by the administration of particular interest groups and individuals. Such 'cutting' did not provoke mass protest because, unusually, those affected were influential and wealthy. Many people seemed content to watch with curiosity, if not enthusiasm, the improbable and intriguing battle between the administration and the commercial lobby, groups generally assumed to be in cahoots.

Immediately after the earthquake, the chief administrator of the district, 'the collector', was transferred to make room for a more experienced administrator. The new arrival became known for his hands-on approach to governance; as he toured the town, he patted and hugged those he saw as victims. He wanted, he said, for the people to feel the care of the state. He had his own understanding of humanitarian governance. By the time of 'tension' and 'cutting', Pradeep Sharma had replaced him in the hot seat. Sharma served in Bhuj between May 2003 and July 2006, arriving just as the new plan was to be implemented. He became a prominent figure in the town, always sharply dressed, and personally involved in overseeing a number of reconstruction projects, most notably a park which became known as the Hill Garden in the new suburbs to the south of Bhuj.

In the main bazaars, damaged shops had been quickly patched up, and reasonable trade was soon restored after the earthquake. The roads were, however, far narrower than the new minimum requirements. The planners from EPC had originally suggested that the main bazaar area should be left as it was and pedestrianised to minimise disruption. The state planners thought differently, deciding that in the interests of safety the area might be improved. Notice was served on shopkeepers in 2002. Much lobbying had ensued to save the bazaar from partial demolition. In winter 2003, ominous red marks appeared on walls—40, 52, 67 and so forth—indicating how many centimetres were to be 'cut' from the front of each shop in order to widen the street.

There was little room for heavy mechanical cutting equipment. Much of the work was done by hand, with lump hammers, hacksaws and grinders. As the demolition crews descended, the atmosphere in the bazaar was extraordinary. There was the palpable excitement of mass disruption and crisis, and the chatter of a large number of spectators. But there was also anger and resignation. The streets were once again quickly filled with rubble and the air with dust; the 'second earthquake' of these few days was greater than a metaphor.

The work was conducted swiftly and without much consideration for safety. Shops remained open, and their keepers wore masks and handkerchiefs over their mouths to keep the dust from their lungs as the rubble fell around them. Sharma made a series of television appearances on an evening news programme, in which he walked through the bazaars with a journalist explaining the logic of the demolition underway. During the day, he could be seen out on the streets supervising the work. I remember seeing him once standing next to his jeep, a foot resting on a rock, hands on hips, surveying the landscape of destruction. His posture seemed to communicate satisfaction.

The demolition improved the sightline of the street, removing most shop-front verandas, forcing business and conversation inside, and changing the character of the bazaar forever. I have also wondered how it is possible to remove a major supporting wall without weakening the integrity of a structure overall.

Sometime later, Sharma took his sense of equity to the prosperous area of Hospital Road in the newer part of Bhuj. There he demanded the removal of the frontage of some six-storeyed buildings because they were in violation of new building codes. The earthquake and TP had left the town familiar with the sights of the intimate and usually private places of family life. Kitchens, hearths, cupboards and other inside stuff of houses were frequently exposed to scrutiny from the outside when walls were missing. Things that were usually concealed behind closed doors became part of the public townscape. The buildings on Hospital Road became the talk of the town, a spectacle. In some cases, apartments were still furnished while surgery was performed to the façade. Even when personal effects had been removed, the exposure of toilets, kitchens and bedrooms attracted voyeurs from far and wide.

Even at the time, this demolition exercise seemed either to be an act of perversion or revenge. There was indeed much speculation as to why Sharma was so motivated. While there might be additional clues in his arrest in 2010 for irregularities in the distribution of land after the earthquake, his acts were commonly understood as being a message for those who had attempted to bypass his authority by taking their issues up through party-political rather than administrative networks.

While these dramatic acts of 'cutting' were remarkable, elsewhere in the town the disruption of everyday life continued to be profound. 'We could not work together, there is no community left here, it has gone, broken by the earthquake and then the suffering that followed. It was all we could do to look after ourselves. Those who we knew to be living were often lost to us as they moved away.' These are the words my friend Saleh used in 2004 to explain the lack of cooperation in his neighbourhood three years after the earthquake. He lamented the dissolution of the networks which had once made it possible to work together, to have collective memories and to participate in political agitations. In a sense, Saleh was nostalgic for the earlier years of the aftermath (2002 and 2003), when, compared to 2004, life was not so bad. For him, life got worse rather than better for quite a stretch after the earthquake.

Eventually, as time passed, the Gujarat state began to prevail. It took an iron grip, divesting people of property, making examples of the defiant, investing in the super-abundance of new bureaucracy and using 'cutting' as punishment. The state itself became a source of worry and confusion for many and, as the nostalgia inherent in the call for a separate administrative status for Kutch revealed, it also became a target for their anger. At first, people felt neglected, and they publicly resented this. Later, the compensation schemes promised wealth. As a result, access to the government's coffers became highly competitive and a source of jealousy, rivalry and suspicion.

In time, the struggle for compensation became a collective preoccupation pursued along non-collective lines. Once the levels and nature of compensation had been set, the general aim was to claim as much as possible. The game with G numbers was only one of the available avenues, which led to a staggered payment system for con-structing new houses for those affected by the earthquake and TP. There had also been compensation schemes for dead humans and animals and lost body parts. In addition, the state offered enterprise grants, and there was a range of financial oppor-tunities in the private sector. Any claim on the state was time-consuming, involving large numbers of documents and numerous trips to various offices.

The immense struggle to maximise compensation claims atomised communities, forcing people to be secretive about the lies they had told. In neighbourhoods all over Bhuj, mistrust ran riot as neighbour stopped talking to neighbour, lest the lies told to ensure compensation or new business and enterprise grants were revealed. Perhaps unsurprisingly, self-interest triumphed over collective endeavours as elementary needs such as housing and dreams of the future took precedence.

At a general level, the pursuit of self-interest contributed to the fragmentation of the separatist movements. At the same time, factionalism and competition increasingly came to characterise the coalition of protestors. The state gradually gained the upper hand and took control as people were lured towards webs of time-consuming procedures and the promises of wealth that they held. In short, the period of collective protest against the state of 2001 and 2002 lapsed into self-interested action in 2003, as the scramble for critical resources began in earnest. Collective action ground to a halt as individuals increasingly began to pursue and protect their own interests.[1]

For example, in 2001, when Kundanlal Dholakia, the veteran Congress politician and resident of Bhuj we met earlier, approached the prime minister of India to urge him to save Kutch from the neglect of 'stepmotherly' Gujarat, his actions were met with great approval and generous newspaper coverage. Two years later, however, he sat down in the compound of a blood bank in Bhuj and fasted for nine days. He expected mass support, but remained practically alone. His overarching complaint had not changed: the state government was destroying Kutch through its failure or unwillingness to understand local needs, conditions and sensibilities, and, therefore, governance should be passed to New Delhi. On the ninth day of his fast, I.K. Jadeja, then minister for urban development in Gujarat, said he would concede to Dholakia's demand for more sensitive town planning, but would not entertain discussions about the incompetence of his own administration or the devolution of the state.

According to others in Bhuj, Dholakia was no longer the hero he had once been. The press coverage too was sceptical. He appeared to be fasting alone because he was alone—everyone else had withdrawn support. Protest and modes of political self-presentation had moved on since the earthquake. Dholakia and his hand-spun clothes and peaceful protest had become a 'museum piece'. According to one particularly cynical but well-informed friend, Dholakia would not let doctors touch him, not because he was prepared to die but because they would see he had been eating. The government sent people to meet him, not because he was influential but because they did not want a martyr on their hands. Why should Dholakia suddenly get involved again in popular protest nearly two years after the earthquake? Was he protesting for the general good of Kutch as he claimed? No, the cynic said, he was doing it because his caste temple was threatened by the town planning schemes. He was now said to be using the façade of public good in the pursuit of personal interest. He might well have been, but at least he attempted something.

SECTION 5

THE WORK OF MOURNING

People began to want impossible things. The king wanted his throne back. Others wanted the earthquake to return their innocence. History became a form of currency. Wonderful rituals took place to purify the land and to begin reconstruction. Umashankar saw an opportunity to put right the things that were wrong. Dilip tried to avoid meeting people. The Bhujians were encouraged to suburbanise. New names were given to old things. Bhuj grew.

Cracked palaces, 2003, Bhuj.

21

NOSTALGIA

The mass destruction of an earthquake is quite a thing. For Bhuj, a hard aftermath followed, and the emergent shapes and sounds of the town served as reminders of the fragmentation of the old ways. The palaces at the core were cracked and then began to collapse. Much of the rest of the old town lay in rubble. When debris was cleared, alarming new spaces were created, rendering old haunts unrecognisable. During these times, nostalgic images and conversations became commonplace. In many ways, nostalgia was also at the heart of separatist agitations. As the population protested, Gujarat was made an outsider to both suffering and history. History was rolled back, and a golden era when Kutch was Kutch and Gujarat did not yet exist became a platform from which people expressed with confidence their anger.

Nostalgia is a form of 'homesickness', and, in quite a literal way, many people missed their homes and the people who had made life what it was. The term 'nostalgia' was coined in the seventeenth century by Johannes Hofer to describe the despondent disease of Swiss mercenaries fighting away from home.[1] In moral philosophy and anthropology, however, nostalgia is more commonly associated with alienation from natural and social worlds.

Nostalgia is often linked to the waxing power of the state or to the sense of decline inherent in Abrahamic religions—a structure given by the expulsion of Adam and Eve from the Garden of Eden, the Fall, and the loss of innocence. A nostalgic person may attempt to recall a general historical loss. Nostalgia may also emerge when simplicity, personal authenticity and emotional spontaneity are denied. As individual freedom and autonomy disappear, and genuine social relationships appear to collapse, then the certainty of what is lost may also be evoked as nostalgia. Finally, the absence or loss of personal wholeness and moral certainty is also again associated with the production of nostalgia.[2]

Nostalgia fits well with the general path narrated in this book, as we begin to move away from humiliation towards self-admiration. Nostalgia is an appropriate response to the humiliation of an earthquake and subsequent deprivations. The death of collective nostalgia, the point at which political protest lost momentum, suggests the dissolution of that society which had made such movements possible in the first place.

If an ancient town collapses, and many people are killed, a sense of historical loss will prevail. In Bhuj, we can see that nostalgia was not a generic response to tragedy, but waxed and waned at very particular points in the aftermath. The passing of nostalgia demonstrated that humiliation has a half-life. The passing of nostalgia is also a direct reflection of the various conditions created by the reconstruction policies: relocation, 'cutting', 'town planning' (TP), compensation and, perhaps more importantly, the uncertainty and then the secrecy and silences of greed.

The nostalgia of historical loss was expressed as a movement for regional autonomy, an expression of collective nostalgia. Protestors called for independence from Gujarat, harking back to an era when Kutch was recognised as 'different'. Without necessarily supporting the populism of such protests, there were others who also held similar views about the distinctiveness of the region, to whom we now turn.

Pragmulji is the grandson of the last ruler of Kutch. He is a proud man with uncommonly well-structured ideas. From his point of view, Gujarat is a political concept with little weight or historical depth. He admires Mahatma Gandhi (and has his autograph) as a representative of what Gujarat stood for. The violence of the modern state has taken Gujarat far from traditional or proper ways. When I met him in Mumbai in 2007, we talked about what had happened in Bhuj since the earthquake.

I knew from earlier visits to his palaces in Kutch that he continued the rituals of the kingdom, much as his forefathers had done. In Mumbai, I was surprised to hear him say that he thought the post-earthquake loss of all that was unique in Bhuj was inevitable, having outlived its time. According to him, then, the changes taking place in the town were too big to fight. Local ways of doing things had not been respected, and this was to the shame of Gujarat. He said that he did not have much time left, and there was little point in worrying about such matters. This final statement, I thought, had the air of something the son of a diplomat would say to a relative stranger, rather than reflecting a deeply held opinion.

Having gone to some length to explain how pointless it was to worry about change because change was inevitable, he then altered the topic and his tone. His grandfather, he said, had been in the habit of setting up temporary camps in different parts of his realm. He did this because he wanted to get to know his people and their land. He was interested in their lives and views, and such expeditions were far more than a ruler impressing authority upon his subjects. The party would engage in hunting or pig-sticking, depending on the terrain. They would also call on nearby villages. There, they would enter a world of wonder, of true personality and unconditional hospitality. The interlopers would learn about the trials and tribulations of rural life. Pragmulji told me that such trips were among the very happiest times of his life.

In 2005, Pragmulji issued a memorandum demanding a new and independent Kutch. He sent the document to everyone he could think of. His main reasons were as follows: the Kutchi language is quite distinct from Gujarati, which has become the standard language of the state. Kutchis have become a linguistic minority, and their language is under threat. Kutch marks its new year with the Ashadi calendar and almanac, while the Kartik system prevails in Gujarat.[3] Kutch possesses a distinct island-like geography, which separates it physically from Gujarat. As Bhuj is such a long way from Gandhinagar, the administrative capital of the state, Kutch finds it hard to get adequate political recognition. Finally, Pragmulji thought, that because James MacMurdo, the first British political agent, had written (in 1820) that Kutch had never been part of the adjoining territories of Sindh or Saurashtra, such separation should naturally continue.[4]

In 2005, Pragmulji had also again started to visit the villages of Kutch to talk to the people he encountered about the possibilities of restoring royal power. His own nostalgia was intense, with the loss of his own childhood, intermingled with the greater loss of his family's power when Kutch ceded to the Indian Customs Union. At the time of our Mumbai conversation, he was around 70 years old and without an obvious heir. He could clearly, and with visible sadness, see Kutch moving beyond his reach. For him, it was not the earthquake that had changed Kutch beyond recognition, but the regime change of more than five decades earlier. The earthquake was the death knell.

The Gujarat Research Society, which worked towards a united and independent Gujarat in the middle decades of the twentieth century, reasoned that it was possible to flatten the differences (the differences Pragmulji had concisely outlined in his memorandum) between the mainland and the peninsula through planned industrialisation and the development of infrastructure. Then, they thought, their Gujarat would be stronger and their internal power greater. The society understood that infrastructure was not a neutral technology; rather, it was something which could be used in conjunction with notions of culture and power to bring about social and political change. The roads and factories they imagined were objects of state-building, rather than aspects of regional development. After a fashion, these ideas were mobilised in post-1960 Gujarat, and intensified in Kutch after the earthquake.

In the past, the perceived under-representation of Kutch in the political structures of the state, of which Pragmulji was of course well aware, had led to previous murmurings of regional discontent. None of these earlier calls for a separate Kutch had amounted to anything, and, although Pragmulji has a small but loyal following, his desire to restore the throne meets with little public support.

For Pragmulji, and some of the others I have mentioned, history is presented as the collapse of the values which once provided unified relations, knowledge and indeed experience. The rate of collapse appears to have been accelerated by the earthquake. State-led development and the apparent homogenisation of cultural life in the name of progress or development have provided fertile ground for the fermentation of nostalgia. The counterpart to this development has been the destruction of provincial religious or cultural certainties through the emergence of an industrial economy and a new town. Thus, with the death of gods or kings, as it were, and the loss of moral coherence, the isolated individual (or property-owning unit) has been increasingly exposed to the constraining social processes of modern institutionalised regulation by the state, which has gradually undermined and strangled a distinct sense of identity and the past. While this sounds like a common and outdated socio-logical argument about the development of the secular state in Europe, it is not; rather, it is the underbelly of the post-colonial reinvention of western India.

The groundswell of collective nostalgia after the earthquake was perhaps also, in part, an attempt to deny the legitimacy and difficulties of present conditions. The state advanced, alienating people from property and routine, and imposing regula-tion, bank accounts, insurance and other new forms of paperwork. The protest move-ments were also a means of coming to terms with new relationships with the past. In comparison to the generalised nostalgia of the separatist movements and Pragmulji's particular restorative vision, the nostalgia that individuals commonly expressed for pre-earthquake Bhuj tended to be immersed in particular relationships and places that no longer existed in any form other than memory. In the initial years after the earthquake, there was a general concern with the people and places of the 'good old days' rather than with life in a 'golden age'.[5]

Friends, relatives and the certainty of the house appeared often in conversations about the past, such as the following: 'I often think of my friend Jatin. He was gen-erous-hearted and, like me, he loved motorbikes. His Hero Honda died with him'. 'My cousin was taken off. With her passing I have lost touch with her family and with part of myself'. 'I learned to play musical instruments in that house as a child. Music was to become the dominating passion of my life. With the destruction of my instruments and my past I am less inclined to play'. 'I think back to when Bhuj was peaceful, before the bulldozers and TP. I cannot believe how lucky we were. We did not know it then'.

For Pragmulji, the desire was for the impossible absence of India, while the general population of Bhuj desired the absence of the earthquake. In both cases, the nostalgic was in search of the absence of trauma or humiliation—itself, I am suggesting, the generating mechanism of this strain of nostalgia. Therefore, in a sense, the nostalgic is a search for a time in which nostalgia or India was itself absent. Nostalgia is, there-fore, what might be seen as an impossible desire for its own absence. The nostalgic person recalls, or at least imagines, a time when the burden of hindsight was not so heavy, and when the individual concerned was unaware of the everyday things they will subsequently yearn for; in fact, they are as yet to understand that they will yearn.

On the third anniversary of the earthquake, Narendra Modi inaugurated two reconstruction projects in Bhuj, one of which was Sharma's bizarrely 'cut' bazaar. As part of his whistle-stop tour, and amid conspicuous security, Modi took the oppor-tunity to announce plans for an official memorial. The BJP cadres had done a good job in motivating the citizenry, for Modi was met with cheering crowds waving flags. The desire of the state to determine how the dead were to be remembered might be interpreted as an attempt to monopolise, institutionalise or fix memories about the disaster. In this instance, the announcement was also an intervention in the history of regional politics that had contributed to the aftermath protests.

Modi was visibly irritated by the troublesome noises being made in Kutch about political autonomy. In his main speech of the day, he told the thousands who had come to listen to him to put the earthquake behind them because the rest of Gujarat had already forgotten about it.

Hundreds, if not thousands of families were still homeless, existing in poor conditions and facing uncertain futures. Bhuj remained a noisy and dirty mess, and much of Bhachau was as lifeless as it had been three years earlier. Despite Modi's suggestion, in urban Kutch it was quite impossible to forget the earthquake, given the general conditions of the day. While the cruelty and pointedness of his remark did not go completely unnoticed, it did not cause the anger one might have anticipated. The cooperation required to protest was disappearing fast.

As people began to see the possibility of a new suburban house, relatively free from the shackles of the past, flare-ups of memory as forms of regional sentiment were perhaps, as the historian of memory Pierre Nora has suggested for France, the final consumption of these memories in the flames of history.[6] Between 2001 and 2004, the state did not have a hand in the design of collective or nostalgic memories. Then, the people were one step ahead of the state, or the state lagged behind. Yet, the state gradually began to take control of the unruly—not through force, but through paperwork and compensation. Pragmulji's attempt to rally his troops came too late because by then the 'stepmother' had won favour through generosity.

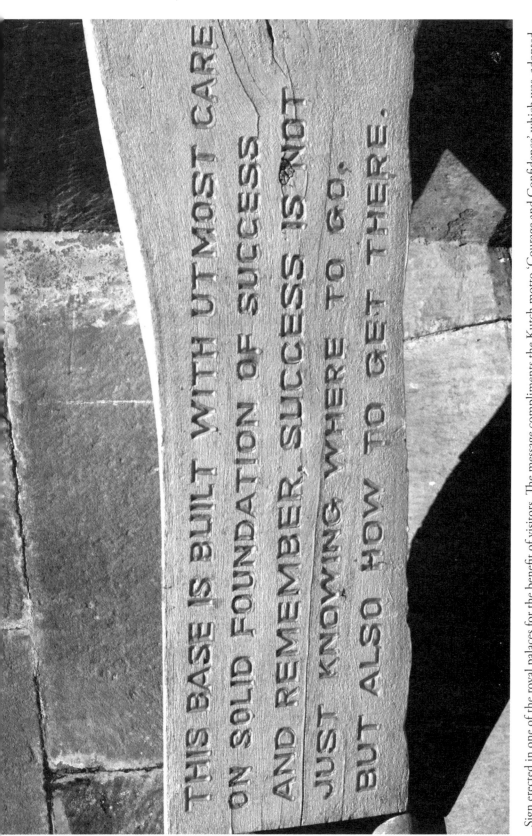

THIS BASE IS BUILT WITH UTMOST CARE ON SOLID FOUNDATION OF SUCCESS AND REMEMBER, SUCCESS IS NOT JUST KNOWING WHERE TO GO, BUT ALSO HOW TO GET THERE.

Sign erected in one of the royal palaces for the benefit of visitors. The message compliments the Kutch motto 'Courage and Confidence' which was adopted, along with a coat of arms, in the late nineteenth century, 2009, Bhuj.

22

HISTORY MAKING

Before and after the earthquake, I have often been directed to men who were experts in the past, as if the past were the only legitimate subject for research. Some were retired civil servants, while others worked for local newspapers and museums. Between them, they authored a large number of articles, pamphlets and self-published books on the history of Kutch.[1] With all respect, their corpus is largely repetitive, as the same wisdoms, heroes and villains are trotted out, often word for word from older sources. Perhaps, for them, history is about authenticity, rather than originality or novelty; or, maybe, there is not enough history to go round, given the relatively large number of amateur historians. While it would be hasty to discard either possibility, it also seems to me that the nature of their repetition reveals other concerns, to which I turn later. For now, it is sufficient to note that these men and their historical productions were given a new lease of life after the earthquake.

As a distraction from the unthinkable horror of mass death, 'history' became even more important in Bhuj. I have already suggested that the emotional and political identification many people had with the place was strong in relation to its ruler's architecture. Despite modern expansion, the walls, gates, palaces and water tanks of the old town, steeped as they were in royal traditions and embellished with myths and symbols, were the pre-eminent and largely encompassing symbols of the town's identity. It was primarily this complex of objects on to which attention fell.

In addition, a culture of heritage was encouraged by some funding agencies. The past was evoked through the collection and display of browning and sepia photographs. Bhuj's past came again to be characterised by the kinds of people and things that appear in old photographs: the ruling classes, their works and the spectacular. Such heritage was in rather short supply, and the business of collecting it became somewhat cut-throat. Some heritage-hunters engaged in petty campaigns against those they imagined to be their rivals. The heritage impulse also fostered competition between local historians, especially when they heard money was available for their contributions towards the collaborative canvas of history-making: history was commoditised.

Men emerged who could recount the history of Bhuj to those who wanted to hear it. They were made to appear as local and authentic by their patrons, as if their indigenous wisdoms had been honed over the centuries along with the town itself. Many of these men were relatively well to do, but their preoccupation with the past was not simply an elite concern, for their histories spilled into the wider world through the media, the circulation of pamphlets, local tourism and, more recently, the internet. The municipality also maintained an almanac, a book of days, which served as a daily reminder of the foundation day, royal birthdays and so forth. Many of these anniversaries were accompanied by public rituals and coverage by the sympathetic local press.

Of course, not all of the historians tell exactly the same story about the foundation and formation of Bhuj. Over the years, however, I have heard one particular form of the narrative very often. This account can perhaps be best thought of as the embroidery on the fabric of the genealogical history presented in Chapter 16.

Bhuj was founded in 1549 when the first ruler, Khengarji, drove a *kili* (peg or stake) in to the ground around which palaces, walls, the town and the kingdom developed concentrically. To this day, a stake marks the centre of the kingdom and the moment of its foundation. Khengarji was passing what was to become Bhuj when he saw a hare fighting with a dog. He was impressed by the courage and strength of the hare. He concluded that the people of this place must also be abnormally able, and so decided to build his capital on the site.

As he hammered the stake into the ground, as part of the rituals to purify the land, it bounced back, the tip covered in blood. The attendant priest believed the king had injured a subterranean serpent. Or, alternatively, the king had been attempting to drive the stake into the head of the serpent to harness its power and to prevent it from writhing and causing disruption to the land. Unsure of whether he had found his target, he again removed the stake, but when blood issued forth from the land he realised he had been successful. When he went to replace the stake, the serpent had moved. This time, instead of pinning the hood of the serpent, Khengarji pierced its tail. From that day onwards, the snake has been writhing in its subterranean home, causing the earth to quake. In order that the snake would remain quiet, it had to be propitiated and, accordingly, a temple was constructed on Bhujia Hill to the east of the modern town.

In the centuries that followed, a succession of kings came to the throne, their strength and munificence loyally recorded in eulogistic prose by bards kept in their pay. Each ruler contributed in various ways to the ceremonial and commemorative landscape, constructing city walls, palaces, gates, water tanks, temples and so on. The king protected his territory and vassals by guaranteeing their safety, prosperity and well-being. Around the rulers clustered service castes, relationships cemented through particular socio-religious institutions. In this sense, merchants, armies, police, bodyguards, educationalists, craftsmen and so on served the interests of the kingdom, itself synonymous with service to the rulers. Ideally, the kings and their consorts maintained the hierarchical caste system, protected the privileges of Brahmins and the rights of all the different castes, confirmed their relative rank, and upheld the authority of caste courts.

Within the kingdom there were smaller Jadeja fiefdoms, autonomous tributaries of the state or semi-independent towns under direct rule from Bhuj, while under them were tiers of lesser headmen with lordship over particular hamlets. Thus, political authority, although having a centre at the royal courts in Bhuj, was hierarchically dispersed throughout the kingdom in provincial political centres, which formed ritual and political microcosms of the ruling Jadeja lineages. Rule was associated with a broad collection of people, buildings and institutions connected to the king and protective deity.

The Jadeja ruler and his goddesses preserved the kingdom. Of the goddesses, two were particularly important. The first is Mahamaya, the great goddess associated with the lineage, and sometimes described as the first ancestor of the rulers. The second is the mother goddess Ashapura, who is the ruler's tutelary goddess as well as royal and state deity.[2] An integral part of ruling power, Ashapura is seen as the source and representative of power in the kingdom and linked to the earth as both fertile soil and political territory. In this sense, she was identified specifically with the lands of Kutch and with the rulers, who were literally seen as the sons of her soil. Vital in the relationship between deity and king was the royal lineage, itself, of course, the pre-eminent form of genealogy, which was also derived from and perpetuated by the powers of the goddess. This relationship was informed by other symbols of royal power (throne, sword, turban, horse, palaces and city walls) and non-Brahmin mediators. As the royal courts in Bhuj were to the lesser fiefs, so the goddess was to lineage goddesses of fief lineages. Thus, gradations of goddesses and territory were hierarchically ordered, but encompassed by the apical goddess and king.

Within this narrative of state formation are the lesser narratives about the origins of each caste and guild, and a chronological history of key happenings. Hindu caste mythology weaves together the social and ritual practices of the present through temples, revered figures and particular places in the landscape. These myths generally identify a divine origin from one of the many characters in the Ramayana or Mahabharata (the two great mythologies of modern Hinduism) and a human manifestation in a noble descent line. This kind of mythology also typically shows arrival in Kutch to have been at the behest of a god, king or holy man, often combined with displacement caused by victory or defeat in battle with Muslims. Once in Kutch, further miraculous events display the affinity of the new arrivals to particular villages and ruling families. The more successful of these myths also connect the caste in question to the kingdom's chronology of significant events. Thus, past battles, invasions, intrigues, successions and so forth became part of the reason for a caste being in Kutch. These sub-narratives implicate themselves in the history of the territory, and by doing so they become indispensable for the narration of the past. The cultural and ritual ethos in the narrative of martial Hinduism permeates every event, moral and outcome.

This ethos is exclusive and attempts to eradicate different geographical origins of the local population, instead presenting them as Hindus of various castes with traceable descent from Hindu deities. The overall effect of this encompassing form of history-telling is that it allows for the different perspectives and stories of caste myths, but ultimately they are subordinate to, and thus complement, the grand narrative of state formation.

The narrative ties different elements of a kingdom together to explain what is already there. This is history moulded from the inside, told in a way that mirrors quite precisely the form of an ideal Jadeja Hindu kingdom in which rule, cosmology and historical narrative coincide and are mutually constitutive. History, in this sense, is a description of the way in which kingship and emergent ideas of sovereignty ideally function in space and over time. The logic of rule, and the narration of the whole coming into being, takes the form of a series of connections between myths, people and places clustered, rather like the physical appearance of old Bhuj itself, around the rulers and their palaces.

The history-makers saw their story-telling as part of the work necessary to put back together the broken and ruined landscape of Kutch. Their story of the foundation of Bhuj is based on the earthquake myth of the writhing serpent, and the ritual complex at the centre of the kingdom in which a metal stake is driven into the earth to hold it in place. We will turn to the significance of the coincidence of stories and events in Section 6. I stress here that the story has been told like this since the nineteenth century, if not earlier—it is not simply a convenient invention following the most recent disaster.[3] Alongside Pragmulji's claim on a distinct language and geography, the history of the structure and composition of a regional identity (which is essentially what the description above is) was at the core of what many people saw being destroyed as the state advanced into Kutch after the earthquake.

In July 2001, Pragmulji's nephews wrote to the government. They were concerned that proposed post-earthquake town planning schemes would encroach on their palaces, particularly in an area known as Soniwad. They wrote:

this part of the scheme militates against the very ethos of Bhuj town, demolishes its history dating back to 1549, affects its excellent architecture, and violates its cultural heritage. Bhuj being the capital town of the former princely State of Kutch, it has given lead to other towns and villages in Kutch in these respects and the proposed destruction of the fort wall will adversely affect the whole of Kutch.[4]

The claim must have seemed peculiar to the recipients of the letter, who may have assumed the demolition would set a poor precedent, or that reduced tourist numbers would be bad for the economy. In order to substantiate their unusual claim, the writers did not appeal to statutes for the protection of monuments or archaeology, which might have been an effective strategy given the emphasis placed on heritage and conservation by the planners and funding agencies. Instead, they put forward a cultural argument about the connections of ritual and power—a claim on what they thought to be true and important. To do this, they explained the significance of the foundation myths of the kingdom. What the writers were referring to was not so much that Bhuj was simply the town of principle importance, but that it stood at the centre of the ritual complex which gave the lesser towns and villages of the kingdom sustenance, power and security. According to them, the proposed demolition of the palace walls was akin to proposing the final ruination of Kutch.

A metal stake was inserted into the earth, just as Khengarji had done to make Bhuj his capital in the sixteenth century, 2003, Bhuj.

23

RITUALS OF RECONSTRUCTION

In February 2003, fifty or so people gathered to inaugurate the reconstruction of Praburai Falia in Soniwad. The area took its name from the Soni caste of goldsmiths who lived there. The area was also home to other high-status castes associated, in former times, with the ruling families, whose palaces abutted Soniwad—and whose palace walls were eventually allowed to stand in the new plan for Bhuj. Among these other castes were the Jethis (a sub-group of Brahmins), whose men were bodyguards and state wrestlers, and whose women were wet nurses for the rulers. Soniwad had been prosperous during the time of kings, but it had fallen into decline as people moved away and subdivided property to accommodate tenants. The old families remaining in the area continued to have sympathy for the royal traditions of the state, although many had also felt their status slip in post-colonial India, as the power of the kings had been undermined.

Pramod Jethi, local resident and curator of one of the palace museums, put it like this: 'Today there are no maharajas, only collectors [district administrators] and government. In the old times, only some families of our area had access to the kings. Now anyone can come to the collector'. The democratisation of governance not only removed the rights of kings, it also stripped the auxiliary communities of their privileges and position. While the immediate effects of independence did not radically alter hierarchical social relations, as the decades have passed, the old guard died off, and those claiming hereditary status due to the services their ancestors performed for the rulers have gradually lost their social standing.

For the best part of two years after the earthquake, Soniwad was practically deserted, as ruins gradually gave way to levelled ground. In Ward 8, which included Soniwad, of 1,502 registered properties, 1,211 were classified as G4 or G5 (some 80 per cent compared to 56 per cent for the entire old town). The damage here was, in other words, tremendous.

Shortly after the earthquake, the planners stumbled into Soniwad and developed a constructive relationship with a few of the residents, who happened to be trained in architecture and experienced in the ways of municipal government. They founded neighbourhood and rehabilitation committees in an attempt to congeal local interests, and to give the planners a body they could talk to about their plans. Such committees, although clearly a good idea, were never very robust and relied on the efforts of a very small number of people.[1]

The boundaries of the wards of the old town were used to divide the plan for Bhuj into manageable sections. Soniwad was in Ward 8, and consequently fell under 'Town Planning Scheme 8'. The committee membership, however, only represented the interests of the prosperous Hindu sections to the south, to the exclusion of Muslim residents to the north. From their association with the planners, the Hindu residents of Soniwad had also learned how to represent their interests effectively.[2] In August 2001, for example, a resident of plot 1,219 wrote to the planners to express his concerns. His house was classified as G3, but he was worried that it would be demolished anyway by TP. He also mentioned in passing that: 'we say that our house land is sacred, as Lord Swaminarayan['s] "footprint" [is] also existing in it. Everyday some pilgrim[s] and visitors are coming to pray at this place'.[3] The writer had judged correctly: the planners were sensitive to what they saw as 'local traditions' and evaluated the claim on the sacred in this light.

Aside from the opportunity to make a speech (a very popular activity in Kutch), the aim of the Soniwad rituals was to bring auspiciousness and prosperity, as well as to reassert the Hindu character of the neighbourhood. As a sociological event, it is a first-class example of how some social and religious inequalities were subtly reinforced by reconstruction, as old Hindu elites stepped up to act as representatives for the whole. We also see in this ritual the more obvious story of how neo-liberal funding regimes inadvertently reinvigorated older ideas of purity and power; this, they did brilliantly. The finance for this ritual came through the local partners of the United Nations Development Programme (UNDP).

The 'residents' of Soniwad had to come from miles around to attend the event. The population had scattered in the aftermath, and TP had rendered much of the area uninhabitable. Former residents were in temporary camps, or staying with relatives elsewhere, while others had moved permanently away but maintained an interest in the property and affairs of their old neighbourhood. The speech-makers had to compete with the endless procession of tractors carrying rubble out of the town, the overhead manoeuvres of military jets, and the warbling of mobile phones. One by one, they were forced to shout about their personal loss and grief, and how the earthquake had laid waste to the holy places of Kutch. They also emphasised a bright future, and described their enthusiasm for the new Soniwad.

The ritual was to prepare Soniwad for reconstruction. The restless and unknown dead were to be calmed, and the land rendered peaceful. At the climax to this remarkable event, a metal stake was inserted into the earth, just as Khengarji had done to make Bhuj his capital in the sixteenth century. Before then, however, the Brahmin priest announced the date, time and location of the ritual so that the deities could find their way. He requested Hanuman and other gods to come to Soniwad to purify the land. He spoke in Sanskrit, the language of the gods, to create the most precise channel through which divine forces could offer their blessings. At this stage, the ritual was cordial, as people wandered through the small crowd greeting friends and acquaintances. Conviviality was important because the gods would see there was a community of friendly neighbours, and would bless them accordingly.

For the briefest moment, the mood grew quiet as the priest recalled the names of some of those who had died. Accidental death, such as earthquakes, car accidents or murder, is considered 'bad death' as lives remain unfulfilled or incomplete. There is no time to prepare for a bad death, and this gives the souls of those so departed a restless and perhaps troublesome character. The ghost of a female gynaecologist, in particular, was supposed to haunt the area. She was the only ghost I heard about to be given the name of an identifiable person. In life, her practice had never taken off, and she largely sat alone in her surgery, only occasionally writing certificates and issuing prescriptions. She had a reputation for moaning and complaining. The earthquake killed her in front of her clinic (I am not sure if it was the clinic itself that fell on her or another structure). The failure and possibly the bitterness which had characterised her life allowed her to become a public ghost, destined to roam ruined Bhuj after dark. In effect, she became the town's ghost.

Then, suddenly, there was laughing in Soniwad as someone spoke up to recall the name of a giant of a man who had fought many neighbourhood battles single-handedly. Distracted by their memories, the attention of the crowd returned only slowly to the Brahmin. He was now requesting every life that had passed away on the land, including the gynaecologist and the brawler, to leave the living in peace, and not to possess them, disturb them or bring them bad luck. In the moment of this ritual, the land was treated as if it were a repository for all past lives and deaths, a site in which all life and death were simultaneously present.

The spot at which the stake was to be inserted into the ground (*kili puja* or stake ritual) had been determined by the reconstruction committee, the Brahmin and a planner who had helped with the map. They had improvised a diagram showing the boundaries of Soniwad and a number of important locations: the meeting hall of Brahmins, the Ashapura Mandir (a temple dedicated to the royal deity) and the house of a respected man called Bapu. Lines had been drawn from these locations to determine the centre of the neighbourhood. This spot, where the stake was to be inserted, they called the *brahmsthan kendra*, or the central place of creation. The principles of the arrangement, the Brahmin said, were derived from *vastu shastra*, the ancient science of structure, widely believed to be a cause of prosperity and moral well-being, and, conversely, when practiced badly, misfortune.

Most of those I asked about the ritual were vague and uncertain about what they had done—but that seems true of most rituals. The manuals on popular spatial theory available in the bazaar were mostly to do with the layout of houses, influenced more by interior design fashions than the ancient science of structure. In libraries in

London I found canonical texts on the ideal relationships between a royal personage and the kinds of space that should surround him.[4] These writings are commentaries on the techniques of *vastu shastra*—treaties on city design, architecture and the proper division and arrangement of space.

The library texts demonstrate how legends and deities associated with a site influence the city's fortunes and well-being (hares defeating dogs for example). Before any construction can commence, offerings must be made to propitiate demons and deities associated with the land (*bhumi puja*, or land rituals). The texts show a number of square diagrams (*mandala*) aligning deities, temples and castes with the cardinal points. Such diagrams range considerably in the complexity of their sub-division. At the centre of all such diagrams, however, is the *brahmasthana* or, as in this case, the *brahmsthan kendra*, the seat of Lord Brahma—the creation deity, and therefore they resemble, rather clearly, the map drawn for Soniwad.

These same principles apply whatever the scale of the construction: a town, a neighbourhood or a single house. The smaller units are ideally architectural and ritual microcosms of larger spatial units. The ideal form then is matched in human and caste terms by mutually resembling and interconnected, but also hierarchically distinguished and ranked components.

As far as I am able to tell, this was the first time in Kutch that such a foundation ritual had been conducted outside the walls of the royal palaces. We see in operation here the creative tension between the invention of tradition and the inventive power of traditions. It could well be that this was a ritual of vernacular democracy: a conservative form of revolution. Given the proximity of those attending the ritual to the traditions of the palace, I do not think it too much of a leap to see this as an appropriation of the foundations of the kingdom from a royal family, which was now seen as degenerate and largely incapable of governance.

In line with arguments already made and those yet to come, however, I favour a slightly different interpretation in which the ritual signals the reassertion of the structures of kingship rather than their appropriation. In Chapter 16, I showed how the Jadeja colonial-centric conceptualisation of Bhuj and its kingdom was adopted in the aftermath as a framework for rebuilding. The focus naturally fell on Bhuj, regardless of the levels of destruction elsewhere. In Chapter 22 I explored how historians were encouraged to promote indigenous notions of history, in which, for various demonstrable reasons, foundation rituals became pre-eminent. In Chapter 8, I discussed how the social fault lines rendered invisible by the consolidation of modern Gujarat were reanimated by the struggles during the aftermath. I have also touched upon the nostalgia emanating both from times past and the alienation of the aftermath. Together, these ideas seem to me to collapse rather neatly into the moment of the Soniwad rituals.

In many ways, the ritual allows everything I have written thus far about the historical and political context of the earthquake to make greater sense. The ritual was a perfect fit for the circumstance: new life was given to old ideas, and death and the regeneration of life were marked in a context which had open but rich meanings. Despite earlier scepticism I had about the contrivances of the moment, I now think that the ritual was brilliant, communicating effectively deep structures of identity and history. If the ritual was indeed a way of placing the neighbourhood back within the broader and encompassing ritual structures of the kingdom, as I am suggesting, then it was simply a practical demonstration of the more abstract work of the political protestors and the amateur historians of the town. Each group was gently attempting to articulate something about themselves which was very difficult to express or explain, for there were no descriptive words available to them—but whatever this thing was, it was somehow deeply important to what was happening to them.

The disintegration of Kutch as a political entity only partially eroded the symbolic power of kingship as a socio-religious institution. This strong claim is not to say that everyone in Kutch is a royalist. We know from the limited support Pragmulji enjoys that this cannot be true. Rather, the ritual, identity and cognitive structures of the kingdom remain important, replicating traditions of the past in the absence of actual political authority. Kutch, then, is a way of seeing and understanding, and not merely a place. While this may well be true for many regions with an isolating geography and a refined sense of themselves, it took the contrasts and battles of the aftermath for this to become apparent.

Gujarat is a relatively recent invention, and its boundaries, at least for a while after the earthquake, had little emotional or symbolic purchase in Kutch. The distinct character of the Soniwad rituals also suggests that there was no plausible mythology or ritual superstructure around which those affected by the earthquake could appeal to the sense of a greater Gujarat—even had they wished to do so. People might not think about kings any longer, but they continued to think in rather fundamental ways about the relations between land, people and gods which underlay the now-denuded structures of kingship.

Much of what makes Kutch what it is to the people that live there is invisible and without words. Much of what links the people to the land and to the past did not therefore appear on the maps and plans drawn up in the aftermath. The sense of power and territory evoked by the Soniwad ritual, for example, suggests a conception of land quite different from that presented on an administrative map in which Kutch might have a boundary and a monotone infill. There are other forms of geography in which kings, gods and ghosts play parts. The land has its own power, which emerges unevenly in the form of quasi-divine hierarchies of place.

The Soniwad ritual suggests that smaller units are the moral and ritual microcosms of larger units, and that the careful ritual maintenance of all levels is essential for the stability and well-being of the territory. The ritual affirms the importance of boundaries and centres in determining the proper relation of people to units of land, ranging from the level of the house to the kingdom. Post-earthquake Bhuj was not a blank canvas. There was no tabula rasa, for the invisible geography remained unmoved by the earthquake. It was not, however, exposed by the earthquake, but by the political contest which took place in the aftermath.

Some years later, a small ceremonial house (*puja kilinu smargh* or *kendrasthan*) was built over the Soniwad *kili* and a modest walled garden was established. By 2008, the structure appeared neglected.

The suburbs spouted at a tremendous rate. The clean lines of concrete houses march towards the horizon, 2008, Bhuj. Compare the same site in 2003 in the image at the start of Chapters 18 and 19.

24

UMASHANKAR'S GREAT ESCAPE

Umashankar was one of the many Soniwad residents who did not attend the brilliant rituals of recreation. He said he could not care less about such things. It was simply a chance for some big men to publicise themselves. I once asked Umashankar whether he thought we lived in the best of all possible worlds. He told me that we lived in 'god's world'. 'Well', I asked, 'is god's world the best it can be? Did god do a good job of making the world?' 'It is not a question of it being good or bad', Umashankar replied, 'this is god's world. If you think about whether it is good, bad or could be better, then you are playing games. We cannot think whether god's world is good or bad. It just is and we are'. I asked: 'Do you mean that we cannot question the world because it is god's world and that is disrespectful to god?' 'No' he replied, 'you do not understand. That is not what I mean. We cannot think enough to know whether god's world is good or bad. It is beyond our limit'.

Umashankar was certain that the earthquake was god's doing. 'Those people who think it was because of evil or punishment', he said, 'what do they know? How do they know what god was or was not thinking?' He continued: 'these are the stories men tell to themselves when they do not understand. God is great!'

From among the people I know well in Bhuj, Umashankar suffered most in the aftermath. The weight of tragedy gradually caused him to stoop. Thick lines of worry appeared on his face. And, although he was never the chirpiest of fellows, he increasingly began to sit for long periods in silence. At the beginning of the book, he stood on the rubble that had been his house near Soniwad and uttered the improbable words 'my rubble', before heading off to find his brother and mother in open ground. Umashankar's 'unconscious mind' (his words) of that time was a mind realising it was experiencing something greater than itself—it was a humiliated mind, and one that had reached its limit.

The search for causes and explanations of the earthquake that had taken place in Bhuj, to which we will come in Chapter 28, were attempts to reinstate the superiority of man over the brute force of nature, and perhaps the uncertainties of knowing what god was doing. Umashankar, however, was of the opinion that any attempt to second-guess the rationale of god's actions was pure folly.

Umashankar had lived in the old city with his mother and brother's family in a house owned by his late father's brothers, who lived in Mumbai and behaved as absentee landlords. I had visited the house before the earthquake, and can recall the fading grandeur and carvings of a once-fine building. As reconstruction work started in Soniwad, we went to see what was going on. There was nothing immediately recognisable to him. His street, which had once been lined with three- and four-storey buildings, had gone. He looked around for familiar landmarks in the distance to work out where the house had stood. He saw the towers of the royal palaces, the Muslim shrine on the hill to the west, and the temple built to propitiate the wrathful serpent on the hill to the east. In that moment, he put himself at the centre of a world that was no more, triangulating the location of what had been with the aid of what remained. When he was certain he had found the right spot (and he had), he traced with his foot in the dirt a rough outline of where each room had once been. I could not help but notice the similarity between his method of triangulation and that used by the ritual specialists to find the centre of Soniwad.

Seeing Umashankar stand where his house and then his rubble had once been was among the saddest of things. He said he had not visited Soniwad since the rubble had been cleared. He could not quite make sense of the fact that nearly everything that had made the place recognisable had gone. But the underlying sense of the place was still clearly utterly familiar to him. He did not cry, but struggled to find the wherewithal to speak. Amid the compacted shards of tile and fragments of brick, we came across a porcelain rim which led down into a drain. It was what was left of his family's toilet, still presumably connected to the broken underground sewerage network. There was something jarring about the discovery. It was the only thing that suggested Umashankar's family had ever lived there. The house had gone. All that was left was the hole through which their excrement passed underground to intermingle with the excrement of everyone else.

Later that day, he took me to other places he used to frequent. He described the relationships he had had with the people at a certain teashop. He recalled how he had played his musical instruments in the evening at a bench in this spot, and how particular people would often come and listen. All of a sudden, as if having to clarify something that was in doubt, he said, 'but we will never come back to this place. We have experienced too many terrible things here and if we come back these things will haunt us'. At the time, I think I assumed he was talking about ghosts of the badly dead, the doctor and her friends, who travelled the area at night. I also thought he might be thinking of the sights and sounds that had congealed as memories of the day of the earthquake.

Indeed, he might have been thinking of these things. By now, however, and some years into this research, I had also learned what now seems blindingly obvious: other terrible things had happened to people in addition to the earthquake, and the earthquake was not always king. As I got to know more about Umashankar and his family, for example, I learned that it was probably the living, not ghosts or disquieting disaster memories, which were at the troubled forefront of his mind. His uncles had been trying to sell the house he had lived in for years. There had been protracted and expensive court cases. Umashankar had managed to secure temporary rights over the property, rights he knew that he probably was not entitled too. The uncles had come periodically to Bhuj and threatened Umashankar. His mother had become unwell with worry over the bitter relations between her and her late-husband's brothers. The uncles had well-placed contacts in their local caste association and had made life difficult, and at times unpleasant, for Umashankar's family. Perhaps it was no accident that Umashankar was unable to find a willing bride within his caste, despite years of trying.

Before the earthquake, I can recall Umashankar explaining to me how his brother was somewhat simple-minded and, although married with a daughter, was not interested in finding work. The brother reasoned that he would never earn more than Umashankar, so what was the point of him working too when he could stay at home and oversee the affairs of the family. Instead of doing this, he had started to attend the sermons and rituals of a devotional Hindu movement which was attempting to expand its support base in the town. Then, before the earthquake, Umashankar thought popular religion was mostly a waste of time and effort.

As a consequence of these circumstances, when the earthquake demolished the Soniwad house, they could neither afford to buy another one nor pay the spiralling costs of rent. Like many other people, they moved far away from Bhuj for a while, staying with other relatives. At this point they were desperate to escape from the collapsed town. Like many other people, they soon found life in a strange city more unbearable than an uncertain future in Bhuj. So they moved back, suddenly seeing the earthquake as an opportunity for a better life. They saw that the promised new Bhuj offered them a way out of their dependencies, embittered relations and financial woes. Quite literally, they suddenly saw the aftermath as a means to escape many of the things which had made them unhappy.

As they sat together in open ground shortly after the earthquake, the saints who came with food and blankets recognised Umashankar's brother and paid his particular huddle of shocked bodies kind and generous attention. A few months later, after their sojourn in distant Baroda, Umashankar and his family moved into a temporary shelter in the extended compound of the movement's temple. The saints promised to look after the family and to provide them with permanent housing in one of the new suburban relocation sites. As a condition, they would have to attend daily events at the temple, and bring friends and other relatives to sermons on Sunday afternoons.

Initially, Umashankar clearly thought he had struck lucky. He enjoyed attending the temple and listening to the moralising about how to live a good life. A year passed, and then two. He, his mother, brother, his wife and pubescent daughter remained in the hut in the settlement which became ingloriously known as 'tin city'. The hut was cramped and leaky, and ill-suited to the climate. They tried, of course, to make it as homely as possible, dividing the space in much the same way as they might have done if they had a larger house with many rooms: kitchen, storage, sitting and sleeping areas. I brought them some plants, which they seemed to appreciate. With the possessions around them that they had managed to scavenge from the rubble, and a bed, and a cooking area, there was not enough room left on the floor for them all to eat at the same time. They were together, but the harsh conditions began to play on their faces.

As we know, the strategy adopted by Bochasanwasi Shri Akshar Purushottam Swaminarayan Sanstha (BAPS) in villages such as Jiyapar had been pointed, but their construction work had been swift. In Bhuj, where the administration moaned and groaned under the weight of difficult decisions, the organisation had less influence over the speed or location of reconstruction. Umashankar had burned ties with his uncles, and there could be no return to Soniwad. There was no choice but to sit it out, to wait and to hope.

Meanwhile, Umashankar had somehow managed to secure compensation for a separate single-room house for which he possessed title deeds in the old town. I asked many times how he had done this, but he never told me and made it clear that this was not a proper topic of conversation. In time, BAPS started construction of a new housing colony in the suburbs, asking Umashankar for half the cost of construction. Umashankar took the opportunity, investing his compensation and a bank loan in the new structure. His gamble appeared to have paid off, but living in an over-crowded metal box for nearly three years was a high price to pay.

As the new houses started to take shape, and roads, drains and car parks began to appear, the emerging suburbs became picnic places. What had once seemed like snake-infested countryside far from the centres of civilisation gradually became areas of attraction. Families would journey from their temporary or shared accommodation to the relocation sites at weekends. There they would sit and take in the air, excitedly imagining the future, their new house, and where they would park the new car they were sure to buy. They would describe how the dust of the building site would make way for beautiful new houses for related nuclear families to cluster together—their houses perhaps divided by a road, and certainly a wall, but not by centuries of oppressive caste history under Jadeja rule.

There are three relocation sites to the south of the old city: Rawalvadi, Mundra Road and RTO (named after the adjacent Road Transport Office). A fourth site to the north and east of the old city, known after the Gujarat Industrial Development Corporation (GIDC), was initially intended for temporary accommodation, but eventually became a permanent site of resettlement. It remains a rather desperate place on the wrong side of the tracks. In contrast, the three sites to the south rank among the most desirable places to live in Bhuj. The popular suburbs are overlooked by the Hill Garden (at present named after Narendra Modi), a haven for flirtation and merriment on Sunday evenings, where visitors can ride on brightly coloured plastic horses, boats and toads.

As the suburbs began to sprout in 2004 and 2005, there was a tangible sense of relief among cash-strapped families such as Umashankar's: they had found a way out of the old town and could say goodbye to its oppressive, dirty and airless streets, its congestion, gossip, hostility and bitterness. The suburbs offered them a clear way to imagine themselves away from the old Bhuj and beginning a new kind of life. I have photographs dating from 2003 and 2004 showing Umashankar's brother posing outside their tin hut astride my own gleaming motorbike. He knew what he wanted.

I also vividly remember visiting Umashankar's new house just after he had moved in. It was a bright and clear day. The sky was blue and the walls of the new house were coloured with the same blue. We climbed up an internal staircase onto the roof. Across other roofs we could see the regimen of the suburbs: clean lines of row upon row of concrete houses, marching towards the horizon. We were in a modernist dream, far away from the dust and grime of both tin and old cities. For the first time, I could see why Umashankar had wanted it.

Dilip takes an evening stroll in the new suburbs, 2007, Bhuj.

25

SLOW DEATH

In France during the early 1940s, the sociologist Maurice Halbwachs asked: 'What would happen if all the members of my family disappeared?'[1] The question was part of his attempt to show that collective memory is not a 'natural' phenomenon, nor part of a mystical group mind. Instead, collective memory is always partial, socially constructed, and part of an individual's dynamic collection of memories.

There were, according to Halbwachs, as many collective memories as social groups. Furthermore, memories of the same fact or incident could be placed in different social frameworks because individuals are necessarily part of more than one group. Halbwachs also saw that memories are brought together as forms of association only by the various ways in which people can also become associated. In this way, the framework of collective memory binds our most intimate of remembrances to one another. For Halbwachs, then, should his family have disappeared, he would for a short while retain the habit of attributing meaning to their first names, and act as if the influence of group pressure was still upon him. He may even have found unknown persons who once knew his kin, for whom their first names would still preserve a meaning. Yet, according to him, the dead retreat into the past not because of the measure of time that separates them from the living, but because nothing remains of the group in which they passed their lives—the group, that is, that needed to name them in order for the group to be.

In previous chapters, I have described some of the ways in which people came together with collective and politicised nostalgia, and how over time the networks that made political protest possible began to fragment. This analysis has been general. If we now increase the ethnographic resolution, we can see similar and correlated processes at work in the lives of particular individuals. If we then think that the same or similar processes must have been at work in the lives of many of the town's other inhabitants, we can then perhaps begin to imagine the intensity of the social fragmentation that survival brought with it.

185

In a town like Bhuj, or for that matter anywhere, not everyone can be associated with everyone else in the same ways. Relationships between people differ in their qualities. Religion, class, caste and gender create particular cleavages in the population and draw other segments together. There are general rules of inheritance and the division of property, and these might vary across religious groups. There remains a strong, but not hegemonic, preference for intra-caste marriage. Public friendships between unmarried men and women are uncommon. Ideally, each person plays certain roles within their immediate kin group, and so forth. The parameters of suitable and possible relationships were not of course fixed in stone, but the disaster shook up what there was, and it took a while to restore a semblance of order. This task was radically complicated by the uncertainties introduced by mass death.

On our travels, and in our questioning of those we encountered, my friend Dilip enjoyed demonstrating to me social inequality, the vanity of philanthropists, and the general futility of what social scientists might describe as 'agency'. He lived in a world of predetermination, or at least in a world in which he knew there were many forces more powerful than him.

I once asked Dilip whether he thought we lived in the best of all possible worlds. He told me that we lived in an 'old world'.

We used to be Buddhists, then Muslims and now we are Hindus. Today, no one here knows these things. Politicians divide humanity, but really we are all the same. Kutch is littered with inscriptions in remote places that tell us that things have not always been like they are now. Have you been to Dholavera [a partially-excavated Indus Valley settlement and the village adopted by Pramod Mahajan for reconstruction]? It is extraordinary! There were cities here in Kutch long before Bhuj was founded. Today, no one here knows these things. Things come and they go, and the people who trouble to be aware of the passing of time are not listened to. I do not know much about the world, but Kutch is a wondrous place.

From Dilip, I have also learned other things about what the earthquake did to social life in Bhuj, which recall, quite directly, the problem Halbwachs faced as a Jew in the early part of the Second World War.

Dilip was also another former resident of the old town who did not participate in the rituals of reconstruction in Soniwad. He said they were 'made up', 'meaningless', and attended by those who liked the sound of their own voices. By 2004, it was quite obvious to everyone that the characteristics of life in Bhuj were changing rapidly. A pre-earthquake edition of a well-known guide book claimed that Bhuj remained one of the few places in India where one might still be offered a lift on a bicycle by a friendly passer-by. There were far more cars and motorbikes on the road, and people raced around honking madly through the dust. The place seemed harder and less friendly. Gandhi and the Ramayana began to seem much less important than mobile phones and share-trading.

By 2005, one was far more likely to be run over than offered a lift. But, behind the visible congestion of new wealth, there were other small signs that some pretty fundamental shifts were taking place. Before the earthquake, the period after the evening meal was a busy one during which groups of men gathered on the streets to talk about the issues of the day. Friends would gather outside shops or on particular verandas in the bazaar to gamble, to talk about what they had just eaten and what they were going to do tomorrow. For me, these were relaxed and memorable times, when my friends were not distracted by work and had the opportunity to talk. I was disappointed to find that the earthquake had mostly killed off this type of sociality. The bazaars were deserted at night, aside from contracted Nepali security guards tapping their sticks on the ground as they patrolled. The gatherings did not appear to have reconvened elsewhere.

By 2004 or so, evening sociality commonly involved going to people's homes to talk over the noise of a television. While the earthquake had allowed many to buy televisions who had not owned them before, there was more to the dissolution of street sociality than the allure of the pixelated screen. Bhuj had turned in on itself and moved behind closed doors. The death imprint of the earthquake remained strong, and the streets were most strongly associated with the fear of falling, and falling masonry. Furthermore, the scattering of the population meant that some of the men who had formed particular huddles at night now lived far away. It was better to stay at home in a family space.

Few people from the pre-earthquake suburbs ventured into the old town with the regularity they used to. Dilip, for example, used to visit family and friends on an almost daily basis. The ruination of the place aside, there are quite probably many other reasons why the old town was less frequented. One of which I am certain is that Dilip, and I dare say others too, feared meeting certain kinds of other people. It was better to stay inside and watch television or to write books about the earthquake than it was to run the risk of bumping into people with whom one now had uncertain or ambiguous relationships.

For a time, there was a tangible reluctance to meet familiar people whose relatives were known to have died in the earthquake. In India, death is associated with ritual pollution. Prohibitions are placed on those who have been bereaved or touched a corpse. Indeed, Hindu cremation grounds are commonly placed at the edge of towns and villages, in part to mark their polluting nature but also to symbolise the separation of death from life. In Bhuj, however, the major cremation ground is close to the centre of town and is overlooked by a school. Too much faith should not be placed in the power of the ideal to organise the practicalities of life. I experienced the unwillingness to be around those associated with death as an expression of 'contagion anxiety'. Not so much the avoidance of impure states and substances, but more akin to the experience of Robert Lifton's Hiroshima survivors: if I come too close to you, I will experience your experience of annihilation and your death. I do not want that.[2]

Alongside this, there was another anxiety of an unnameable type. This anxiety was associated with encountering once-familiar people, only to learn from them that mutual acquaintances had died in the earthquake. News of death in close circles was mostly easy to come by. That, after all, is a major point of social life, although people might have been unwilling for the heaviness of suffering to rub off on them. The second type of anxiety came from meeting those associated with distant family or old friends, neighbours or colleagues whom one might not have seen for several years, given the disruption of the aftermath. People were scattered all over the place, and networks and the knowledge of the health, wealth and location of distantly meaningful others was fragmented. Three years after the earthquake, in Dilip's company at least, chance encounters with once-familiar people were to be avoided, if at all possible. During such meetings, the earthquake had to be recalled in order to re-establish a relationship. Contagion anxiety contained within it the essence of this second form of anxiety, but the second form itself was also visible given the chaos of the town.

Such encounters did not provoke macabre reflections on the nature of physical destruction, or even on the nature of an individual's death; rather, they recalled the person or people who had allowed those involved in the encounter to know one another. Consequently, such encounters were often quite intense, revealing in a single laconic moment some of the shifting contours of public morality.

I have described in previous chapters how the physical form of Bhuj allowed people to experience and understand the world in particular ways. Once the town had collapsed the struggle for survival and the desire to see familiar things caused mass disruption. Instant confusion only gradually gave way to the restoration and transformation of the senses. In the case of the social landscape, the damage, unless obvious, was mostly invisible at first, and it was only much later that the gaps in old networks became clear.

I asked Dilip about the pages of death notices in the local newspaper in the weeks after the earthquake. Did these not tell you who had died? Did these not bring your social inventories up to date? They might have done, he said. I remember some of those whose deaths were announced, but those were difficult times and it was impossible to remember so many dead people in one swoop. Those announcements were of course to tell others that a cherished one had died, but there were just too many of them. Dilip probably knew upwards of 500 people in Bhuj at first hand. Even with such a broad knowledge, he still only knew less than 0.5 per cent of the adult population. Given his inevitably partial knowledge, the significant number of deaths, and the inter-relatedness of the population, there were many unknown connections between the living and the dead to be wary of.

When meeting the distantly known, there was the awkwardness of having to recall a constellation of people, some of whom would inevitably be dead or have suffered terrible misfortune. Oh yes, such and such was taken off by the earthquake. Or, such and such is paralysed from the waist down and lost an arm. These encounters contained an additional peril because they could also leave those having the conversation in the position of quite suddenly not having a legitimate way of knowing each other because the linking person had died.

We know that there are different kinds of deaths. The death of a mother, a sibling or one's child brings with it different forms of grief, not only for the person and the relationship that has gone but for the expectations one had, perhaps unconsciously, for life. Death within families also brings subtle rearrangements of existing relationships, the burdens and joys of which inevitably shift, given the new absence of one of the people who made the collective relationship what it was. I have a relationship with my sister, but this is also mediated by our separate relationships with our mother and with other people. Should my mother die, then my relationship with my sister cannot remain the same. We will be changed.

The casual encounters Dilip tried to avoid could leave inappropriate or impossible relationships with a once-familiar person because those who had made those relationships legitimate have disappeared. Once, Dilip and I bumped into a woman whose husband Dilip had worked alongside many years ago. Dilip had attended their wedding and eaten the food he had been offered. Before the earthquake, Dilip used to see the man quite often, but had not seen him since. Visibly hesitant, Dilip inquired about his friend and was told that he had been killed. Dilip sucked his teeth, the conversation fizzled out, and we parted company with the woman. At the beginning of the conversation, Dilip thought himself to have a legitimate and good relationship with her—by the end of it he did not. Had the woman died in the earthquake and it was her husband we encountered, then Dilip could have expressed his condolences, patted the man on the arm, and departed knowing that his friend was still knowable.

On another occasion, we met one of Dilip's former neighbours whose daughter-in-law had been part of a women's organisation of which Dilip's wife was also a member. The man told us the story of how his son (the young woman's husband) had been crippled and how, unwilling or unable to cope with the burden of care, the woman had returned to live with her parents in Mumbai.

Through both of these encounters it became clear that there was no longer any way for Dilip to have a legitimate relationship with the old woman, as married men do not freely associate with widows, whatever their age. There was, frankly, little point in continuing to know the man with the runaway daughter-in-law as the person who allowed Dilip to know him through his wife's association had disappeared, leaving a hole. Dilip was primarily friendly with the young woman through his wife as a way of encouraging the activities of the association.

Before moving to the suburbs in the 1980s, Dilip had lived in the old town, and he still had family and acquaintants there. I know he used to go there frequently—but, by 2004 or so, he seldom visited. The restless doctor did not deter him, but he feared the living he no longer knew. Parts of their relationships were dead. Often the deceased part of such relationships was significant enough to make the relationship improper (as in the case of the old woman) or hollow (as in the case of the man who lost his daughter-in-law in the aftermath).

The earthquake did not simply make people dead. To deaden them properly took quite a few years, as the knowledge of their death was not known to all who had known them. Their deaths were re-enacted in chance encounters, as the town and the routine channels of communication were at sixes and sevens. To the best of Dilip's knowledge, many of the dead were actually alive until a chance encounter killed them off. So it was, that in time, the dead gradually retreated into the past, not because of the measure of time that separated them from the earthquake, but because nothing remained of the group in which they passed their lives and which had allowed them to exist.

Together, the alienation of the aftermath, the secrecy required for successful corruption, the fear of unpredictable encounters, and the tendency to close the doors at night contributed to the new Bhuj of the suburbs. Through these processes, the will and possibility of nostalgic collective action fragmented. It is at this point, as it were, that the characteristics of transfer between individual and collective narratives finally broke down. Any form of collective narrative failed to repair and thus sustain itself because memories could be brought together as forms of association only by the various ways in which people can themselves be associated. Thus it was difficult for individual memory to be part of collective memory because it relied on a social milieu which was no longer what it was or of which many key parts were missing. In this, we see one aspect of the fragmentary qualities of survival as it unfolded in Bhuj.

While one might object that it is perfectly possible to have a creative and meaningful relationship with another living person through the shared memory of a dead person or even a town, the evidence from Bhuj suggested, then at least, that people actively went out of their ways to avoid this kind of association.

Like many other people in the neighbourhood where we both lived, Dilip observed absolutely meticulous daily routines; you could almost set your watch by them. He left his house at particular times, following certain routes to perform preordained tasks. He did so before the earthquake, but in the aftermath these routines seemed to gain in importance, as he attempted to minimise the risk of losing further acquaintances to chance encounters.

In the normal run of things, his community of Nagar Brahmins held a simple ceremony when someone died, often advertised in local newspapers. Fellow caste members and distant family would sit for a while with the immediate family of the deceased in the caste's community building. The event acknowledged the death and, in a sense, allowed for the reconfiguration of relationships that death entailed. In the mass death of the earthquake, this procedure had not been followed in an orderly fashion. Widespread death, compounded by the conditions of disruption, made accurate news of relevant deaths hard to come by. In this sense, mass death was a greater terror than if fate had picked people off one at a time, because long after the disaster the dead continued to die.

Gandhi behind bars which display the ritual Urdhva Pundra mark of the Swaminarayan Sect, 2005, Bhuj.

26

VALUES OF CITIZENSHIP

Mahatma Gandhi was upended by a bulldozer. His white marble feet were left pointing to the sky, his face caressed the rubble. In the same part of town, a library was cut down the middle to make way for a road. The librarian hastily tossed his collection to one side of the hall, while the bulldozers clawed and bashed at the other. The dust of progress settled forever upon the vellum and within the folds of a literary heritage. At about the same time, a leaflet was widely circulated to explain TP to the population of Bhuj. The dominant image shows a man dressed in a suit, walking down a computer-generated suburban street. Parked on the road is a Porsche sports car. All over the town, new names for old things began to appear.

We know that Gandhi was toppled to make way for new heroes, but in this case his plinth was required for a musical fountain. His statue was later rescued and placed on the boundary of a park reserved for Bhuj's retired and senior citizens. Gandhi was put behind bars bearing the symbol of a Hindu sect. The destruction of the library, which contained a large collection of aging Gujarati language books, took place without public anxiety. I have often felt as if those displaced by TP in Bhuj were allowed to imagine they would get the rendered software road and the Porsche. I think Umashankar continued to imagine something very similar after he received the keys to his new house. Roads, too, served as an opiate, a source of marvel and awe. I surveyed opinion, and, amongst it all, roads were regarded as the overwhelming signifier of the modernity and development which had been brought to the town.[1] Bhuj was enthralled by the new tarmac necklaces.

Millions of tonnes of concrete were poured into the mould of new Bhuj—not so much the rise of a phoenix as the slow spread of a slick. At first, the remains of the old town cowered at the centre of a huge web of new ring and radial roads. Places that did not yet exist were connected by tarmac, and islands of possibility appeared in the spaces between new roads. Speculators speculated, some successfully, others built white elephants. The surrounding countryside gradually began to take on a new

193

shape, which made it possible to imagine a good life in what was recently jungle. As Bhuj grew, its centres of influence moved further to the south, away from the old town. In 2013, Bhuj had not yet filled its infrastructural boots. Hundreds of acres of planned housing colonies to the south and east remained scarcely inhabited, sometimes uninhabited, and roads protrude from red dust like partially buried skeletons. But, these outlying efforts, which once seemed so distant from the town, are gradually being drawn into the orbit of urban life.

As I have said, Bhuj had been expanding for decades, the population gradually settling outside the walls, tentatively at first, and then in something of a rush. There was more to this than the weight of numbers, for the expansion also reflected changing ideas about power, citizenship and the ways in which people understood and ordered themselves. Moving outside the walls was to pass beyond the authority of the traditional ruler as the citizen of a democratic state. By the 1960s, the chances of being molested by brigands outside the town were much reduced, and some of the most influential post-colonial citizens began to settle in new housing colonies. Long before the earthquake, aspiration led many to look longingly towards the suburbs. After the earthquake, the pace and scale of the town's expansion increased as suburban life became an almost universal possibility. It often appeared as if suburbanisation was a state command.

On the whole, things were replaced like with like, although the new was generally heralded as bigger, better and safer. Bhuj was equipped with a new hospital, government offices and so forth to replace old ones. A new university was founded, and the airport was reconstructed—granted, both given new names to aid the toppling of Gandhi. But these projects had been on the cards before the earthquake. In light of the grand designs often proposed elsewhere in the world after a disaster, is it surprising that there was to be no monumental parade, no extravagant urban building programme to testify to the might of the state, and no systematic state-led attempt to give the town a new social identity? There is the new Hill Garden with its ride-on toads, but that was surely trifling.

In Lisbon, Pombal built magnificent wide boulevards (resembling those of Paris) and grand squares (resembling those of northern Italy). In Lisbon today, his statue surveys the city he created from the top of a grand column. In Gujarat, there has been little attempt by the state to incorporate new things into the fabric of the town, other, it seems, than roads (not boulevards), names and suburbs. As we will also see in Chapter 34, attempts at creating a memorial have also been rather half-hearted. Does this mean that the state is above such vanity or lacks conviction? Perhaps also it once again signifies the peripheral nature of the affected district to the political project of Gujarat. In the big cities of the east, there are statues and monuments to past heroes and critical events. There are regional precedents; it is not as if there is no culture of monumentality. There might not have been enough money, of course, but the absence of a dramatic ideology may well have contributed to the disguise of all the lesser assumptions contained by the plan. Looking back, changes to the town allowed for the emergence of an acquiescent and more homogeneous citizenry.

In the new Bhuj, the palaces and those they represent have been consigned to the heritage industry, as the centre of most influence has been moved beyond the walls. The planned-for citizen is connected to shopping centres, government offices and the Hill Garden by roads. This citizen is no longer connected to a caste-specific temple or marriage hall, for such routes were either invisible or of secondary importance to the planners. The design of new Bhuj, while mindful of obvious 'heritage' issues, has contributed to the partial redundancy of the old town and the waning authority of some of its institutions. To engage with the older places of tradition generally means a short-lived journey back to a landscape associated with collapse and failure, and caste and kings.

Those who have been planned for the most, as well as those anticipated into being by the work of the planners, were to lead particular kinds of life. Inhabitants were to be part of suburban nuclear families and dependent on fossil-fuel for their mobility. These lives were to be largely devoid of pre-earthquake history, and free from parochial and superstitious traditions. In this, Umashankar's family is typical: freed from the shackles and ties of caste, they moved to one of the new suburbs, their house allocated to them on the draw of a lot. There, and with varying degrees of commitment, they embraced the teaching of the sect which had part-financed their house.

Roads, as public spaces, created new links and divisions between people and places. They connected the new airport to the best hotels, and the wealthier suburbs to the lakeside parks and new temples. For others, roads have become obstacles to their daily routines. Some roads were built in the face of public protest, whilst Muslim cemeteries, most notably, as well as other religious sites, were bulldozed. A structure for communal prayer (*eid garh*) was reduced in size to accommodate a sharp turn in a road, much to the dismay and anger of its Muslim managers.[2] I am not inclined to think that the demolition of Muslim grave architecture solely demonstrates the communalism of the state. Instead, and more interestingly, the enormous spread of graveyards indicates the sustained and important role Muslims must have played in the development of the town. Their influence has, however, been largely written out of history by modern politics, but remains to be rediscovered.

Although the state's plan for Bhuj was thin on overt ideology, the religious sects that renamed key locations in the town had other intentions. Some sects already had a strong presence in Bhuj, others came with ideas for the future of the population, which often dovetailed neatly with those of the Gujarat state. They also saw the importance of Bhuj, not as the capital of a dynasty, but as the site of the second of six sacred temples built by their divine leader in the early nineteenth century. Bhuj had been chosen by god, and, as the planners had discovered, his footsteps were preserved in the soil of the town. Lord Swaminarayan's original temple was damaged in the 2001 earthquake, although, miraculously, the idols survived unscathed. This temple stood adjacent to the palaces of the former rulers. After the earthquake, the temple was shifted to the area of important government offices, and well connected to the new road network. The structure took seven years to construct. It is built from a staggering 126,000 cubic feet of quarried marble. It radiates an enchanting white light, as the strongest single statement of power and influence in Bhuj.

In the years after the earthquake, there was an extraordinary promotion of the leaders and teachings of two of the main Swaminarayan sects, on what amounted to the town's permanent advertising hoardings. As roads were widened, new names began to appear: Shri Swaminarayan Road (in Hindi, other signs of similar appearance directed people to Shri Swaminayaran Road); Mundra Road became BAPS Pramukh Swami Maharaj Marg (in English and Gujarati); Alfred High School Chowk became Shri Narayan Dev Circle Alfred High School (in Gujarati). The town's gates were also given new names in return for uninspired restoration works: Mahadev (Shiva's) Gate became Shri Muktajivan Swami Bapa-Mahadev Gate, after the twentieth-century leader of the Ahmedabad branch of the movement; Patwadi Gate became Shri Sahajanand Swami-Patwadi Gate (Sahajanand is another name for Lord Swaminarayan). And so on.

Of course, erecting black marble slabs with gold lettering is not quite the same as implanting a name deep within collective consciousness. Dilip said the long-winded names would never stick. As far as I know, none of these re-namings have yet been officially adopted, but the signs were not forcibly removed. Over the years, some signs have been lost to traffic accidents and scrap dealers, but others were cemented in place and will be around for longer.

Naming roads after deities or revered personalities is common practice in India, as it is elsewhere. It might also be seen as the privilege of a patron. Changing the names of places (Bombay to Mumbai) is not novel either. However, this is only done to remove the negative associations of colonialism or the influence of now unfashionable religious traditions. In other words, renaming is a deliberate act of effacement, as well as self-promotion. What past were they attempting to efface in this instance? The past of a princely state, of non-Gujarati sentiment, and all of the other things I have described as being ridden roughshod over in the name of post-disaster intervention. The counterpart to which is that they were in search of dominance, and used the moments of shock and SHOCK to push this goal home. In addition to the maps and bulldozers of the planners, other kinds of cartographic knowledge were called upon to reconstruct Bhuj. Sacred geographies and aspirations inter-mingled with bureaucratic and technical plans.

For many commentators, the spread of new forms of Hinduism in Gujarat has been taken as evidence of state authoritarianism and chauvinism. From a very different perspective, political Hinduism may also be seen as a maturation of post-colonial ways of doing politics—with the version of secularism inherited from the colonial government gradually replaced by a system altogether more indigenous in inception. Either way, or together, political Hinduism, institutionalised devotion and variants of integral humanism have become increasingly popular.

Hinduism is not a unified religion and comes in many forms. As with other religions, sects are rivals for a limited pool of potential followers. In Kutch, and Bhuj in particular, there has been extreme competition for supremacy. In the process, the population has been bribed and pulled away from their old deities towards those embedded in the sophisticated structures of trans-regional and global sects. The renaming of things in Bhuj is part of this process, as rivals have attempted to map their own version of the good life onto the new town. In the process, many of the traditional marks of power and tradition have been effaced.

The language of devotion of these influential sects is Gujarati, which contributes to the erosion of the importance of the Kutchi tongue, and furthers the integration of the region into the state. In theory, some of these sects, albeit in different ways, also lack straightforward prohibitions on the initiation of people from different castes. Many of the practices of these sects are congregational, events at which people of all castes (but not sexes) mix freely. As the population was redistributed after the earthquake, the ordering of castes through the town—which was never neat and tidy, but was broadly thought to be known by all—was re-determined by the lottery of property. Those most vulnerable to the vagaries of circumstances, and therefore the most likely to end up in a mixed-caste resettlement colony, were the poorer middle classes. The wealthy had more influence on their destinies. Many of the poorer places of the town were materially unaffected by the rapid expansion of Bhuj, and people largely stayed where they were.

The power of caste to order people and give them political power and corporate identity has been diminished. In the past, particular castes and groups of castes were influential in elections and in the configuration of party politics. Hindus were often divided by caste interest. They were also divided in their sectarian affiliations, with many powerful religious institutions being the exclusive domains of particular caste or class configurations. As I have stressed, the dominant political project in the early years of the aftermath was to create the impression of an undivided Hindu vote bank on which the ruling party could rely for support. The denuding of caste through the suburbanisation of Bhuj, and the permitted spread of congregational sects, for whom membership is not predetermined by caste, serves as a pincer movement in this project.

The modernisers did not have it all their own way. Their work was prominent, publicised and endorsed by the regular visits of the highest politicians in the land. Every now and again, however, there were tell-tale signs that other people had other ideas. In 2003 and 2004, the words Shri Kalika Road appeared as graffiti along one of the new loops in the old town. The road passed through areas strongly associated with mass death and wholesale destruction. I asked many times who was responsible for the graffiti. The artists remain unknown, but their work resonates with what had happened in Bhuj. Kali (of Kalika) is the black consort of Lord Shiva, associated with death, time and change—apt indeed, but the evocative name did not stick, nor was it allowed to remain unofficially, for officials painted over it. Unlike other re-namings, this one did not have the institutional clout of a major sect to support it. Today, Kali's Road is called Ashapura Ring Road, after the tutelage and territorial goddess of Kutch, perhaps reflecting other conversations I was not privy to.

SECTION 6

HOPE

A comparative excursion reveals great similarities in earthquake thought across space and time. Kant is shown to have been practising what he preached. The Bhujians come to terms with the changes going on around them by describing to themselves who they are. Concrete weathers, grass grows in cracks, and children grow up with no first-hand memory of the earthquake.

The faces of the dead clipped from newspapers on display at an event to mark the fifth anniversary of the disaster. The earthquake did not simply make people dead. To deaden them properly took quite a few years, as the knowledge of their death was not known to all who had known them. de Beausobre asked the question: is death a greater evil when it strikes at many people simultaneously, rather than removing them at intervals? 2006, Bhuj.

27

ALL IS GOOD?

Published in 1759, *Candide* is widely acknowledged as Voltaire's pessimistic master-piece. Two chapters narrate what happens when a storm engulfs Candide's ship off the coast of Lisbon. In the commotion, one of his companions tries to save a sailor who has almost fallen overboard. The companion saves the sailor but is himself swept into the sea. The sailor does nothing to help him. The ship sinks. Candide, Pangloss (a philosopher in the style of Leibniz, to whom we will come later), and the brutal sailor struggle to the shore and walk towards the city.

As they enter Lisbon, the earth shakes violently. The sea rises in the harbour and the city collapses into flames and ruins. The sailor finds some money, gets drunk, goes to sleep and finds a prostitute. Later, the groans of dying and buried victims rise from the debris. Pangloss and Candide help the wounded. Candide is himself injured by falling masonry. Pangloss, an optimist, attempts to comfort the victims by telling them the earthquake has occurred for the best of all possible reasons. One of the officers of the Inquisition accuses Pangloss of heresy because an optimist, such as he, cannot possibly believe in Original Sin. The fall and banishment of Adam and Eve from the Garden of Eden, the Inquisitor claims, proves beyond doubt that everything is not for the best because things were once better. In reply, Pangloss attempts to defend his theory of all things being for the best, including the drowning of the hapless companion, the wrath of the earthquake and the general suffering of Lisbon. Voltaire is writing to mock the position the philosopher represents, and therefore Pangloss is not allowed to succeed.

After the earthquake, the Portuguese pundits cannot think of any better way of preventing utter ruin than to hold a splendid *auto-da-fé* (the ritual public penance of condemned heretics and apostates that took place as part of the Spanish and Portuguese Inquisitions). The University of Coimbra declares that the spectacle of a number of people being ceremonially burnt over a slow fire is an infallible way of preventing a further earthquake. They choose to burn one man because he had married his godmother, and two others because they refused to eat bacon. The authorities also hang Pangloss for his optimism and flog Candide for listening to the philosopher with an air of approval. Against their expectation, the collective punishment brings about a further tremendous and noisy earthquake.

Candide, terrified almost out of his wits, covered with blood and trembling violently, utters the following famous words: 'If this is the best of all possible worlds, whatever must the others be like?'

The novel careers disastrously on. At the end, after adventure, jeopardy and intrigue, Candide asserts that it is best to tend our own gardens (he has of course had to travel far and wide in order to reach this conclusion).

Even in instances unaccompanied by mass death and the collapse of things, the evidence suggests that an earthquake is among the most terrifying of all possible events. Unlike trees or birds, almost all the ordinary actions of our social lives require that the ground should remain motionless under our feet, our settlements and our philosophical systems. The literature abounds with references to the overthrow of mental security that results from the ground moving and quaking, as well as with reference to the nervousness, restlessness and tranquilisation that accompanies survivors. If we also add the unpredictable suddenness and potential ferocity of such events, the instant consideration that one is powerless in its face, and the dreaded possibility that it might happen again at any time, we can perhaps begin to understand why earthquakes have such an impact on the lives of those who witness and survive them. Earthquakes are capable of rubbishing the best achievements of humanity and levelling the vainest cultural ambition. Consequently, earthquakes make people think.

Given these extraordinary powers, we might sensibly ask what thoughts earthquakes have prompted in the past. In history, the sublime reach of catastrophe has led to speculation on the possible purpose of mass death and destruction in the grander scheme of things. In particular, the catastrophe of an earthquake may provide opportunity to reconsider how men should properly relate to their gods, or prompt additional speculation on god's supposed intentions.

The 1755 Lisbon earthquake is much written about by those seeking to understand the debate, enlivened by the disaster, on whether optimism or pessimism was the underlying philosophical condition of eighteenth-century Europe. Looking at the earthquake with hindsight, historians have wondered whether the shock of the disaster pushed the Enlightenment in certain godless directions. Some say it did; others believe the paradigm shift from god to rational science was already underway.[1] But what of the moral and philosophical content of the debates provoked by the earthquake? Do these have relevance for thinking about earthquakes elsewhere? Can we think comparatively about the thoughts people have in the aftermath of a disaster? Or, do the thoughts earthquakes provoke only belong to a particular place and time, in this case Lisbon and the Europe of the mid-eighteenth century?

Lisbon was a prosperous mercantile centre. The destruction of its inhabitants and wealth by an earthquake and ensuing floods and fires reverberated across Europe.

Lisbon was also known, as we know, for its inquisitors and idolatry, which added a sharp edge to proceedings in the aftermath. The Protestant clergy in northern Europe asserted that the earthquake happened because the people of Lisbon were Roman Catholics. The clergy of Lisbon, on the other hand, felt that the shock was the result of divine anger at the presence of certain Protestants in the town. The heretics were forcibly baptised, and, as we know, a splendid *auto-da-fé* was held, with a view to preventing further disaster.

Lisbon, too, boomed after its destruction, and the new glory sat uneasily with the images of loss, wrath and human sacrifice that accompanied the initial news of the earthquake. The tugs and contradictions of the destruction and the prosperous after-math detained some of the foremost thinkers of the age, Rousseau, Voltaire and Kant among them, as well as the lesser-known Louis de Beausobre. Their desultory dia-logues led them to consider the possible death of god, whether god's design for the world was the best of all possible designs, and, if so, what place there was for the terror and destruction of an earthquake. Is chance or fate the general principle of universal operation? De Beausobre in particular asked the intriguing question: is death a greater evil when it strikes at many people simultaneously, rather than remov-ing them at intervals?

It is worth considering their thoughts further, for these are the very questions earthquakes beg, and I cannot see any other place or time in which such questions have been addressed so candidly or clearly, and documented so comprehensively.

In the last years of the seventeenth century, long before the earthquake struck Lisbon, the French philosopher Pierre Bayle put forward the following radical thesis: the universe is not all for the best—evil is present in the world and is largely in control of the things that matter.[2] In response, Leibniz put forth a case for the opti-mism Pangloss represents with a metaphysics grounded in a rational proof of god's existence and goodness: from the very idea of god, it followed that the universe he created was, famously, 'the best of all possible worlds'.[3] Leibniz thought that god, after considering the different worlds it was possible to make, created a version in which there was more good than evil. God had therefore decided that a world with no evil would not be as good as this world, a world with some evil. Once a world had been created in which evil exists, it follows that god cannot intervene to prevent it from fulfilling its appointed role because this would imply that the world god created was not the best of all possible worlds.

These ideas were given renewed vigour in Pope's *Essay on man*: reason proves that evil can only exist for the sake of a greater good.[4] Pope argued that no matter how imperfect, complex and disturbing the universe appears, it functions in a rational fashion according to natural laws. Such laws operate a universe that is the perfect work of god. It is only because humans have limited intellectual capacities that the world appears imperfect. If we accept our position in the vast chain of being, only then is there the potential for happy and virtuous lives.

De Beausobre's *Essai sur le Bonheur*, written after the Lisbon earthquake, is in the *tout est bien* mode.[5] For him, there was pretence and hypocrisy in the grief of those crying in the ruins. They say, he wrote, that god's providence has failed them, but in their shock they have forgotten the blessings and happiness of normal life. The earthquake victims are dead; but death is not a greater evil when it strikes many people simultaneously than when it removes them one by one at intervals. Why then should death suddenly be deemed so awful when it is accompanied by the quaking of the earth? Similarly, he reasoned, the riches of the city are lost, but the city can be rebuilt. In his view, a great calamity is just a multiplication of the ordinary calamities that may happen to anyone without causing any general alarm. Suffering simultaneously with others does not make suffering worse, and all that can really be said about an earthquake as an evil thing is that it causes a greater total amount of grief on one occasion than a single accident. We may be sorry about this but, after all, and in answer to his own questions, plagues, war, famine and earthquakes are divine punishments on humanity, and we cannot sensibly expect them to be pleasant.

In England at the time there was also much discussion about the causes and meanings of earthquakes following a remarkable series of tremors in London. One Reverend Stukeley argued from his pulpit in St George's church in Bloomsbury that earthquakes are 'singled out above all natural phenomena by their majesty and dreadful horror to mark an immediate operation of god's hand exercised in His divine anger'. Stukeley was clear that, whatever the natural causes might be (he theorised some form of electrical intervention), earthquakes are god's instruments.[6]

On the other side of the Atlantic, in New England, earthquakes were also the prominent trope though which the 'rational' and the 'supernatural' were theologically ordered.[7] Counter-intuitively perhaps, earthquakes were seen in Puritan eyes as rational events, their cause here again attributed to divine retribution for the sins of humanity. Some even argued that in the absence of sin earthquakes would disappear. In this view, earthquakes are not irrational or random acts of a god without purpose. On the contrary, they are supremely rational and calculated to induce fear.

For all those mentioned here, earthquakes were wondrous things, not only to behold, but with which to think. Earthquakes shake certainties as well as foundations, and therefore they necessarily became part of the discussions of theologians and philosophers. For Christian theologians, earthquakes were instruments of fear, operating either as a routine and indiscriminate part of the divine order of things, or as divine instruments of fear and punishment, which could be distributed when appropriate. Consequently, not only in Europe but in many parts of the world, aftermaths have often spawned the rise of new religious forms, as the beleaguered have become zealots, transforming their fear, guilt, trauma, felicity or rapture into improved forms of devotion, or into ritualised apologies for their wrongdoings. In Peru during the 1970s, religious resurgence took the form of a battle between different currents of Christianity.[8] The discussions that followed the Lisbon earthquake, although not restricted to that disaster by any means, marked another kind of critical shift, and added momentum to thinking in the Enlightenment mode.

Voltaire had initially aligned himself with Leibniz and Pope (his reading of Bayle had already taught him to doubt the perfection of the universe), but the Lisbon earthquake of 1755 broke his faith in the doctrine of 'whatever is, is right' (the *tout est bien*). In his first poem on the earthquake, written before *Candide*, Voltaire attacked the optimism of Pope, 'come, ye philosophers, who cry, "All's well,"/ And contemplate this ruin of a world'.[9] Voltaire mocked: whatever happened must have happened for the best of all possible reasons! In Lisbon, the heirs of the dead will benefit financially; the building trade will enjoy a boom; animals will grow fat on meals provided by corpses trapped in the debris; an earthquake is a necessary effect of a necessary cause; private misfortune must not be overrated; an individual who is unlucky is contributing to the general good. Is this the best of all possible worlds? Is there not as much evil in these sentiments, Voltaire asked, as in the earthquake itself?

For Voltaire, man could not hope for a safe life with the benevolent protection of a Providence rewarding virtuous behaviour. As T.D. Kendrick, author of an eloquent book on the subject, notes of Voltaire's thought:

Man was weak and helpless, ignorant of his destiny, and exposed to terrible dangers, as all must now see; the optimism of the age must be replaced by something that is not much more than an apprehensive hope that Providence will lead us through our dangerous world to a happier state. *Un jour tout sera bien* [one day all will be well] should be the new limit of optimistic thought.[10]

For Voltaire, the saddening truth is that we know nothing of our origin, purpose or destiny. Nature has no message for us. God does not speak. The bodies of men are made for decay and our minds for grief.

Rousseau was unhappy with Voltaire's views on our fate. He said that at a personal level the optimism Voltaire attacked had helped him to endure the very things supposed to be unendurable. For Rousseau, man must recognise evil as the consequence of his own nature as well as that of the universe. A benevolent god desired to preserve man from evil, and, of all the possible systems whereby god's creation might be ordered, god had chosen the one that contained the least evil and the most good. Put bluntly, said Rousseau, the reason why god had not done better for mankind was that god could not do better.

Voltaire argued that an omnipotent god could have prevented evil from tarnishing the world, and the fact that god did not do so means that the only discoverable reason for our existence on earth is that we are here in order to suffer and to die. In contrast, Rousseau maintained that moral evil originated in man himself, not god, and that, even though physical evil is a necessary part of the Creation, the majority of physical evils are man's own fault. According to him, it was not nature or god that had congregated twenty thousand houses of six or seven storeys in Lisbon. If the inhabitants of the city had not lived in crowded and dangerous buildings, the damage would have been less. Had they departed the city after the first shock, then they could have been saved. Instead, they stayed obstinately on the spot, worrying about their money and their possessions. For Rousseau, there was sociology in the disaster as well as theology and philosophy.[11]

Rousseau thought Voltaire's pessimist to be a bourgeois and intellectual. Had Voltaire asked a hard-working Swiss peasant, then, on the contrary, he would not find one willing to exchange paradise for his simple existence and the chance to be reborn so that he could go on living his accustomed, uneventful life forever.

After a number of drafts, Voltaire concluded his poem with a concession to hope:

A caliph once, when his last hour had come,
This prayer addressed to him he reverenced:'To thee, sole and all-powerful king, I bear
What thou dost lack in thy immensity—
Evil and ignorance, distress and sin'.
He might have added one thing further—hope.[12]

Rousseau saw Voltaire's variety of hope as vague and dubious. If correct, then the worldly happiness and prosperity such as he enjoys was worth nothing. Therefore, he was a pessimist. Rousseau, in contrast, possessed hope of another kind, strong and certain, a hope that he saw as illuminating and beautifying everything in his life. He could tolerate no doubt on the subject of the immortality of the soul and the heavenly recompense that he would receive for his suffering on earth. God is kind and *tout est bien*.

Rousseau also observed that, for the pious, Providence is always right and for the philosophers it is always wrong. Men have a conviction one way or the other, and this conviction cannot be altered for one party by pointing to the unjust death of innocent people, or for the other party by observing that premature death saves its victims from a gruesome death-bed agony in old age, and sends them to heaven unembarrassed by the sins that they would have committed had they lived.

For Voltaire, the suffering of the earthquake indicated that we do not inhabit the best of all possible worlds. Optimism is for duffers (such as Rousseau). Voltaire took the criticism forward into his fantastic *Candide*, where, as we know, a storm overtakes Candide's ship off Lisbon, and Pangloss is humiliated for his senseless belief that all things happen for the best.

What if Candide's ship was instead bound for the East and had sunk in a terrible storm off the coast of Gujarat? What if Pangloss, Candide and the brutal sailor had made their way inland and were entering the city of Bhuj when the earth began to shake and the town began to tumble? Would Candide have witnessed the same debates taking place in the ruins?

Eighteenth-century Europe and twenty-first-century India are clearly very different. Earthquake debates in the two places do not share an obvious intellectual or political provenance. Yet, Candide would have recognised a great deal of what was said in Bhuj from his time in Lisbon, as he would have done if he had visited Peru with Barbara Bode in the 1970s. In the ruins of Bhuj, Candide would have met those pondering their responsibility for whatever order there may be outlined in our life, having been faced with the enormity and incomprehensibility of nature. He would have entered into intractable discussions about why the earthquake happened in Kutch, and why it did not strike elsewhere. He would have heard people around him asking: was the earthquake a divine form of communication? If so, what was our deity communicating? Are earthquakes things that just happen or are they given by god? Is human life governed by fate or chance? Is the world a place of optimism or pessimism? He would have heard blame cast in terms of rival religious orthodoxies. He would have met people discussing the exact same question posed by the Frenchman de Beausobre some 250 years earlier: is death a greater evil when it strikes at many people simultaneously rather than removing them at intervals?

In Bhuj, the answer was most unequivocally 'yes', as Dilip has shown us. For de Beausobre it was 'no'. Candide would have seen, and as Rousseau observed, that the religiously and philosophically minded were not, for the most part, moved from the primacy of their convictions by the earthquake. He would have marvelled at the boom following the disaster and the rejuvenation of the stricken city. He would have witnessed these things, but he would also have seen other things as well, including a splendid *auto-da-fé*, of sorts, in 2002.

Lord Krishna looks on with interest as his lovers, the Gopis, are brought back to life by a temple artist, 2002, Ratna

28

EXPLANATION

Over the years, I have read a great deal about earthquakes and disasters. Along with other scholars, I was taken by the graceful and witty arguments that took place across Europe in the aftermath of the Lisbon earthquake of 1755. When taken as a whole, from the vantage of the early twenty-first century, the literature suggests that the earthquake moved the cultural foundations of Europe. The debate between Rousseau and Voltaire, for instance, is so clear and touches on some of the enduring qualities of humanity—what, for example, is hope? The earthquake also seemed to take hold of Kant. And, as he struggled to come to terms with what he could not understand, he developed a critique of reason which would change the way we see things.

I was shaken from my thrall by Edward Paice's recent revisionist history of the Lisbon disaster.[1] He recounts how, in 2004, a mass grave was uncovered beneath the courtyard of the former Franciscan Convento de Nossa Senhora de Jesus in Lisbon (now the Academy of Sciences Museum). It contained the bodies and body parts of at least 3,000 people. They had been buried without any ceremony, a discovery which shocked the modern and deeply Catholic country. Skulls had been crushed, others had exploded due extreme heat. Many of the dead had been subjected to violent trauma inflicted by the hands of compatriots. Skulls had been pierced by lead shot, and a huge number of bones had cut marks. The numerous shallow cuts on the skull of a child suggest that before dying it was used to extort something from a parent. The knife marks on a thigh bone imply cannibalism. It is thought that these bodies date from the time of the Lisbon earthquake.

The conditions that allowed these deaths and the unceremonious disposal of the remains are simply missing from the well-known philosophical discussions. The works of Rousseau, Voltaire and Kant are brilliant and soothing. They are also attractive and readily within our grasp. They fill our minds. They make us feel clever, alive and smug. They are far away from the murdering, burning and cannibalistic aftermath suggested by the mass grave. Kant's discussion of the sublime, it now seems to me, has done the work that it is itself a theory of. Until recently, the Lisbon earthquake was generally remembered for its thoughts, not its terrible violence. The thinkers of the age recovered from their humiliation through self-satisfied contemplation, which, in turn, became a foil for the human dignity of Europe. Kant and others restored the power of reason over nature through explanation. In the process, the real earthquake, the one he could not comprehend, was forgotten. These, it might be said, were the foundations of the Enlightenment, as in the following decades a new age of reason was ushered in.

For much of my fieldwork in India, many people I know were interested in explaining the disaster. As we have seen, people made great efforts to apprehend the actions of the state, but they also took the time to consider the earthquake. What caused the disaster? What meaning did it have? Why had it happened? For a while, those who survived the earthquake could not leave it alone. Shivang was often drawn back to those moments when the earthquake struck. You will recall that he had been in the bath, and was temporarily convinced of his own madness as his family abandoned him. For him, hope came in the form of a blue penholder. The Harijan journalist, also from the beginning of this book, too often found his mind wandering to the sights and sounds of that day: the head he had seen sticking out of the hospital. In 2003, he described what he was experiencing as being 'caught in a trap'. His mind was drawn to the past and the images of things it could not let go, while, at the same time, the spirit of reconstruction was forcing him to anticipate and to look forward, as newness was once again being endlessly produced.

In the aftermath, the disaster took its particular shape because it simultaneously had an impact on everyone. There is a way, as we have seen, in which the death of a similar number of people, dying their individual deaths, was not so great as if they died together. The whole was more than the sum of its parts. It was a momentous rupturing event—on this, I think, there would be consensus, if such a poll were possible. Having experienced only one small vantage point on the catastrophe, in the aftermath, Shivang and many others eventually heard of different stories, experiences and understandings. In the process, they recreated the earthquake and turned it into a narrative. In ways similar to those I have attempted in this book, they constructed the disaster by connecting particular events and making chains of causation and justification. They turned it into a story, and this helped make it go away.

Individuals explained their own survival by the correctness of their lives, the habits they cultivated and the care they displayed towards others. People talked about sin, and the thousands of unknown sins that had died along with the dead. My friends also sought to explain the disaster by recourse to things that were wrong and out of place. In this sense, responsibility lay both with individual sin (known or unknown), but also clustered around broader notions of legitimacy and social order. As the disaster was understood through the lens of the aftermath, categories of people became pitted against one another in explaining the earthquake: foreigner against native, Gujarati against Kutchi, eastern against western, crow against human, Hindu against Muslim, and urbanites against rural folk.

The disaster affected the whole of Kutch, and, with guilt and conflict flourishing in the aftermath, explanations of the tragedy grew to take in all of the sociological complexity of the region. Much of what was shaken by the earthquake were the submerged structures of meaning and distinction given by history. As I have shown, the story of the decade following the earthquake is inseparable from a longer story of struggle and conflict. In this sense, explanation went beyond accounting for oneself and other selves; it sought to account for the ties that bound people together and kept them apart. My friends interrogated their institutions and the nature of bonds that cemented them together as a broad population. Was there something wrong with their values, ambitions, political organisation or religious practices?

In time, explanations of the disaster came to resemble a description of the society the disaster had affected. Caste, religion and history were drafted in as forms of explanation for the tragedy. Event and society merged to form a unique 'disaster identity', the form of which I have described in this book. The earthquake gave cause and time for people to consider why things happen as they do. What are the purposes of life? Are human lives governed by design or chance? Was the disaster a consequence of man's provocation of the universe or god? In a broad sense, the ensuing discussions were tinged with guilt as those who survived were also forced to reflect on why they were in safe places at the time of the earthquake. What was it in the long chain of events that caused their life not to be taken or their body not to be dismembered? Why had they lived while others had died? People thought thoughts they had never had before, as they weighed and measured what had been and what might have been.

The straightforward question asked most often was: 'why had this happened to Kutch?' The language matters here. The earthquake was seen as having happened to Kutch and not in or to Gujarat. The initial newspaper headlines I described in Chapter 1 said it all. The battles that would come were perfectly signalled: 'Gujarat, including Kutch, has experienced a major earthquake: further shocks expected'. A front-page editorial had asked, 'Why is the god of death so annoyed with Kutch?' Implied always in this question was: 'what had Kutch done to offend god (however so conceived)?' Answers to this grand question sought to identify what had gone so horribly wrong. Prior to the earthquake, there had been drought, and the earthquake was described as a continuation or an intensification of the suffering god granted Kutch. Whether Shiva's dance of destruction, Allah's displeasure or the machination of some other god of death, causation was, again almost universally, traced back to the wrongdoing of humanity, through the slippage of geology to god. For many people in Kutch, attributing the earthquake to god was a rationalisation of the cause rather than a mystification of the event.

If the earthquake was a straightforward manifestation of divine displeasure, then there must be something or someone to blame—pure chance was insufficient. As we know, the stories of the foundation of Bhuj became important once again. Had the rituals of propitiation simply been neglected or performed incorrectly? Yes possibly, but, far more commonly, the foundation story was used to explain how the moral and ritual structures of the kingdom had declined in the post-Independence period.

211

The power of the ruling family, around which the castes of Kutch and the history of the kingdom were arranged, had fragmented and grown impotent, creating disequilibrium between the divinely sanctioned kingdom and its socially degenerate inhabitants. The tremors caused by the writhing serpent were wrapped in a pervasive sense of political decline and the loss of the power of kings in post-colonial India. The physical damage the earthquake brought was a cruel parody of the hastening impotence of past powers, causing most intense destruction to the old town, its palaces, walls, religious buildings and the traditional caste neighbourhoods clustered around the royal palaces.

The serpent may have been inspired to move by the decline of the traditional order. In the aftermath, the old orders were further levelled by those who intervened with their notions, villages, politics and memorials. Once the capital of a feudal and ritually elaborate kingdom, Bhuj was redrawn by planners as a post-colonial town in which transport corridors and shopping centres, rather than the palaces of its rulers and the location of its religious sites, oriented the lives and imaginations of the population. Populist electioneering took on communal overtones, as political leaders attempted to present Hinduism as a unified religion, and therefore Hindus as a natural vote bloc defined by common enemies (most commonly Italians, Muslims and secularists).

There is something distinctive about the ways in which blame operates in the aftermath of a natural disaster. In politics and communal violence in India, as we have seen in this book, it is common to blame an 'other' for wrongs in society. After a natural disaster, blame must be cast inwards, rather than outwards, for to seek a cause in the existence of an 'other' would be to grant efficacy and power to the deities of those others.

There were those who attributed the earthquake to divine displeasure regarding the existence and habits of Muslims. In their view, the carnal and craven Muslims were matter out of place, violating the purity of the land and undermining the wishes, purposes and sovereignty of the gods. In this sense, however, the earthquake was not divine revenge against Muslims, but more a reflection of the divine disquiet of Hindu gods and people. The failings of Hindus brought calamity, which was then entwined with the politicised concepts of xenophobia and rule (of the type seen in the sovereignty of *dharma*).

In contrast, a number of Sunni Muslims told me that the earthquake was sent to those who had forgotten how to approach god correctly. Their candidates for blame were not Hindus but other Sunni Muslims. Over the years, I have been increasingly aware of factionalism among Sunnis, which, in some instances, has divided once-unified marriage circles. On the face of it, the nub of dispute is a sectarian one, with the increasing influence of reformist groups undermining the hegemony of older and local sources of authority in the region. In practical terms, the major difference in thinking is about the powers and legitimacy of the cults of saints. The reformists reject the saint as an unnecessary and sometimes illegitimate intermediary between people and god. The traditionalists, for want of a better term, venerate saints, but they also regard them as conduits and active agents of charisma and grace.

I was rather taken aback by the force with which this schism was discussed in the aftermath of the earthquake. One of my friends told me bluntly, with no hint of irony, and perhaps even a mild gloat, that the reformist Muslims associated with organisations called Tablighi Jamat and Ahl-e-Hadis in Anjar and Bhuj had suffered the highest mortality rates of all who had died in the earthquake. According to him, they had forsaken the traditions of protection offered by local saints and their shrines, and mass death was the consequence.

In the past, I have heard stories of how particular saints have deflected and absorbed the power of lightning strikes to save nearby settlements. The pre-eminent and encompassing shrine in Kutch is that of Haji Pir, who, among other things, is remembered as having died while attempting to save some cows. The shrine is strongly intertwined with a general Kutchi sense of identity (along with Ashapura, goddess of kings, who lives remarkably close by), and with Kutchi Muslims in particular. The annual fair at the shrine attracts Muslims from all over Kutch who walk the long road out to the west of the district (rather as Hindus do to the abode of the goddess during Navaratri).

Many Muslims I know will visit the shrine before leaving Kutch to seek the saint's blessing and to ask for protection. The saint thus has a strong territorial identity, and is closely associated with the welfare and conditions of Kutch. The reformists, by contrast, turn to what might be considered a universalist form of Islam, divorced from local territorial and spiritual concerns. The conflict between reformers and traditionalists is therefore also about the relationship between territory and religious practice. For the traditionalists, the cult of saints roots them firmly in the local landscape, its conditions and history.

The friend who first provided the explanation (I later heard it in a similar vein from others) as to why some groups of Muslims died in higher numbers than others was of the opinion that the earthquake was a way for Allah to remind Muslims not to neglect his agents—the saints—as the conduits of his love and intermediaries in divine intercession. In their misplaced zeal, the reformists had lost contact with Allah.

In other words, in some ways, all of the explanations of the earthquake and of human error in relation to divine intention are also commentaries on profane social trends, divisions and schisms that were well established before the earthquake. Such narratives are also critical commentaries on other unfolding social anxieties and alienations. When understood in this way, we can see that they are replete with all the inconsistencies and expediencies of normal social life, including hypocrisy and transference. Relations between colonial and post-colonial society, Hindus and Muslims, and Muslims and Muslims, were being reconfigured in the aftermath of the earthquake in significant ways, much as was happening elsewhere in the region without the catalyst of an earthquake. What initially appeared to me as explanations for the catastrophic moment (for that was the way they were presented), are, with hindsight, also attempts at coming to terms with rapid social change in the aftermath of the disaster. Needless to say, these narratives were also part of the process of creating divisions and reinstating order in things.

It was widely remarked that, in addition to reformist Sunnis, Jains and the Shia group known as the Daudi Bohras suffered disproportionately in the earthquake. This might have had something to do with the location of their businesses and houses in the older parts of the worst-affected towns, but it was generally taken as a sign of dire portent. The plight of these successful mercantile classes became part of a general narrative about the decline in standards in Kutch. Greed and the self-interested pursuit of profit had replaced more decent values of community and philanthropy. This narrative stood separately from those others which blamed the degeneration of the kingdom and the abandonment of proper pathways to god.

This type of narrative is commonly found in the literature on disasters. In this case, the main features of decline are: weakening of the caste order, exogamous marriage, the commercialisation and abandonment of ritualised relationships, and the focus on consumption rather than spirituality and devotion to higher causes.

Although the story of decline masquerades as an explanation for divinely sanctioned catastrophe, it also rather accurately described some of the dominant social processes apparent in the years of the aftermath. The public narratives of explanation therefore sit at the nexus of abstract religious doctrines and the socially sanctioned ways of discussing change and division. In this sense, they are quite ordinary explanations for an extraordinary event.

The explanatory narratives I have detailed came from members of different religious communities, but across them there is an almost consistent sense of divine accountancy for the actions of man, and a similar architecture of ideas: some group (usually one's own) was doing something against the prescribed order of things, or had allowed something bad to happen, and the earthquake served as a mechanism of corrective justice. Here, however, the earthquake was seldom seen as 'punishment' for individual or even generalised sin, thus distinguishing the narratives to a degree from those of the puritans in New England. In contrast, the blame was cast through sociology and a weakness in relation to those who followed other paths towards god. The explanations people provided in Kutch come to terms with the sublime of catastrophe and the personal ambivalences it induced by variously casting blame through the well-rehearsed structures of religious identity politics in the region.

Significantly, in all of the narratives I have presented, the category 'Kutch' is given agency. Sometimes this ascription represents a human collectivity. More commonly it represents a moral and quasi-divine category, capable of intercession between humans and supreme gods, and, indeed, capable of delivering justice to its inhabitants at the behest of higher deities. Land and territory here become part of a moral order, and not just an anodyne matter of territory or geography. Kutch is ascribed an active moral character, and, in a way that speaks volumes for identity politics in the region, it is the only unit of moral territory regularly evoked in this type of discourse. Gujarat remained hollow in both divine and cathartic orders, partially, of course, because its history is recent and it lacks the elaborate ritualised identity of the former princely state of Kutch. I do not think Kutch has vanished in the aftermath of the earthquake, but many of the features that made the people what they were have been undermined by reconstruction. The earthquake proved to be an opportunity for what political scientists call 'sub-national integration', as a distinct district of the state of Gujarat was cowed.

In addition to mass grief and the severe and long-term disruption to life that the earthquake brought to all in Kutch, many people now have to live with themselves and others quite differently. An unknown woman gave herself improperly to god, and her actions were televised: how does she find adequate and sustained meaning in the everyday? A business man experienced madness and saw the abandonment by his family all at the same time: how does he stop curiosity drawing him back to madness, or contempt from forcing him away from his family? The face of a stranger took up residence in the head of someone who claimed to be an atheist, and has accompanied him on and off through life for many years, often making its presence felt at night.

Of the business man, Shivang, I can say that he suffered from severe headaches, before turning to regular fasting, irregular exercise and visits to his lineage goddess. For some time, the atheist found solace in one of the busier Muslim shrines in Bhuj. He thought his homunculus was a Muslim, and therefore he had more chance of getting to know him in the presence of a saint. I do not know who the woman was who appeared in the remarkable footage of the moments after the earthquake, but the loss and terror marked on her face continues to haunt me.

The directions in which individual fear takes the affected is given by the contingencies of personal lives and empirical experiences of the disaster, and these are diverse. The reverberations are irregular. In contrast, public narratives of blame and explanation have been used to rationalise the catastrophe, giving the disaster, in quite a literal sense, the same form as society in Kutch. Existing religious and social divisions in-the-making in Kutch have been used to articulate, explain and thus to represent the disaster. In this way, narratives of the disaster resemble what the disaster affected. The explanations of the earthquake I have discussed here have been given structure and meaning by the structure and meaning of divisions and hierarchies in local society. Everyday and political divisions in society have provided the building blocks of difficult discussions of the sublime and the inexplicable. The answers to the greatest questions have not been found in the minds of professional metaphysicians but in the everyday conflicts and tensions that made society in Kutch what it was becoming. The disaster descended into the ordinary: political contestation, rituals, relations within families, routines and names.

Today, Shivang has forgotten the extraordinary story of the blue penholder which saved his life. When I attended his wedding in January 2011, I asked him if he still had it. He had absolutely no idea what I was talking about, even when I pressed him. I wondered how it was possible to forget something which had given him the presence of mind to live. It was the mundane object somehow imbued with those qualities which had allowed his mind to acknowledge defeat. I have since listened again to the recording I made of him in 2002. His account of an everyday and ordinary object taking on all the significance of life is as compelling now as it was then. I realise now though that the blue penholder was his humiliation and part of the disaster's death imprint. I could afford to dwell upon it without an unbearable cost to my day-to-day well-being—he could not. Shivang's displacement of the penholder marked the passage from shock to self-admiration. It had stayed with me as an example of the ways in which the movement of the earth can shake priorities and reassign hope (Rousseau's hope). Meanwhile, Shivang had learned how to forget. His amnesia suggests, I think, that these days his sense of vertigo has receded. I often wonder what he disposed of first: the penholder in his mind or the one in his office.

Cutting, 2008, Bhuj. Compare with the same site shown in the first image of Chapter 20.

29

INHABITATION

At various points I have permitted hope to appear. Businesses opened in the forlorn spaces of 'town planning' (TP) acts of 'cutting'. Picnics and excited speculation took place on relocation sites. Umashankar had a sky-blue moment on the roof of his new house. Such instances shone fleetingly through the dust, stress and dreary politics. Time slowed and confusion halted as hope concentrated the mind.

In 2004, I spent a day in the village of Nutun Chitrod in eastern Kutch, which had been reconstructed by a caste association from Mumbai, with financial assistance from the governor of Antwerp and the 'Indian diamond community in Belgium'. High walls had been placed between the new houses, seemingly as a hasty after-thought because the structures had been built close together and the recipients were not happy with the enforced intimacy. These walls were made from cast concrete, manufactured on site. Straight from the mould, the blocks had been laid on sheets of newspaper to dry. The newsprint merged with the concrete to form a resilient skin. The comic result was that the entire village was covered in old news, upside down advertisements and un-done crosswords. In time of course, the paper washed away to leave only an ever-fading trace.

When I look back on that period, I wonder what it was really all about. What consequences did the frenzy of intervention and opportunism have for those who remained? What stuck? What, like old news, faded away? Did those who came to intervene know what the consequences of their actions would be?

Villagers were brought into contact with strangers and new ways of working and decision-making. Jeeps, spreadsheets and brochures brought with them the language of development and rights, gender-awareness programmes and micro-credit unions. At the time, it was straightforward to build a village based on the politicised fear of Muslims. The names of Hindu sects were already associated with wealth and power, and they too found an easy path into rural life. Had an intervener attempted to introduce pork as a staple food or insist that all men should wear pink suits and convert to Judaism then they would, I imagine, have been uniformly unsuccessful. In general, interveners met with success when what they intended for the future had already been imagined in the village.

Alongside these experiments with rural aspiration, there was also the intensification of expectation and competitive greed. These characteristics were not born of the earthquake but given new and particular forms. The interveners set the bar high: how many villages could they adopt? How fast could they reconstruct them? How big could their promotional signboards be? The atmosphere was frenetic.

In villages, stories of financial spillage were common. Headmen, big-men and brokers of other kinds often emerged with distinguished accommodation. Some houses were too badly built to be inhabited, constructed for a kickback or a contract; in other locations, entire settlements remain uninhabited to this day. Villagers became greedy in relation to what they saw or imagined others to be getting. In many instances, this made them reluctant to commit to offers of village adoption in case better offers came later. When consensus over an arrangement with a particular adopting agency could not be reached, it generally led to the division of the village, mostly, but not always, along pre-existing lines. The shock of inaction caused by disaster was exacerbated by the paralysis and divisions of greed, which were built firmly into the procedural architecture of the public–private paradigm.

The run of events in the villages outlined in previous sections represents different ways in which reconstruction policy partnered the promotion of political ideas in the countryside. In 2003 and 2004, enquires took place in the USA and UK after it was alleged that money raised in those countries had funded what was termed 'hate' and 'social exclusion' in Gujarat. In the UK, it was claimed that the Leicester-based organisation Hindu Swayamsevak Sangh (HSS) had strong links with the Rashtriya Swayamsevak Sangh (RSS) in India and had channelled money donated by the British public to RSS causes in Gujarat. Funds raised by Sewa International (mentioned in Chapter 12), a section of the HSS, were shown to have been used to glorify the RSS in the name of the earthquake.[1]

In 2005, a British parliamentary commission investigating 'terrorism and community relations' received written depositions from the Swaminarayan Hindu Mission further to oral testimony to the Home Affairs Select Committee, which alleged that the Vishwa Hindu Parishad (VHP) was operating from the Bochasanwasi Shri Akshar Purushottam Swaminarayan Sanstha (BAPS) temple in Neasden, north London.[2] The allegation, especially in conjunction with use of the word 'terrorism', which was unsubstantiated, understandably caused great offence to BAPS. The temple strenuously denied links with the VHP and presented evidence and testimonials to the Select Committee, including its Guinness Book of World Records entry for the most vegetarian dishes served during a particular festival and supportive statements from former President Clinton.

BAPS further asserted that it was a victim of terrorism at Akshardham in Gandhinagar (although why that particular temple was targeted was not discussed) and detailed to the Committee a list of charitable works it had undertaken. Yet, there was no account of their plan for becoming a national movement in India, no exploration of their designs on the Gujarati diaspora, and no analysis of their particular presentation of Hinduism and history, which is clearly on display for all to see at their main temples.[3]

A vast literature on housing in post-disaster contexts addresses the intractable problems of balancing immediate and longer-term needs, tradition and modernity, and cost and benefit.[4] Participatory planning is very much in vogue in development circles, focused on delivering development to complement culture, local knowledge and capacity-building. The reconstruction of Gujarat suggests that while participatory planning for post-disaster housing may seem like a sensible idea in the abstract, in practice it opened a Pandora's box of choice, leading to social divisions which were otherwise latent and ill-conceived.[5]

Understanding the layers and streams of culture in an Indian village takes time—time which an aftermath does not allow. Anthropologists working in villages generally assume that it takes a year to comprehend the basics. An experienced eye might see as much with a more rapid appraisal, but irregular and unpredictable patterns of disaster do not lend themselves to having such experience at hand. However, once you understand something of the cultures of the village, then you will also understand that managing the expectations of everyone equally is quite impossible. Many of the things people want, or think they want, will impose upon or negate the wishes and rights of their neighbours. And while 'participation' can mean much more than 'choosing', engineering the kinds of relationships where joint, guided or informed decision-making can take place is also very time consuming.

Rural Gujarat is inhabited by a vast range of different castes, classes and occupational groups. No amount of sociological vision could have smoothed all the concerns that emerged in relation to rural housing. Villagers do not simply do this or that; they have a range of ways of doing things and of arranging their lives and genders. There is no normative villager. Any attempt to plan as if there is one will not reach all villagers in the same way: the effects will be differentiated.

Some scholars have argued that grid-patterned villages often built after disasters pay too little attention to local conceptions of social organisation and settlement. Such disruption of a community's spatial organisation, they reason, may lead to its 'social disarticulation'.[6] In such reconstruction programmes, it has been argued that there is no space between the intervening agency and villagers for negotiation, advocacy or internal learning. Instead, the focus for the agency is on implementation, direction and control—a passive project-oriented management that is linear, teleological and ethnocentric.[7] There is also a strong objection to 'matchbox housing' built on city-like grids. Instead, the argument goes, houses should be reconstructed to ensure 'cultural continuity': houses should be built to fit the needs of the way of life of the people.[8]

In the short term, the Gujarat material would appear to support these criticisms. In the early years, the 'grid' villages looked horrid; the atmosphere was far from chirpy. Uniform lines seemed incapable of accommodating the wonderful diversity of rural cultures. In the longer term, however, some of those villages which initially resembled neglected concentration camps have fared very well, and I would argue that a great sense of 'community' now prevails—in part, perhaps, because it had to be remade afresh. In contrast, many of the villages in which 'consultation' and 'participation' took place often fragmented from the outset. Projects in which villagers were treated as if they had equal rights to the resources of the adopting agency 'failed' most frequently. Participatory planning engaged most firmly with the divisive politics of the period, encouraging social division and the laying out of caste and religious hierarchies in concrete—not always, of course, but often. Villagers were presented with choices which in the normal run of things were neither there nor theirs to be made.

Additionally, I think that the critics of housing reconstruction in Gujarat have simply not understood that many organisations building houses imposed their own frameworks of meaning on the grid, and that the grid was far from value neutral. Many organisations did not simply build a grid and let villagers get on with it. They spent time explaining and encouraging people into certain ideas, training them how to think in particular ways, and how to live in the grid as political subjects. In this sense, political Hinduism offered a straightforward planning paradigm.

Had I brought this research project to an end after five years, I would probably have sided with the arguments against grid housing outlined above. Villagers were mostly unenthused too, but they publicly complained about building materials, rather than the disagreeable new sociology. Surveys and media reports repeatedly found dissatisfaction with the quality of houses. If you ask a villager how satisfied they are with the quality of their new house, then the answer has already to a great extent been preconfigured. Leading questions aside, some pretty fundamental struggles over meaning were taking place in the countryside, as adoptees and adopters got to know one another. I cannot help but think that the reported complaints about shoddiness, leaks and flakes were one way of translating deeper disputes into a language that journalists and development workers could understand and be moved by, while keeping the underlying chauvinisms and struggles veiled, perhaps because they were difficult to figure out in words.

Like others, I was initially dismayed by the unimaginative and barrack-like nature of many new villages. I have often asked myself why I should have felt like this: the prejudices of a certain class-based upbringing in Britain, an inherited and vague disdain of modernist architecture and the idea of the suburb, and perhaps, the remnants of a utopian view of village life (although having grown up in a village I know that utopia is always found in the next village over the hill, and so on). I cannot help but feel that similar unexplored prejudices arise in the post-disaster housing literature more generally. What was being built in Gujarat was not conceived of as a 'barracks' but as a 'colony', the word used for desirable low-rise suburban and urban housing developments. As we have seen in Bhuj, many of the town's elite lived in colony-style suburban housing, and the general craze in the town was towards suburban dwelling. Therefore, for some people, the construction of colonies in the countryside was an extremely positive development, speaking of modernity and progress, and giving new respect and status to villagers.

On the tenth anniversary of the earthquake, I visited Keshavnagar, the place of Togadia's hate speech in which he had shouted about barking and hanging. The entrance gates had faded and were shabby. I noticed for the first time that the list of donors included the Dayanand Saraswati Association of New Jersey and Pandit Din-dayal Upadhyay House of Ohio. I had not fully appreciated the significance of these names during my first visits years earlier. Saraswati was founder of the Arya Samaj, an anti-Gandhian, broadly in favour of the rationalisation of popular Hinduism and an associate of Shyamji Krishnavarma (he of Chapter 10). We already know of Upad-hyaya's integral humanism and religious governance.

It was the first time in five years that I had been to Keshavnagar. I remembered it as a desolate and depressing collection of concrete boxes grafted onto a barren hill-side. It was the place which, at first, most typified the cynicism of the aftermath. Such interventions had openly served the interests of political strategists and power, rather than the beleaguered. Something hard had been encouraged in the hearts of people who had earlier been gentler. I had always seen this village, and many others, as an effort to naturalise certain social and political differences. It had been an attempt at engineering a society through planning regimes and strategic social exclu-sion. My final visit in 2011 prompted me to sit down and finish this book, before the research seemed too far out of time.

As I walked into the village, I found it difficult to recognise my own memories. Compound walls had been constructed around houses and clusters of houses; decora-tive doors in the traditional carved style now welcomed visitors. Earlier, the houses sat on the public hillside; now, they nestled in private spaces. Gardens had been planted. To the eye, which is not the same as a survey, the place was verdant and looked wonderful. Those families without the means to construct walls had created fences from bundles of dry prickly foliage, just as they would have done before the earthquake brought them to Keshavnagar. Indeed, the village provided houses for many families whose collective resources had previously prevented them from inhab-iting anything that resembled a house. Many houses had been modified, which completely dispelled the sense of mass uniformity. One house had a second storey painted bright yellow; many others had balconies and staircases leading up to roof-top drying and threshing areas. There were animals in the compounds, stores of fodder and produce. As a community of farmers, the village seemed to be thriving following the construction of water tanks and dams as the VHP had continued to invest in the development of resources.

Given such blossoming, the most straightforward solution to mass rural housing, given the resourcefulness of the population at large, and that people could not always rebuild their own houses where they were, might have been to provide a standard core structure, which could later be modified as required and with the participation of the occupants. In practice, such modifications have been made to many thousands of houses. Had this concept been formalised, the purpose of a core structure explained, and additions linked to further compensation payments, then much of the unhappi-ness associated with the provision of mass rural housing might have been avoided.[9]

Of course, houses built in the wrong places with inappropriate materials are undesirable—but this is basic sense, rather than a refutation of the idea that houses cannot be built for people. Likewise, those building houses should be aware of who is living in them and what they do. Also undesirable is the assumption that pre-earthquake settlements were harmonious and wise, and that the culture found there should be unthinkingly preserved. While untouchability, bonded labour and child marriage might not be the things those arguing for cultural continuity would wish to preserve, how can such things simply be divorced from broader religious, agricultural and caste traditions? Also to be avoided, I think, is the idea that this thing often called 'culture' is so obstinate that it cannot flourish in new forms of housing. It took ten years for these newly constructed villages to become so well established. Perhaps planners and architects know that such things take so long; I did not. This is one of the major lessons I have taken from doing this research. The second flush of the aftermath takes time to gain confidence. To decorate, modify and redesign things given to you by strangers is slow going, especially so when a culture of uncertainty is made to prevail.

Back in Keshavnagar, I was soon joined by a small group of children. They told me proudly that a house in their village had just sold for a princely sum. They attended the local primary school, and when the time came they would walk to secondary school in neighbouring Lodai, the original settlement. They had friends and maintained close connections with neighbouring villages. As we walked further into the village, women distributed sweets, not because it was the anniversary of the earthquake but because it was Republic Day.

These children had grown with the village. None of them had first-hand memories of the earthquake. They knew it had been a significant event. In their time, the lines of buildings had softened, weeds and weather had worn the faces of the concrete, and paths had been trampled into the hillside. These routes rebelled against the perpendicular, taking people where they most wanted to go. With their own ways of dwelling and decoration, the inhabitants had reclaimed the place from the draftsman's board. I listened to the children explain that on one side of the temple lived people of the Ahir caste, on the other lived Rabaris, and beyond them were now a few families of Harijans. Of course, they said, there were no Muslims in this village! The grid might not have stuck, but the ideas that had put it there had taken root.

SECTION 7

AMNESIA

The disaster is related to forgetfulness—forgetfulness without memory, the motionless retreat of what has not been treated—the immemorial, perhaps. To remember forgetfully: again, the outside.

Maurice Blanchot, *The writing of the disaster*

The earthquake prompted reflection on the past. As the past was gradually recalled, the fragility of life was increasingly exposed. Some towns and villages had previously fallen, repeatedly. The British arrived in Kutch two hundred years before, accompanied by a terrible earthquake. This dual disaster led to a regime change and gave rise to the modern diaspora. A section of Anjar had been demolished by the quaking earth in 1819, 1956 and 2001. Despite sorrowful and angry protests, people were again drawn to inhabit the site of repetitive mass death. Only later did scientists suggest that this was not a good idea. People came to erect monuments to the dead, to themselves and to the earthquake. Their inscriptions were failures. The state commissioned two adroit memorials as part of its nation-building project. The latest earthquake began to be forgotten, and in the process a new India was being born.

The plaque showing details of reconstruction following the 1819 earthquake, 2007, Anjar.

30

SHOCKS OF COLONIALISM

The earthquake of 2001 uncovered material evidence and neglected memories of previous earthquakes. In Bhuj, the bastion of the inner fortress shed its outer skin of roughly hewn stone, poignantly revealing an older and elegantly-ornamented façade of marching elephants and other portentous signs. The bastions had been encased and strengthened following their partial collapse during an earthquake in 1819. The layers of history and meaning vividly displayed by this exfoliation return us to the beginning of the nineteenth century, when convulsions of the earth coincided with the arrival of British colonial power and an unorthodox regime change in the palaces of Bhuj.

From the beginning of the nineteenth century, it was British policy to 'settle' western India. In order to do this, the colonial government attempted to determine the boundaries between the many states, so that regimes of tax and treaty could be imposed. Through such means, colonial influence gradually seeped from Bombay into what were to become its provinces. Kutch signed its first treaties with the British in the early years of the nineteenth century.[1] At the time, the territory was divided by internal war and feud. Perhaps as a consequence of these conditions, the treaties were poorly observed. Unrest and sporadic raids on cattle and property continued, especially in the area known as Wagad or Wagur between Kutch and Saurashtra to the east. During one such raid, the camp of the colonial officer James MacMurdo was attacked. This, and other events which need not detain us, led to the application of military pressure on Kutch. So it was that Colonel East crossed westwards across the Rann with around 4,000 troops in December 1815 and took the fort at Anjar. MacMurdo was installed as political agent, following an additional treaty in 1816. For a while, Bhuj remained outside the sphere of colonial influence. Tension persisted, resulting in further treaties.

Once established in Anjar, MacMurdo built himself a fine bungalow on a rocky outcrop in the shadow of a fortified tower. Some say the bungalow was modelled on his family home in Dumfriesshire in Scotland. He decorated the interior walls with beautiful frescos depicting scenes from the Ramayana painted in the local *kamagari* style. At one time, the structure may also have had an earthen terrace on which those in repose before dinner might have sat in the evening breeze. The sensitivity to local ways of life evident in this building, as well as the ethnographic depth of his writing on the region, has fuelled speculation about how MacMurdo could have known so much in advance of his arrival.

In Kutch, it is generally accepted that MacMurdo had first visited disguised as a holy man in order to collect political intelligence and to learn the local languages. There, he sat in penance, chanting stories about the god Ram in front of the Madhavra temple in Anjar. He became known as Bhuriya Bawa. Recently, one of the erstwhile ruling family told me that MacMurdo's disguise had been uncovered. He had been dragged naked by the hair through Bhuj by an indignant crowd. Such public humiliation, unsurprisingly, does not find its way into the colonial record.

Even from the partisan colonial accounts, it is obvious that the British were not welcome. These sources tend to depict Rao Bharmul, then the ruler, as a figure deranged by lust and violence, and addled by opium and spirits. James Burnes, who was surgeon for the Bombay establishment in Bhuj in the 1820s, wrote of how Rao Bharmul was infatuated in this hatred of the British and how he never spoke of MacMurdo in anything but the terms of the grossest abuse. Rao Bharmul's hostile attitude, although focused on MacMurdo, extended, it is pretty clear, to the entire colonial presence in Kutch. The British sources suggest that Rao Bharmul's defiant opinions were only expressed with the aid of Dutch courage. This explanation is partial at best, for Rao Bharmul also used other means to make things difficult for the British. Notably, he strangled the trade of the Anjar merchants through tax and various other restrictions, which reduced revenue for the colonial government and presumably contributed to discontent in the town. Burnes also records that Rao Bharmul publicly boasted he would have MacMurdo assassinated.

Under these tense circumstances, MacMurdo paid a visit to the palaces of Bhuj in 1819, or thereabouts. They were jostled by the troops and attendants as they passed through the courts of the palace; their salutations were not even returned; and the populace appear to have been instructed, or, at all events, permitted, to assail them with ribaldry and abuse. The Rao himself was found intoxicated on every occasion of Captain M'Murdo's waiting upon him … and the resident left Bhooj without having gained any one object.[2]

Despite Rao Bharmul's resistance to British military advances, for that is clearly what they were, rather than the actions of someone simply deranged, after a series of skirmishes and near skirmishes between Kutch troops and the British, the Marquis of Hastings, the governor general of India, proclaimed Rao Bharmul to be a public enemy and declared war against him. Rao Bharmul was deposed, his infant son was nominated by the lesser ruling families of Kutch as successor, and the colonial administration established a residency in Bhuj.

James Burnes wrote of these events when they were recent and raw, and were yet to have the sharp edges taken off them by apologists or by those seeking to rectify prejudices of the colonial gaze. He wrote:

The tyranny and injustice of Rao Bharmuljee had scarcely been crushed, and a new and better order of things introduced through the means of the British government, when the hand of Providence seemed to join in depriving Cutch of some of the instruments of cruelty. A violent shock of an earthquake, attended with some extra-ordinary circumstance, levelled with the dust nearly all the walled towns in the country, and anticipated an intention, which had often been conceived, of dismantling some of these nests of discontent and treason. The desolation of which can scarcely be imagined.[3]

MacMurdo, by now holding the titles resident of Bhuj and collector of Anjar, was sitting with some friends on an earthen terrace in front of a house in which the party was to dine. It was 16 June 1819. The hot day had given way to a serene and clear evening.[4] His attention was suddenly attracted by the slight motion of his chair. Before he could ask 'What is that?', his chair again moved. Realising an earthquake was upon him, he ran for open ground.

MacMurdo later recalled:

My feelings at the moment were such as for an instant to deprive me of all presence of mind and power of reflection; and when self-possession did return, my mind was too deeply occupied with the awful and appalling spectacle of the face of nature in a state of excessive agitation to admit of other thoughts or impressions.[5]

As he watched buildings crumble, so too did his conviction in the strength of man over the natural order. He also records his reaction to the visitation as a 'kind of gasping anxiety', of which the prominent symptoms were 'weakness of the limbs' and 'sickness of the stomach'. Among Europeans and natives alike, he observed restlessness and the disinclination to be alone or to attend to the usual occupations. Over the following weeks, the 'natives' (as the colonials called the Indians) insisted to a man that there was almost a constant undulating motion in the earth, such, we might suppose, was the fear of falling again.[6] The language is not dissimilar to that used in the accounts of the 2001 earthquake at the start of this book.

As MacMurdo wandered in the ruins, the people he met were chanting the names of the deities Ram and Krishna, seemingly, he thought, unconscious of what they were saying. He observed that, 'half of the town, which is situated in low rocky ridges, suffered comparatively nothing; whilst the other half, upon a slope to a plain of springs and swamps, into which the town is drained was entirely overturned'.[7] Later, there was wonder and speculation as to how two sections of the same town, so proximate, could be so differently affected by the earthquake.

In Anjar, of the 4,500 houses MacMurdo counted in the town, he reckoned 1,500 were destroyed and 1,000 badly damaged. The calamity was general. Money could not buy labour, and the wealthy sat around helplessly near their collapsed properties.

Elsewhere in Kutch, fire was seen to issue forth from the land, and at least one fireball exploded from a hill near Roha.[8] Wells overflowed, and dry rivers filled to their banks with fresh water for periods of minutes. In places, red rivers gushed and brimmed; natives said the red colour was blood. MacMurdo assumed the colour had been absorbed from the soils through which the waters had been pushed.[9]

In Bhuj, elephants broke free from their pickets and rushed through the town, until falling houses obstructed them. Horses on the hoof lost their equilibrium: one Colonel Miles initially attributed the tickling he felt in his stomach to the odd movements of a sick horse—at least, that is, until he saw the walls of Bhuj begin to collapse.[10] There, the fortifications suffered damage, as did the tombs of the former rulers of Kutch, 'the principal ornament of the sterile plain of Bhuj'.[11] In Bhuj, nearly 7,000 houses were damaged and some 1,000 to 1,300 people were killed.

Placards appeared from unknown quarters foretelling further misfortune for those who did not feed their priests, or those who persevered in sin. MacMurdo found a paper stated to have been sent from the holy Hindu city of Benares warning that the age was changing and that sinners would be swallowed by the earth. Those spared would be the charitable and virtuous, those who depend on god, give alms and fear the consequences of bad actions. Muslims acquired scrolls from Mecca warning them to be pious. Mullahs stated the cause of the earthquake to be the Prophet Mohammad's horse or mule 'Dooldool' pawing for his food. Strict injunctions were issued to all good Muslims to send a certain quantity of grain and grass to satisfy the horse. These supplies, MacMurdo remarks, were appropriated by the leaders for their own private emolument.[12] The Hindus attributed the earth's motion to a quarrel among the Dyets and Dewas (presumably deities or spirits of some kind). In short, MacMurdo complained, at least when he presented his account to the genteel audience at the Bombay Literary Society, 'there was a superabundant display of everything absurd or extravagant that could be advanced by ignorance and presumption, deceit and superstition'.[13]

In 1839, Marianne Postans speculated how the natives must have begun to think the world was fearfully increasing in sin, as other parts of India had been affected by quakes in recent years. She wrote:

As the favourite Hindu tenet connected with the subject is, that the world is supported by an enormous, many-headed snake; that only one head sustains it at a time; and that, as the snake becomes fatigued, he slips it off upon another, which produces a corresponding effect of motion on the surface of the globe, occasioning earthquakes of greater or less force, according to the weight of the earth, and the effort the snake makes to change its position. Now, say these ingenious theorists, the earth becomes heavy in proportion to the sins of men; and as crime increases, the supporting head of the snake becomes more frequently fatigued, and earthquakes of course more frequent.[14]

Far away in Ahmedabad, almost as if the city were connected to Kutch by some subterranean structure, both minarets of the Juma Mosque were thrown down, depriving the whole city of its greatest ornament. The acting judge in Ahmedabad at the time petitioned the colonial government to reconstruct the minarets. He reasoned that rebuilding them would win the gratitude of their subjects because both Hindus and Muslims 'respect and venerate' the memory of Sultan Ahmed, the founder of the city, for their protection. The East India Company declined on the grounds of expense.[15] How different it is now when many Hindus call the city Amdavad so as to efface the memory of the Sultan? Others want to rename the city altogether.

While Burnes saw Providence at work in the destruction of Kutch—the earthquake enabled the acceleration of the 'good work' of the colonial project—others too saw the earthquake as an opportunity to intervene. The early colonial residents in Bhuj record the disgruntlement of the Amirs of Sindh that Kutch had signed treaties with the British, fearing the consequences of British influence and design on their own borders. Again, and at least according to Rushbrook Williams, there was talk in Hyderabad that while Kutch was in ruins it ought to be invaded so that the British could be turned out.[16] In the end, the idea came to nothing other than a weak demand for the secession of parts of western Kutch to Sindh.

In sum and in short, the earthquake was part of the confluence of extraordinary events in Kutch: the consolidation of British rule was well underway (a process clearly speeded up by the disaster), the ruler had very recently been deposed, and an infant under the supervision of the British regency had taken over the throne. By now, Kutch was changed forever.

In the aftermath, the elegant walls of the old regime were encased in anonymous and roughly hewn stone. The young ruler, tutored in the ways of righteousness by the regency, grew up to head a tributary of the Bombay Presidency, and became a favourite of Queen Victoria. His long rule over Kutch was thus appropriately regarded by the British as intelligent, amiable and dutiful.[17] Under the 'stabilising influence' of rule by the residency, even his disagreeable, and now cloistered, father became 'temperate, even to a degree'.[18] MacMurdo died of cholera the year after the earthquake; he was thirty-five.[19] At the beginning of the twenty-first century, as was the case more than a 150 years ago, his grave is a site of veneration for those in search of a boon.[20] In Anjar, an inscription (a memorial of sorts) was erected recording that during the minority of Maharaj Rao Daisul the British regency ordered the reconstruction of the fort. Through this work, the inscription states, 'the subjects were made happy, and the city was rendered flourishing'.[21] Later, another inscription was placed inside the fortified tower adjacent to MacMurdo's bungalow.[22]

The available material on the 1819 earthquake is colonial in inception. It is unfortunate that other accounts do not exist to cast this remarkable confluence of events in different terms. To me, it is inconceivable that the military and diplomatic invasion of the British, the dispossession of the ruler and the calamitous events of the earthquake were not linked together in popular accounts of explanation and blame. The deposed ruler's mother is reported to have perished in the ruins, a fact which adds a further inauspicious layer. In such accounts we can imagine it was not Providence that caused 'the angel of destruction to sweep over this devoted province' but indigenous protective deities—those that gave life and sustenance to the kingdom—expressing their anger at foreign intervention and the dismantling of their regimen, or, perhaps, their dismay at the failure of their own subjects for permitting such terrible things to occur.[23]

In the aftermath, MacMurdo, who clearly had an exceptional understanding of the region, wrote: 'there does not exist even a tradition of an earthquake of any violence having occurred. The natives, therefore, were perfect strangers to such a phenomenon, and were terrified in proportion to their ignorance'.[24] Similar sentiments were expressed by the light-penned Marianne Postans in the 1830s. 'The natives', she wrote, 'during this confusion, were terrified at the phenomenon, in proportion to their inability to account for it'.[25] She also notes the conspicuous fact that earthquakes do not form part of any local legends or tradition.

In the late 1990s, I remember meeting two individuals in Kutch who held to the memory of particular earthquakes and who were aware of the unpredictable danger they posed to the safety and prosperity of the region. With the exception to which I turn in the following section, there was a general silence on the possibility of an earthquake. Perhaps in an area such as Kutch there has to be such silence because living with the permanent fear of falling is too terrible and paralysing. Yet, when recent earthquakes are examined side by side we can see the remarkable consequence of this collective 'not remembering', the amnesia of my title.

The list of donors giving more than 100,000 rupees to the Ramkrishna Mission's earthquake relief and rehabilitation efforts. The names are displayed on the entrance gates to a village 'adopted' by the Mission. The locations of the donors, many of whom are Gujarati, reveal the global reach and imply the wealth of the diaspora, 2002, Dhaneti.

31

EARTHQUAKE DIASPORA

The slight role of earthquakes in the myths and legends of Kutch is striking, given the seeming frequency of their occurrence and the sometimes awful consequences. Stories of subterranean serpents and collapsing towns may give the impression of an organised corpus of material reflecting the perennial threat of an earthquake. I have, however, had to dredge for this material, and by bringing it together in a single piece of writing the result is not ethnographically representative of the weight earthquakes are given in daily life in Kutch. There were no signs, paintings, cartoons, warning notices, safety campaigns—in fact, no indication at all that there was the possibility of collapse, save, that is, for a neglected plaque in Anjar and a couple of small signs in a village named Jawaharnagar.

Since the early colonial writers claimed there were no earthquake traditions, the 1819 earthquake has gradually become one of the principle organising motifs of modern history. When I was conducting research in Kutch before the 2001 earthquake, I was often made aware of the 1819 calamity—not because of the damage it did to Bhuj or Anjar, but due to the appearance of a mound of earth in Sindh which supposedly halted the supply of fresh Indus waters to Kutch. This unusual feature, variously known as the Allah or Ullah Bandh (dam), has attracted the attention of a large number of those with a geological inclination. After due investigation, it has been variously suggested that the dam was thrown up by the earthquake, is a product of hydro-mechanical action, or is an illusion caused by a depression.[1]

After nearly two hundred years of speculation in the pages of scientific and political journals, the role of the dam in the desertification of the northern reaches of Kutch remains uncertain. In Kutch, there is no such doubt: the 1819 earthquake created the Allah Bandh; this feature diverted the waters of the Indus; the fertile lands of Kutch withered; the population moved away, overseas and into commerce. Until very recently, the newspaper shop near my house in London was run by a family originally from northern Kutch. They told me this story with as much certainty as

235

many in Kutch have done. In this sense, the appearance of the dam is the starting point for the narration of a history in which the central focus is overseas trade and migration, rather than the succession of kings and political agents through time: the earthquake raised a dam; in turn, the dam gave rise to a diaspora.

Before the coming of the British, Kutch and Sindh were frequently at war. Following a battle in the eighteenth century, when the slopes of the hills 'ran red with blood', Mir Ghulam Shah Calora returned defeated to Sindh. In a stroke of vengeful genius, he constructed a mound of earth, or *bandh*, across the branch of the Indus which fertilised Kutch. The dam diverted the waters into dry portions of his own territories and into other tributaries of the great river. Through this act, he destroyed a large and rich tract of irrigated land in Kutch, converting productive rice country into a sandy desert. This original dam did not entirely prevent the waters of the Indus from reaching Kutch, but impeded the progress of the stream to the point that all agriculture depending on irrigation ceased. Later rulers of Sindh built more dams, often out of self-interest rather than malice, contributing to the further reduction of the supply of water to Kutch. The once fertile rice lands of Kutch gradually became part of the abutting salty Rann, or so the story goes.

According to Alexander Burnes, the destruction caused by the 1819 earthquake was trifling when compared to the alterations brought about to the landscape.[2] The sun was setting when the shock was felt at Sindri on the banks of what had been once the eastern branch of the Indus. The little brick fort, which had been built there for the protection of merchandise and Kutch revenue officers, was overwhelmed with a tremendous inundation of water from the ocean. The saline waters spread on all sides, completely flooding the country, which had previously been hard and dry. The inhabitants scampered up the towers of the fort as the structure filled with water. Eight years later, in 1827, and to his undisguised amusement, Burnes found fish to be swimming within the structure.

It was soon discovered that the deluge was not the only alteration effected by the earthquake. The inhabitants of Sindri observed that a few miles to the north a mound of earth or sand had appeared in a place where the soil had been low and level. The mound was around sixteen miles long and passed completely over the Indus channel, separating the river from the sea. The natives called this 'Allah Bandh', or the 'dam of god', because it was not like the other dams on the Indus, which were exclusively the work of humans.

At the beginning of the twenty-first century, the effects of Allah's dam are undistinguished from the other artificial earthworks which were introduced as hostile measures by the rulers of Sindh. Without going into the historical merits of the case, it is striking that the only well-known story about the earthquake of 1819, that just narrated and which is frequently found in local newspapers and pamphlets, is focused on events that take place on the margins of Kutch and outside its boundaries. The collapse of the towns had been erased from common knowledge to the point that there was genuine surprise and marvel in Bhuj when the older walls were revealed in 2001. As with the most recent disaster, the 1819 earthquake is displaced and projected in the same light as the hostile earthworks of rival rulers. In 1819, Mir Ghulam Shah Calora, Allah and political hostility were incorporated into the earthquake narrative. In 2001, as we have seen, Pakistan and *jihadis* were made to become part of the narrative, as the shock was projected outside and onto the fantasy of an epi-centre in the Rann. This, I stress, is a form of narrative driven, in the first instance, by new colonials and, in the second, by those who came to intervene in the aftermath of the earthquake in 2001.

The name of the Allah dam probably originally reflected the attitude of those humbled by the awesome power of god. In Kutch, the significance of the name is different today, although not without ambiguity. If earthquakes are a form of repri-mand, which as we have seen in Chapter 28 they often are, then by locating the nega-tive effects of the earthquake outside Kutch, the citizenry absolve themselves of wrong-doing; however, they later suffer as the fresh waters of the Indus dry to a trickle and then to nothing. Is this suffering a secondary form of punishment from god? Or, is it merely an incidental and unfortunate consequence of the primary punishment by the Sindhis? Furthermore, there is also a second displacement with a communal overtone: the dam carries the name of the god of Islam, indicating that only Muslims were being punished by the earthquake; god, generally, does not reckon with the believers of other gods; therefore, the dominant Hindu population of Kutch, whose public sphere it is that keeps this story alive, has had to suffer yet again for the bad behaviour of Muslims.

We might now also cede that the earthquake is an extraordinary metaphor for the ruptures which accompanied the establishment of British colonial rule. It is usually only the starting point in the narration of a mercantile history of the region. In this sense, the earthquake brings a new ethos and way of life to Kutch, just as it was shown to bring new loyalties and forms of rule in the previous chapter. As agricultural lands withered, the population of Kutch turned to trade, commerce and international migration for its fortune. The earthquake produced a new kind of people and society. This adds a further layer of ambiguity to the earthquake-as-reprimand story. Although the lands of plenty turn barren and an age of innocence is lost to the disaster, this history is one that explains triumph, success and wealth. This is the history through which the Kutch I knew before the earthquake largely explained itself to itself. It is also the version through which the people who would occasionally sell me a news-paper explained to me how they happened to be in north London. Might it not be the case that this narrative is of the form in which self-satisfied contemplation replaces the double humiliation of an earthquake and colonial takeover?

Rupji was a farmer in north-western Kutch, loyally tilling his lands to ensure the survival of his family and the payment of his tithe. In the 1820s, the soils dried up. Of the reasons for this desiccation we are now aware. Threatened with starvation, he and his son, Devji, decided to seek their fortune in the coastal town of Mandvi. Rupji laboured and brokered small deals in the agricultural-produce market. In time, with their savings, Devji tried his hand successfully at trade. In 1830, or thereabouts, he went by sea to Muscat, Oman. After some years, he had saved enough money to buy his own small ship. Devji never settled in Muscat, but his son Mulji, who took over the business, started to stay there for a number of years at a stretch. By the 1840s, Mulji and his sons Khimji and Bhimji ran a number of ships, and took turns to stay in Muscat while the others conducted their business from Mandvi. Soon they opened a small office in Zanzibar, and decades later in Bombay and Karachi.

Of course, as the generations passed, and the nineteenth century wore on, the family spilt, arguing over business and property. Different clusters of family maintained commercial interests in many of the port cities of the western Indian Ocean. Their networks remained strong, as did the importance of their ancestral village. They returned regularly to Kutch for their rites of passage, sometimes for Navaratri, but more often to visit their lineage goddess and their sect's priests and sacred sites. They financed the construction of a dovecote and a rest house in Kutch. They lost their offices in Karachi at the time of Partition, and in Uganda in the 1970s when Idi Amin expelled the 'Asian' population. Those who held British papers from the East African protectorates were able to settle in the UK, where, after some initial difficulties, they again prospered. London and Leicester then became firmly connected to Kutch.

Rupji and his descendants are real people, whose fortunes are representative of thousands of families from Kutch. There can be no doubt that life in Kutch in the first half of the nineteenth century was often dreadful.[3] I also think it fair to say that the consequences of the 1819 earthquake are empirically exaggerated but rhetorically, politically and intellectually compelling. The population of northern Kutch was never great enough to fill the Indian Ocean with entrepreneurs, and the turn towards overseas adventure seemed to grip the entire littoral of western India, and not just those sections deprived of their prosperity by an earthquake. Furthermore, migrants were not only escaping misery and starvation, for they must also have been attracted by the rise of colonial Bombay. Kutch was taken over by the British regency, which may also have had consequences for the freedom and privileges of merchants. East Africa was largely governed from colonial Bombay during the nineteenth century, and Indians were actively encouraged to settle there, which they did from Kutch in very large numbers. Kutchis in Muscat, as elsewhere to a lesser extent, actively facilitated the passage of trustworthy young men from Kutch to work in their firms and offices. From these origins, migration rates from Kutch probably reached a peak at the beginning of the twentieth century. In sum, it is often said, and for good reason, that as many Kutchis live outside Kutch as within it.

Many of those who originally left Kutch, and their overseas descendants, continue to gaze lovingly upon the lands of their forefathers. When the earthquake struck in 2001, communities of global migrants watched in terror as news of the ruination started to arrive. Through caste and temple associations, trusts, charities and political organisations, these people invested heavily in the reincarnation of Kutch, often projecting the forgivable nostalgia of the migrant onto what was rebuilt. Many of those who gave also knew of the role that an earthquake had played in their own family's history of migration and success. Therefore, their generosity was perhaps also tinged with guilt for those who had been left behind.

Nehru's village, with the Rann stretching out in the distance towards Pakistan, 2003, Jawaharnagar.

32

NEHRU'S VILLAGE (TWICE)

At 9.30 pm on 21 July 1956, an earthquake destroyed 1,353 houses in Anjar and killed 115 people.[1] Most deaths occurred on the slopes to the east of MacMurdo's bungalow, just as had happened in 1819. As in both 1819 and 2001, hot springs were reported, on this occasion at the village of Khengarpur.[2] In 1956, eyewitness reports said the devastation was terrible, donations from the outside world were tremendous, but the state failed to take suitable relief measures (these remain the principal themes in modern press coverage of disasters).[3] Prisoners were so moved that they contributed money to the relief funds.[4] In Bombay, a 'Quake Ball' was held at the Taj Hotel to raise funds, with Mickey Correa, 'the Bombay Jazzman'.[5] The Khar Gymkhana hosted Chic Chocolate.[6] The YWCA held a Halloween dance featuring the music of Hal Green. Elsewhere in the swinging city, R.N. Joshi, chairman of the Indian Institute of Engineers, spoke publicly about how the same part of Anjar had been destroyed in both 1956 and 1819.[7] Minister for Revenue Rasiklal Parikh boldly told the Bombay legislative assembly that the plans prepared to rebuild Anjar included the provision of 'quake-proof' houses.[8]

Prime Minister Nehru visited Kutch in mid August to offer words of cheer and condolence. He asked how did you count the number of houses destroyed? How did you assess the exact damage? How did you remove the debris and excavate the dead? Have people who left property in their houses claimed their valuables back? How much of such property has been recovered? These questions were reported as being extremely satisfying to the people of Anjar.[9] He addressed a large crowd in Bhuj and told them:

This and other natural disasters should not dishearten people. They should attempt at utilising the occasion, good or bad, to bring about some good results. The deaths and destruction were a matter of great sorrow. However, the sufferers should rebuild the devastated areas themselves and in a better way. Make them better places to live in.[10]

241

During this visit, Nehru also inaugurated a rehabilitation centre at the village of Zoran or Jhuran; the villagers, it was reported, insisted the new village be renamed as Jawaharnagar, after the leader of the nation.[11] Two years later, the new village was inaugurated.[12] The *Times of India*, whose relief fund had partially financed the reconstruction of the village, carried a piece celebrating the success of the post-colonial government in bringing modern facilities to Kutch. The article triumphantly concluded: 'That is Kutch[:] out of poor earth its people coax their crops. Amid scarcities of fodder and water they tend their cattle. From the rubble of an earthquake they raise a Jawaharnagar'.[13]

In addition to Jawaharnagar, it was determined to build a new Anjar to the west of the old one. Here, too, Nehru laid the foundation stone and the settlement flourished.[14] It was reasoned that the old town was built on dangerous ground and that the earthquake provided an opportunity to construct a well-planned and modern settlement in a safer location. Despite the dangers, the land immediately to the east of MacMurdo's bungalow was not neglected; on the contrary, it also prospered again, becoming the town's principal and busiest bazaar. The subjects were once again made happy, and the city was rendered flourishing.

The similarities in the press coverage of the 1956 and the 2001 earthquakes are striking, as prisoners show kindness, water emerges from parched soil, deep connections between Bombay and Kutch are revealed, and personal relations are formed between political leaders and villages in the name of charity and reconstruction. There is also a remarkable recurrence of deadly destruction, for on 26 January 2001, Jawaharnagar, whose name had once meant 'shaking', again collapsed. In Anjar, on the land immediately to the east of MacMurdo's bungalow, nearly 200 children parading through the streets waving the national flag with pride were among those who were crushed as the whole area collapsed with the shock.

Dilip and I have repeatedly made the trip to Jawaharnagar—the village Nehru had 'adopted' after the 1956 earthquake—to talk to the villagers, a few of whom had taken a liking to our company. Try as we might, we had not met anyone who had anything but praise for Congress, who had once again stepped in to rebuild the village after the 2001 earthquake. This time, reconstruction was conducted in the name of Sonia Gandhi. Those working on her behalf did a good job, the houses are neat and robust, and sensibly laid out. There was no irony we could find, no mirth to be had from the fact that the village kept falling down, only to be reconstructed by the latest leadership of the same political dynasty. Again, the rubble had been cleared, a new village planned and constructed, and promises had been made for a quake-proof and prosperous future.

Dilip found it noteworthy that the plaques marking the first reconstruction of the village had been preserved and installed adjacent to the new ones. The juxtaposition of these vain signs indicated to him that there were greater forces at work in the world than politics. Even promises made by a man as great as Nehru seemed small, silly even, when held up against time and god and nature; for him, the juxtaposition created a meaningful and successful memorial. Dilip incessantly questioned those we met as to why, after the 2001 earthquake, caste Hindus had been given big houses near the road while Harijans had been housed at the far end of the village in smaller houses. Was Congress's India a country of caste inequality? Did Congress of Gandhi today support untouchability? The caste Hindus we were talking to at the time looked at the floor, kicked the dust, smiled conspiratorial smiles, but did not respond with words which could later be repeated.

Dilip also found it worthy of comment that the new memorial listing the dead doubled as the main shady sitting area in the centre of the village. In the midst of life, the villagers were sitting on the memory of death—a rather improbable arrangement of ideas and objects given the circumstances. Dilip asked the men we were with at the time what it meant to them to be sitting, smoking and spitting on a memorial to the dead of the village. The question embarrassed them into focusing on what someone else had originally intended for the object, for a short while at least, before normality returned.

Sitting on the memorial, we talked about the problems of rain-fed agriculture, government rural employment schemes and labour migration—subjects on which the villagers were keen to share their views and experiences. The earthquake, they said, was god's will. They could not say why god had commissioned an earthquake. God shakes the earth, Congress puts the village back together again. There was unmistakable pride in the relationship they shared with the Congress leadership. The man speaking at that moment then shrugged, turned his cupped hands, fingers crocked and spread, to the sky—a locally recognised sign of resignation—and laughed, loudly. His wife, we already knew, had been killed in the earthquake. His laughter marked the end of all that it was possible to discuss.

On the journey home that evening, I stopped the motorbike by the side of the road to rest and admire the view. Dusk was falling and things were beautiful. Dilip turned to me and said, 'I do not know what it is about this land, but it is a part of me, it is in me'. As we stood in the gloom, I felt the warm air on my goose bumps. I thought that Dilip had admitted something profound, and I thought then that I understood something of what he meant. He had been born in Kutch, had lived there for most of his life, and perhaps looked forward to dying there too. We were a part of the earth, and inseparable from the forces that animated all of the things in the universe. But, the earth of Kutch was distinct from other earths, its people had a particular character and did things in particular ways. These differences were not simply due to the will of humanity, or to be explained as part of a 'culture' imposed on humanity's natural self, but were part of the divine and true order of things.

The view to the east of MacMurdo's bungalow after the rubble was cleared. In the far left, the parading school children were crushed. Use the small temple to the right as a point of reference in photo essay that follows the text of this chapter, 2002, Anjar.

33

PLANNING TO FORGET

On 31 January 2004, I accompanied the hunger-striker Kundanlal Dholakia to Anjar to meet Dr Shyam Sundar, the letter-writing protester. At the time, it felt mischievous—an anthropologist meddling in the affairs of others. I had thought it possible that the meeting of the two leading protestors might lead to bigger protests. I booked a rather fancy car for the journey, imagining it would complement his stature. When Dholakia saw it, he looked dismayed and then irritated, and told me that I should have brought an Ambassador, the lumbering Indian version of the British Morris Oxford which remains one of the most recognisable symbols of Nehru's protectionist era. The car remains a sign of pride for some, and of India's then backwardness for increasingly greater numbers of people. In 2004, rather like successful Congress politicians, these vehicles were already few and far between on the roads of Kutch.

I was first introduced to Dholakia by Dilip in 2002. Although he was in his 80s and frail, Dholakia had an unexpectedly firm grip and a scrutinising stare. He was also a compelling speaker, readily recounting his political life and the twentieth-century history of Kutch. In the 1950s, he had gone to England as part of a delegation and had met Clement Attlee, which had left a fondly remembered and lasting impression on him.

On the day of our visit to Anjar, he was dressed in a white hand-spun *dhoti* of the kind associated with Gandhi and the Congress of old. When at home he did not dress like this. At home, he allowed himself to laugh. As we travelled towards Anjar, his face grew increasingly grave. I remember being surprised at the attention he paid to setting his expression, his irritation with the car, and his carefully selected Gandhian battle dress: the appearance of simplicity required much work.

I had met Shyam Sundar earlier in the year. Then, as we had talked in his home, in front of a large poster of a ferocious-looking god from South India, there were constant interruptions from the busy hospital below. He would leave to conduct minor surgery, pronounce someone dead, receive a crash victim to the emergency

245

room and so forth. He would return, unflustered, remove his ring, wash his hands, place the ring back on his finger, and the conversation would resume. Like the god watching over us, he was originally from Andhra Pradesh, and had lived in Kutch since the 1980s. On that occasion, in 2004, he said there were now two parts to Kutch: the towns and the villages. In the former, people have lost a lot and gained little, while in villages the opposite is true (a neat summary of the consequences of the initial division of work made by the development banks). Three years after the earthquake this was a claim, and source of irritation, I heard often.

At the time of the earthquake, Shyam Sundar had been in the bathroom. He could not understand what was happening and suspected he might be unwell. By the time he had gathered his senses and family, the earthquake was over. Outside, there was little damage and no one seemed distraught. Then, as the dust cloud began to rise over the old city, the screams began. At first, he treated patients in the hospital, but later moved to a tent. He remembered that it was the kind of tent usually reserved for the joy of marriage parties. In twenty-five years as a doctor, he had not certified as many people dead as he did that day. The things he saw then, he said, inspired him to continue to fight the government.

According to him, the desperate condition of Anjar three years after the earthquake was primarily due to the profound corruption of the administration. The government had actively encouraged the economy of the town to collapse by providing merchants with rows of red metal cargo containers for temporary shops. The market was so unpleasant that those who could do so travelled further afield to shop. He had a point, for the market was congested, hot and did not encourage either loitering or browsing. The market was a poignant and daily reminder to him how everything in Anjar that had been done since the earthquake was a temporary and inadequate measure.

Shyam Sundar said:

This town has gone to the dogs. The government could have rebuilt Anjar quickly. It could have taken some land, built some roads and some houses, and given the people the keys. They did not do this, they have given in to pressure from the development banks to build infrastructure. Why do we need infrastructure? Town planning? Within only a few days of the earthquake most of the town had water and power. I see no reason to spend millions of dollars in Anjar. What reason could there be for this kind of waste?

The question was rhetorical.

I had come to ask Shyam Sundar about his involvement in the early protests against government inaction, and in the formation of Group 2001, which sought to coordinate protests in the town. I had seen some of the spirited letters he had written demanding transparency in decision-making and the construction of the new new Anjar (the first recorded new one was built after the 1956 earthquake): 'It is a shame for the Govt. of Gujarat, it can't even provide a shed for the affected people even after two months. Only God knows when your Govt. will be able to provide permanent houses'.[1]

Although he was outspoken about inaction, he was also a BJP man and keen admirer of the work done by the RSS in the aftermath. By 2004, he was more interested in talking about his current preoccupation, which was to stop the rebuilding of Anjar on the land to the east of MacMurdo's bungalow.

I have appealed to everyone I can think of to make them see sense. The government conducted soil tests in the three wards in Anjar where 90 per cent of the casualties occurred. They kept the results secret and then released false data. We paid for our own soil samples and dug four bores to a depth of sixteen metres. In the last two earthquakes, this area collapsed completely while other areas remained standing. The area is a 'paleo lake'. They are planning a cemetery, not a town.

As I was leaving Bhuj with Dholakia, I began to wonder whether these two formidable men with very different political views would find common ground on the subject of injustice. As the car passed through Kutch, Dholakia talked about how long the same journey had taken in previous decades, and how he had helped the village we were then passing through to develop its water supply system in the 1960s. In Anjar, we first visited the offices of someone he knew. He sat cross-legged on the floor. We had arranged to meet the head of the town's Area Development Authority to discuss planning matters. Someone whispered in Dholakia's ear that the officer had been called away to Gandhinagar. Instead of cursing him, Dholakia said to those gathered around him that because he had seen the terrible state of the town he now refused to meet the officer. A series of the town's notables were summoned. They bowed as low as they could, as they reached to touch the old man's feet. They spoke only when they were asked to do so. Such, it seemed, was Dholakia's reputation.

Later, we moved to the government rest house where we were brought some stiff tea and soft biscuits. We sat in a grey room which contained too much furniture. Shyam Sundar arrived sometime later to make a formal representation of his complaints. Dholakia fixed his stare and gestured for him to speak. The issues they discussed were the plight of tenants, corruption, slothful administrators and the fortunes of land speculators. In Anjar, tenants fared relatively well with a private organisation providing them with land at low cost to compensate for the failings of the government. As elsewhere, 'G5 people' faced particular problems: compensation was released before land for reconstruction was allocated. Much of this money had become part of the local consumer boom, leaving people without the resources to build the plinth which would entitle them to the second compensation payment. In a large number of cases, after three years those affected by the earthquake of 2001 and the subsequent town planning schemes were yet to be allocated an alternative plot of land.

At the time, Anjar was strewn with pathetic objects which actively recalled both the earthquake and the causes of Shyam Sundar's anger. Aside from the market, which had something desperate about it, there was the brute fact that half the town was flattened and the other half was not. This was made all the more obvious as the area to the east of MacMurdo's bungalow had recently been levelled by bulldozers, and the foundations for roads and drains were being laid. On the hill next to the bungalow lay a crushed car and a tangle of other metal, which recalled quite directly the weight of falling masonry. I believe these things had not been taken away for scrap, as all other such damaged vehicles had, because they were government property. Daubed on the wall next to the dark blue 'protected monument' sign outside MacMurdo's bungalow were the red marks of planners, which indicated that a 6 metre-wide road was to pass through the middle of the historic building. Elsewhere, seats from the town's devastated auditorium had been retrieved from the rubble and laid out in rows on open ground: a staged metaphor for the condition of Anjar.

Talk in Bhuj about the misery of Anjar had encouraged Dholakia to come and see things for himself. The following is extracted from the conversation that took place between him and Shyam Sundar:

SS: The government does not care for this town.

KD: [interrupting] In this room we all know this. What are the problems Anjar is facing? Has the collector ever been here?

SS: I have not met him many times. No one has given me any information for the last two years. We are never told if people from the outside are visiting. The government does not want us to tell them what is really going on here.

Let me tell you something else. The townsfolk have contributed to the destruction of the town. I am not in a position to only accuse Keshubhai [Patel] or Modi for the condition of Anjar. Every time something is proposed the ignorant townspeople get it cancelled.

KD: The people of Anjar?

SS: Yes. When the original draft development plan was approved, G5 people were to get land and financial compensation. Some people did not like it, or thought they could get more, and they got the plan cancelled. Now the town is in this mess. I have shut down my medical practice for the last one-and-a-half years. I have been running around all over the place and getting qualified scientists to test the soil. Everyone has told me that part of the old town is built on a 'paleo lake'. If there is an earthquake within 300 kilometres of Anjar, the town will collapse again.

KD: I have read that. But are the people willing to go to the place when you tell them that the area is dangerous?

SS: If I told the people the land was unsafe, do you think they would believe me? The government says it is okay. I say it is not. I am a doctor not a scientist. Dr Arya is an earthquake expert in Ahmedabad. He says it is a 'paleo lake'. There was a person called Ravi Sinha from IIT-Bombay who knew that it was a 'paleo lake'. The government would notify him in such a way that it was impossible for him to attend planning meetings for Anjar. If there was to be a meeting on the 12th then he would be sent notice in the afternoon of the preceding day. By the time he got here from Bombay, the meeting would be over.

KD: The situation looks dark. What should we do?

SS: If we go to Modi there will be fifteen officers with him feeding him wrong information. It is the non-Gujarati officers who are ruining Gujarat.

KD: I have fought for many problems in my life. I am ready to fight for Anjar also.

SS: I am ready to hunger strike and all that, but who is going to explain these things to the public? Most of the people are ignorant about their rights and are largely responsible for their present poor condition.

KD: How is the chairman of the Area Development Authority?

SS: It is better not to talk about him. In Bhuj the town planners are not corrupt, the collector is good and the person in charge of the Area Development Authority is cooperative. That is why development in Bhuj is good. In Anjar we have a dictator. He does not see eye to eye with the chairman of the municipality, and there is a complete lack of coordination and communication between them.

KD: What about your parliamentary representatives?

SS: After the election these people do not care.

KD: I am proud to be a politician. What do you want me to do?

SS: Take the head of the Area Development Authority from here and send us the good officer from Bhuj. All our problems will be solved.

KD: I have to go now.

SS: Nothing has been done here sir. You will go away but I have to live here.

The above extract does not do justice to the encounter, which, from my point of view, was high drama. A veteran Gandhian politician, pretending a power he did not quite have, and one of Anjar's most influential and controversial men discussing things that then seemed of the greatest importance. Dholakia was composed; Shyam Sundar was exaggerated. At times, he pleaded with his whole body for Dholakia to see his point of view. Shyam Sundar's Anjar was bleak. For him, neglect by the government was noteworthy, not the resourcefulness of the citizenry. On this occasion, nothing was done.

Dholakia had come in search of a clear injustice against which to demonstrate. In the discussions earlier in the day, it had become obvious that none of the principal issues at stake was clear cut: the business community had temporary accommodation and were not starving; a private trust had found a solution to tenant housing problems; the town planning schemes were not quite finalised but, when they were, many of the remaining problems in the town would begin to come to an end.

As for the transfer of the head of the Area Development Authority, Dholakia probably also knew that he did not have sufficient leverage. As for Shyam Sundar's claim that Anjar was to be rebuilt on a dangerous 'paleo lake', Dholakia said he did not know enough about the subject. Who did? He could not start a protest on the basis of evidence he did not understand. In the car on the way back to Bhuj, he told me that he thought Shyam Sundar was meddling with matters he did not comprehend. I never got a clear answer from Shyam Sundar as to why he thought the government was hell-bent on building on land that it knew to be unsuitable. Sometime later, a cynical friend in Mandvi told me that Shyam Sundar was running around Anjar barking like a dog in order to build support for a future career in party politics. I thought his energy, organisational skills and vision would probably serve him very well.

As we approached Bhuj that evening, Dholakia told me that he was putting the finishing touches to his long life, and was nearly ready to die. He died peacefully on 7 March 2011.

By the time of Dholakia's death, life had returned to the 'paleo lake'. The development authority determined the area safe and laid new infrastructure. Gradually, although with hesitancy, life has returned to that sad section of the town. Dilip and others mounted a campaign to save MacMurdo's historic bungalow from demolition to make way for a road—they were successful.

You will recall from Chapters 30 and 32, and earlier in this book, that habitations on the eastern side of the bungalow have repeatedly been terminated when the earth quaked and buildings collapsed. On the face of it, and given no shortage of land around Anjar, it is remarkable that the site was not respectfully razed and abandoned. Perhaps the engineers were confident that stricter building codes would withstand a further turn of the subterranean serpent. Perhaps the government's soil tests really did say that the land is safe. Whatever the science may have said, the inability or refusal to remember past events also permitted the town to be rebuilt where it was. Occasionally, I cannot help but wonder what will happen with the next earthquake. Will the houses built on the 'paleo lake' stand firm as the government vainly promised in 1956?

It might be that the repeated reconstruction of the stricken area of Anjar points to the profoundly attractive qualities of fear. Or that, through the act of re-inhabiting the sites of ruination and loss, the power of the earthquake is depleted by the rein-statement of everyday life as the healing of routine and daily anxiety takes over. Separately or together, these explanations might account for the displacement of an earthquake from history and memory.

The repeated collapse of Anjar might also suggest that earthquakes cannot be remembered because they are too big and too terrible to comprehend. In this sense, we might speculate that earthquakes are forgotten in their true form because they literally cannot be remembered. Our minds and thoughts are not earthquakes, and therefore our minds convert the real earthquake into other shapes which fit the contours of what our minds are capable of. We are unable to comprehend the enor-mity of the event. When we realise, and we do realise, that we have reached the limits of our capacity to comprehend, we make smaller earthquakes in our minds. These lesser earthquakes make us happy because we have created them and can comprehend them. In the process, the true earthquake, the one that shook things to the ground and killed people, is lost from view.

Subsequently, two teams of scientists have carried out studies in Anjar. They con-sidered what are called 'site effects'—that is to say, how the geological and alluvial characteristics of a place may influence the impact of an earthquake on the built environment. The first team was supported by the French Embassy in Delhi, the Centre for Mathematical Modelling and Computer Simulation of Bangalore, and the

French Insititut de Recherche pour le Développement. They measured 'ambient variations' in the soil using 'microtremor measurements'. According to them, greater destruction had been observed in one zone than in others. Consequently, a greater earthquake intensity had been attributed to that zone and the anomaly had been explained by 'site effects'. This, they suggested, was incorrect because their results showed little 'ambient variation' across the whole old town. They concluded that 'the 2001 event has simply been one earthquake too many for the old city, and the difference in damage when compared with neighbouring sectors is not an indication of a higher intensity [of earthquake impact] in the old city'.[2] According to them, buildings collapsed because they were old and poorly constructed, not because they stood on a particularly vulnerable spot.

The second team of scientists was from India and Japan, and funded by the Gujarat State Disaster Management Authority (GSDMA). They published their results in 2011. Using satellite imagery to assess patterns of damage in Anjar, they too noted particularly severe damage to the east of the town—in an area residents believed had been a lake some centuries ago. The new scientists were critical of the methods of the previous ones and, to compensate, deployed additional measurements (multichannel analysis of surface waves). The second team found considerable variation in their results between damaged and undamaged areas. They cautioned that any explanation of damage should take into account both the seismic motion on the ground and the condition of particular buildings. They also suggested that because the area of severe damage in Anjar was so small, the characteristics of the 'input motion' from an earthquake occurring 30 kilometres away would not have differed greatly across the town. Therefore, the patterns of seismic motion in the town had been most probably determined by the 'site effect' of Anjar: the shape of the land and the nature of its underlying soils. Hence, they concluded that, besides the poor quality of buildings, 'site effects' (lake-like sediment) also contributed to the severe damage found only on the east side of old Anjar city'.[3]

Rebuilding old Anjar continues. The future destruction of the town appears to have been made certain.

The temporary bazaar of shipping containers—now firmly established. The market was a poignant and daily reminder to Shyam Sundar of how everything in Anjar that had been done since the earthquake was a temporary and inadequate measure, 2003, Anjar.

On the hill next to the bungalow lay a crushed car and a tangle of other metal, which recalled quite directly the weight of falling masonry, 2003, Anjar.

Foundations for a new road layout are bulldozed into the earth to the east of MacMurdo's bungalow, 2003, Anjar.

A 'motor grader' works on the road network in an unseasonal downpour. The temple is now in the middle of the shot as we look from the right of the first image in the series, 2002, Anjar.

Daubed onto the wall next to the dark blue 'protected monument' sign outside MacMurdo's bungalow are the red marks of planners which indicate that a six-metre wide road was to pass through the middle of the historic building. The sign reads: 'This monument is protected ... [any] person who destroys, removes, impairs, alters, defaces or imperils this monument in any manner is liable to a punishment'. A campaign led by concerned citizens saved the building, 2004, Anjar.

Seats from the devastated auditorium had been retrieved from the rubble and laid out in rows on open ground: a staged metaphor for the condition of the town, 2003, Anjar.

The creep of inhabitation. Commerce returned to the gaps and holes of the bazaar. A woman and daughter trade in basic foodstuffs in a collapsed structure, 2004, Anjar.

The view to the east of MacMurdo's bungalow. The temple is centre shot, obscured by the many new buildings that have 'come up' in the area, 2008, Anjar.

નિષ્ફળતા નો શિલાલેખ

"લખજી લ્યાનત આય અસાંક"
અમે એક વર્ષથી પરેશાન થતી કચ્છ ની
ભૂકંપ પીડિત પ્રજા
૨૬, જાન્યુઆરી ૨૦૦૨ ના બાવનમાં સાતાક દિન
દીનતાપૂર્વક જાહેર કરીએ છીએ કે પ્રજા તરીકે
અમે કોઈ સત્તા ધરાવતા હોઈએ એવો અનુભવ
આજે અમને થતો નથી
કારણ કે સ્વતંત્રતાના ૫૪ વર્ષ પછી પણ અમે
કાર્યક્ષમ, નિષ્ઠાવાન સારા નેતાઓ મેળવવામાં
વહીવટ તંત્રનો ભ્રષ્ટાચાર ઘટાડવામાં
અને સંવેદનશીલ નોકરશાહી બનાવવામાં
પૂર્ણ રીતે નિષ્ફળ ગયા છીએ.
અમારી આ ઘોર નિષ્ફળતાની કબૂલાત રૂપે
અમે આ નિષ્ફળતાનો શીલાલેખ ભાવિપ્રજાના
માર્ગદર્શન અર્થે નિષ્ફળ ગયેલી પેઢી રૂપે મુકીએ
છીએ જેથી તેઓ અમારી આ ભૂલમાંથી પ્રેરણા લઈ
યોગ્ય ભારતનું ઘડતર કરે.
ભુજ - કચ્છ - ભારત

The 'inscription of failure' was erected in 2002 at the height of the organised protests against delays to reconstruction, 2003, Bhuj.

34

MEMORY

Deciding what form of object will commemorate a disaster is a difficult task. Who does it, how and where are typically moments marked by profound and prolonged disagreement. The historical literature shows that it often takes decades after a disaster for a consensus to emerge over a memorial—or, more commonly, that people no longer care enough to continue to argue. In highland Peru, for example, after the earthquake documented by Bode discussed in the Introduction, the government of the country initially erected a shell fountain which looked like a vagina. The locals felt the monument was disrespectful of their loss and wanted to blow it up.[1] It took twenty-five years for the state to erect a satisfactory memorial to the thousands who died in the earthquake and landslide of 1970. Such a gestation period is not uncommon. Similarly, negotiations in Gujarat are ongoing and this chapter, as we move towards the end of the period documented in this book, records some of the 'pre-memorial' twists and turns of a protracted process.

Most existing public memorials for the earthquake have been gifted by politicians and state governments. Memorials are yet another way in which disasters can be played with by those who chose to intervene in the aftermath. An extensive literature rightly suggests that memorials are social objects, products of particular times and places, and open to constant reinterpretation.[2] Memorials may well be associated with specific events, but their relationship to the memory of those events is anything but straightforward.

The object itself cannot remember. People and rituals enliven it, and people are different and the repertoire of possible rituals is considerable. A memorial may evoke or remind, but it will typically engage with a diverse audience who will bring with them inchoate and grotesque memories that take individual forms. In this sense, a memorial might be regarded as a public representation of the different experiences of many individuals.

The memorial may allow names, dates and sometimes images to become the focus of public attention, replacing the altogether more troubling smell of blood or the haunting image of a parade of dying children. The memorial flattens the extremes of individual memory—replacing it, and therefore in a sense denying or pacifying it, with something altogether more palatable, if not anodyne. This is perhaps one of the principal capacities of a memorial: a neutralising device to think about an event. The successful memorial translates the unthinkable into the thinkable, and the event becomes accessible to others. Various configurations of objects and memory are also possible. Memorials allow for the persistence and engagement of individual memories. When a group of people gathers before a memorial, the object can override the ambiguities that characterise their relationships and their diverse experiences of the memorialised event.

In Gujarat, I have not seen memorials succeed. I have not seen congregations gather at memorials. Instead, the landscape is littered with neglected memorial devices, which reflect the now-forgotten concerns of those who put them there. In other words, despite the grave events and emotional extremes of the things with which memorials are associated, memorials can fail. The emotional pull of a disaster, however great the depth and form of its death imprint, does not ensure that all objects dedicated to such memories will contain them in the survivors' eyes.

Two presumably well-intentioned memorials erected to the dead of the 2001 earthquake have already disappeared. One in Bhachau, a sombre black marble plinth, was bulldozed to make way for a rather gaudy statue of a subaltern political leader and some permanent advertising for a new ceramics firm. The second, again a black marble plinth, constructed by the government of Maharashtra, stands in a state of irreversible dilapidation.

In what might be thought of as the 'pre-memorial era' in Gujarat, the space between the disaster and the closure promised by an official memorial, there have been countless lesser memorialising events.[3] Bill Clinton unveiled a small and controversial memorial in Anjar in 2001. Subsequently, there was a dispute about the ownership of the land, and the structure now stands rather ignobly between the poles of an electricity transformer by the side of a busy road.

Many other memorial devices are personal, such as photographs of the dead in domestic shrines. Some have preserved particular objects, once the possessions of the now dead. Other memorials have been organised along community lines to coincide with reconstruction projects, such as the rituals and small commemorative garden marking the reconstruction of Soniwad. On some of the earlier anniversaries of the disaster, photographs were displayed of those who had died in particular neighbourhoods. In some parts of Bhuj there are commemorative benches dedicated to the memory of particular individuals. Congregational temples hold annual memorial events, and Muslims visit graves on death anniversaries. Books have been published to commemorate the lives and times of dead fathers. Schools have been constructed in the names of dead sons.

At various times since 2001, there have been debates in Bhuj about the appropriateness of different kinds of public memorials. Prominent ideas included the preservation of a ruined neighbourhood or a traditional house filled with possessions of the dead. Neither of these ideas is particularly novel. They are inspired by memorials for the Holocaust and for other earthquakes. The impetus for these projects stalled once the possibility of international funding receded. Although no memorial was built, the discussions encouraged people to place the suffering of Bhuj in a global landscape of loss and tragedy, as sympathies with the earthquake nations of Japan and Turkey were expressed publicly.

A poet constructed a model of a pagoda-like structure decorated with images of crushed and bloody children, which, he thought, when built as a full-size memorial would serve as a practical reminder of the horrors of the earthquake for a forgetful population. Under the images he wrote: 'The mothers of the children did not know they were saying "bye bye", "see you" for the last time. They will never see their children again! They happily got them ready for the rally [that killed them]!' The only memorial of which I am aware that came from the local population is an 'inscription of failure'. It was erected in Bhuj in 2002 at the height of the organised protests against delays to reconstruction. It reads:

We deserve to be condemned for ever.

We the people who have been suffering from the effects of the earthquake for one year in Kutch meekly announce on this 26th January 2002 the 52nd Republic Day that we have not experienced any empowerment because after 54 years of Independence we do not have competent, honest leaders who may be able to rescue us from rampant corruption. They have failed to develop a compassionate bureaucracy.

We are placing this inscription as an admission of our gross failure for the guidance of our future generation so that they take a cue from our utter failure to make our motherland a better place to live.

Bhuj, Kutch, India.

Despite the critical and angry tone of the inscription, the local municipality has not had the courage to demolish the structure, although, over the years, it has been increasingly hidden from view by a cultivated screen of foliage.

With these anomalous exceptions, local people have been quite unenthusiastic about public memorials. It was primarily the various state governments and political parties from elsewhere in India that financed the construction of memorials as integral parts of their own reconstruction projects. On the outskirts of the colonel's Indraprastha (the village discussed in Chapters 14 and 29), for example, is a monument to the dead built on top of a small hillock, now known as Tiger Hill. Set into the foundations of a pole for the national flag, the formal plaque lists the names of those who perished. The slopes have been planted with sweet smelling flowers and, power and water permitting, a fountain trickles down an artificial watercourse.

The significance of this monument is that it fabricates a direct connection between those who died because of the earthquake and their sacrifice for the nation. The bloody, partially televised, battle for Tiger Hill, adjacent to the Srinagar to Leh highway in Kashmir, was a turning point in the border skirmishes between India and Pakistan in 1999. Soon after the Indian army captured the peak, the press was full of images of the Indian tricolour planted on the summit. The Indian soldiers who lost their lives became the most celebrated of martyrs. The memorial lists the dead in Hindi, their names in formal rows, as if they too had sacrificed themselves for the nation (rather by the weakness of the nation). In 2012, the memorial continued to be well-maintained, but had been closed to the public because it had become a popular haunt for miscreants and lovers.

Taken as a whole, there has been no purposeful attempt to build an encompassing or totalising memorial in the region. If you know where to look, there are many memorials scattered throughout the district, but most of these are as incongruous as the one on Tiger Hill, with no local precedent in terms of design or sentiment. Each tends to reflect primarily the agenda and intervention of an outside agency in the reconstruction process. The government of Maharashtra, for example, built a black marble plinth and water feature in a small memorial garden in the village of Vondh. Today, the water has drained away and the marble coating has fallen from the memorial, leaving an unsightly concrete stump. There is no memorial of any kind at the epicentre of the earthquake—neither at the nationalists' epicentre, nor the scientists'. Last time I visited in 2011, there was no permanent structure to mark the spot where the 200 children died in Anjar—discussions there are ongoing too.

The failure of specific memorial objects in Gujarat of course shows that the intentions of the memorial-makers do not always mesh with the cultural compulsions of those affected by the earthquake. There is also the clear sense that memorials have been imposed on the landscape by outsiders, and that memorials inscribed with militaristic or governmental fonts do not resonate with the graces of the local population. This does not mean that memorials in Gujarat are simply redundancies; rather than being symbols of meaning, memorials have become an effective medium of communication. Failed and failing memorials are nodal points of contestation articulated in the language of loss, bereavement and politics. Some writers have suggested memorials bring people together.[4] In Gujarat, they have mostly kept insiders and outsiders apart. Memorials have marked the limits of the success of outside intervention.

Those who built the Tiger Hill monument were attempting to fold the names of those who died in the earthquake into the memorialisation of the national struggle against Pakistan in faraway Kashmir. The dead were to become martyrs for the nation. While it might seem far-fetched, we have seen elsewhere in this book how readily others endowed the disaster with political animus. From the perspective of the people who remain in the village (those whose kin are memorialised), the object is alien, and has become a place synonymous with visiting politicians, the media and Republic Day, but not the earthquake dead. It is not even that there is no tradition of erecting memorials to the dead or for thinking about sacrificial forms of death. A great many villages in Kutch have collections of 'hero stones' on their outskirts. These commemorate the sacrifice of widows who committed themselves to the pyres of their husbands and male warriors who lost their lives for meritorious causes. There is no tradition of the collective facing an object that names a group of dead people, regardless of who they were.

At the grassroots level, many of the debates surrounding memorials, their authenticity, and legitimacy that have been taking place have been informed by patterns of social hierarchy and political contest that long preceded the earthquake. The reanimation of pre-existing social patterns, as we have seen, has been accompanied by a mining of the past for images and metaphors to accommodate and mediate expressions of mourning and loss. Disaster is clearly also a break with the past, at least in terms of personal memory, but also because of the renewed importance of the past more generally. There has been, as the content of this book reflects, more past in the present than there was before. The structure and presentation of nostalgic pasts, and the ways in which they are projected onto the landscape as ideas of particular kinds, led, as we have also seen, to the increasing importance of regional identity as a platform for protest, and a campaign for regional autonomy in the worst affected part of the state.

The chief minister of Gujarat first announced a memorial for Bhuj in 2003, when he came to inaugurate the widened old bazaar. Four years later, two projects were finally sanctioned. The first was a plantation on the outskirts of Bhuj, containing a tree to mark the life of each of the 13,000 dead. The park was to be designed around open spaces for contemplation. The atmosphere was to be calming and meditative. The plan was devised by a firm of architects from a faraway urban centre. Fantastically, it was proposed that different species of trees were to represent different castes and religious communities.

The plantation was planned for a large hillock just outside Bhuj, until someone pointed out that there was insufficient water to support tree growth. For a while, there was a search for an alternative site. The search was abandoned because the hill in question was demilitarised and opened to the public for the first time in many decades. The old fort walls and paths that criss-cross the steep slopes have become popular, if extremely vertiginous, places for recreation. New architects have been commissioned to design a less thirsty memorial park on the slopes of the hill.

The panoramic views from the summit over Bhuj are a stark and exciting reminder of the ways in which the town has expanded in the years since the earthquake. The hill has made a spectacle of the new Bhuj, providing a panorama worthy of wonder and contemplation. Furthermore, the opening of the hill fits persuasively into the post-earthquake master narrative planned for the region by the state, in which the traditional signs of authority and legitimacy in Kutch have been weakened. The fortified hill was home to the British colonial military garrison and synonymous with the ruling families of Kutch, whose temple dedicated to the propitiation of the wrathful serpent is on the lower slopes. The opening up of the hill to the public in the name of the earthquake further contributes to the weakening hold that older forms of power have on the town, as the space of the former rulers has become the space the state permits its citizens.

The second state-led memorial project involves the preservation of the ruins of the village of Adhoi, in the east of Kutch. At first glance, the eerie shells of houses and silent emptiness of the now almost uninhabited village evoke the tragedy of the obliteration of life. Gazing through jagged gashes in buildings and into the places where families once cooked and watched television is salutary and quietening. For these reasons, I visited Adhoi frequently because I have found it good to think with; however, I have seldom met anyone else casually visiting the place.

On display in Adhoi are not simply the tragic ruins of a village devastated by an earthquake. The first part of the illusion is that Adhoi was atypical of villages in this part of the district. The haunting ruins are predominantly the large second homes of wealthy families resident in Mumbai. Many of these structures are, importantly, still standing, and thus can appear as dramatic ruins—unlike in other villages where poor quality buildings collapsed leaving unimpressive piles of rubble. The second part of the illusion is that most of the damage that moves the visitor was caused by the pillaging of building materials after the earthquake, and not by the earthquake itself. Finally, the houses of the poor, which formed less impressive ruins, have been cleared and their occupants resettled at some distance from the original site, contributing to the feeling of empty desolation in old Adhoi.

Pillaging aside, on the surface, the unusual silence of the site suggests a commitment among local people to the idea that the village should be left to stand as a memorial. Probe just a little deeper and it is clear that the project allowed some influential property owners to receive compensation from the state. The project has bitterly divided the villagers, and there have been court cases and slanderous battles waged in the classified section of the local newspaper. And, despite various government orders, and the high-handed tactics of some local men of influence, life has returned to parts of the ruins.

As with the opening up of the hill in Bhuj for the marvel of the citizenry, a political edge accompanies the Adhoi site. Although the village is within the modern district of Kutch, it was never part of the pre-Independence ruler's territory. The village belonged to their rivals in neighbouring Morvi, who, in effect, maintained a small island of territory within the kingdom of Kutch (a 'thorn in the side of Kutch', as it was called in political correspondence). As a consequence, relations between the two states were rancorous, and Adhoi is often seen as an enduring symbol of the weakness of the Kutch state. Not quite a vagina, but to select the site for a monument to an earthquake which so damaged Kutch is really to bury the knife deeply into the old order of things.

As the next earthquake lies in wait for things to again assume their beauty and relevance, a post-post-colonial India is being born.

Detail of a painting commissioned for a memorial competition showing children being crushed and bloodied in Anjar. The inspiration for the memorial came from the poet and entrepreneur Jaysukh Parekh 'Suman', 2007, Bhuj.

AFTERWORD

An earthquake does not conclude. It lives in metaphor and history, passing in and out of popular consciousness. The 250th anniversary of the Lisbon earthquake met with a flurry of publications and awe. When Anjar falls again, as the evidence suggests it might, the earthquake will be evoked as an element in a sequence of numbers: 1819, 1956 and 2001. These are numbers in which nature and politics have been inextricably linked. Other earthquakes in the region, which were born without political upheaval, are forgotten. In 2002, a man from Anjar made the headlines for having lost his parents in the earthquake of 1956 and children in 2001. I have heard people laughing loudly at the absurdity. What else could they do? Earthquakes are remembered, but in other ways they are forgotten; occasionally, forgetting and remembering touch one another.

I had been conducting research on the earthquake for six years or so when I took my two-year-old son to Gujarat. We stayed in a building in Bhuj that I had previously known, but had seemingly then forgotten, to have been badly damaged. The owner, fearing financial ruin, had procured insincere safety certificates to prevent demolition. I was awoken in the night by a tremor. I cannot say whether I was more shocked by the vibrations, or that I had unthinkingly put my son to sleep in a dangerous building, or by the fact that the possibility of an earthquake had not been in my mind at all. 'The disaster is related to forgetfulness—forgetfulness without memory, the motionless retreat of what has not been treated—the immemorial, perhaps. To remember forgetfully: again …'[1]

Writing about an earthquake is akin to bringing together the different descriptions of an elephant given by the blind men in Saxe's poem in the Preface. The result is not an elephant! Depending on which part of the beast they touch, the men are variously reminded of walls, spears, snakes, trees, fans and ropes. Similarly, relevance in an earthquake is perceived in remarkably different ways. The crushed, dispossessed, thieves, architects, councillors, bystanders, politicians and administrators necessarily see their lives and duties in the earthquake/elephant/aftermath in disparate ways, as will you.

The homeless demanded and prioritised things quite differently from those responsible for the financial consequences to the exchequer. We know that understanding the purpose and design of the neo-liberal and neo-corporatist restructuration of Gujarat was not a priority on the streets of Bhuj. Likewise, a senior Indian economist saw no value in the 'nice little stories of people's lives' that I had collected. For him, the earthquake was an exercise in federal fiscal transfers and inter-state borrowing arrangements, as well as an opportunity to experiment with the slide transition menu of PowerPoint. The stories these people eventually learned to tell about the earthquake often shared no language or an agreed sequence of events. The disaster became competing and contradictory forms of knowledge.

While this might all sound perfectly obvious, significantly it was often not at all obvious in Bhuj, where most 'problems' in the aftermath could be put down to various 'perspective gaps'. The homeless and economists (to continue the example) both saw themselves as being at the centre of all that was important, and struggled to see beyond their own immediate concerns. It was their earthquake, their experience. It is to 'perspective gaps' such as these that 'participatory planning' and schemes to translate policy into vernacular words and languages are offered up as mechanisms of information transfer in post-disaster settings. They are both principled and sound ideas, intended to bridge differences in understanding and explanation between different people and institutions. There was a great deal of information sharing and collection in Gujarat. Some of it was very effective; some was in the wrong language, and so on—all the usual arguments apply.

One of the main points of this book has been to show that the type of information being shared did not shed light on much of what was happening or what might have usefully been explained. I suspect that this is a conclusion with near universal applicability in post-disaster settings, related more to the incidental and reverberating powers of bureaucracy and policy than a straightforward conspiracy of interests. Leaflets about G numbers or grades of compensation did not explain the recoil people were experiencing against Kant's sublime. The creative potential of mass grief was bludgeoned by fumbled policy pronouncements, funnelling collective energy into conservative and obstructive forms of protest. Nor did the pamphleteers account for the giddy feeling of Mill's hyper-consumption, as first entropy and then life itself was accelerated. Where were the information campaigns about the rights and wrongs of industrialisation or the politics and consequences of re-naming things? Those producing leaflets mostly could not see that their actions were part of what should probably have been explained to the local population, whose ideas about authority, rights and place were being firmly trodden upon.

On the whole, reconstruction activities in Gujarat have been presented as a general success. Of course, such a judgement is a subjective and political measure, and there are many ways of calibrating the scale. A great deal of money was spent on new roads and suburbs, and tax concessions and other state-subsidised incentives led to a booming industrial economy. If these are measures of success, then indeed that is what reconstruction was. It is also the case, and I think uncontroversially so, that the work required heavy borrowing, spawned new inequalities, fragmented public services, further entrenched an oil-oriented economy, and led to severe and worsening environmental degradation. In these regards, measures of success should be cause for open debate about what the future might hold.

Earthquake experiences are visceral and profound—attached so firmly to our bodies and minds that they become personal truths to defend. It is also the case that an earthquake is good to think with, and to get other people to think about things in particular ways. It is easy to attach meaning to an earthquake because it is shocking, enormous and tied to profound emotional churning. An earthquake may also consequently serve to legitimate ideas and actions which may not be allowed to fly during non-earthquake periods. Of the many earthquakes in the Bible, for example, notable ones are always accompanied by changes to the law and leadership. New politics may be made to appear. In time, these ideas and actions may then also become part of the personal truth of the disaster that people work hard to defend.

In Bhuj, traces remain of the grief, alienation and anger of the early aftermath. You can find jagged walls and empty building plots, but you have to have an experienced eye to know these things were made by an earthquake and are not just the by-products of daily life in a provincial Indian town. Plate glass and tarmac are reminders that the surface of things has changed. Events planned to mark the anniversary have met with limited support. In the end, the political will of amnesia made it possible to go on. Why cling to destructive memories?

Elsewhere in the world, earthquakes are not made to be forgotten as they have been in Gujarat. In Chile, for example, the threat of earthquakes has been drawn into the popular culture and daily routines of the nation.[2] Earthquake films, public art and evacuation sirens and signs punctuate life. There, people and the state live together with earthquakes as an open secret. In Chile, to forget an earthquake is seen as risking death; in provincial India, not to forget an earthquake is seen as risking life.

Elsewhere in the world, the Gujarat earthquake continues to strike terror. In 2012, I attended a ritual to mark the start of work on a new Hindu temple just outside London. The transnational religious organisation is supported by people of Gujarati origin. Over lunch, one of the ascetics of the order told me how, shortly after the earthquake, launches set sail from Pakistan loaded with Muslim desperados hell-bent on looting and raping amidst the ruins. I nearly choked on my chapatti. I had never before heard mention of this outrage. Sensing my incredulity, a fellow diner interrupted, assuring me that it was true, and was well known among the congregation of the temple. This conversation took place in view of the highest spiritual leader of the movement, who had come from India for the function. His presence contributed to my sense that there was no reason to think that these people were deliberately lying or testing me.[3]

It is as if a pathogen or fractal has entered transnational Hindu thought. Many have fallen into the trap of their own thinking. History and society can only be recast in terms of victimhood and the predatory actions of sexualised Muslims. Logic, 'facts' or even well-established history no longer seem to matter, as otherwise sane people

265

uncritically and endlessly reproduce these discourses. Sociological literature suggests that rumours relating to natural disasters are often hopelessly out of kilter with realities.[4] Rumour sprouts in situations of social change, ambiguity and uncertainty. However divergent from reality rumours may be, they are real in and of themselves. They snatch our attention and can be used to incite emotion and to deliberately make politics. It scarcely needs pointing out that most of those who descended on Bhuj in the aftermath of the earthquake in Gujarat were not Muslim and none of them were from Pakistan; there were reports of minor looting, but none of rape.

In time, ideas drift together, colliding with such gentleness that no one notices the new meaning that emerges; or, maybe they do, and when they do they give the new meaning a deliberate shove to help it on its way. I have tried to imagine who first told this story to someone else. What did they hope to achieve? Did they believe it to be true? Did it emerge from guilt, or as justification? What would Freud have said?

More than a decade after the disaster, the earthquake continues to serve political masters. Fantasy and fallacy appear proper because they are presented against a backdrop of magnitude and mass death—things so grave that they should surely only warrant the truth. Similarly, the claim to 'success' only stands when it is made far from the epicentres of the disaster. In Delhi or the World Bank, or even in the big cities of the east of Gujarat, it is easy to proclaim success—who would know any different? In Bhuj, people are generally pleased. In Anjar and Bhachau the idea of 'success' would not be easy to maintain. It would take a hard-nosed person to stand up in these towns and crow.

Many people in Kutch will recognise some of their own experiences in what I have written. However, many people who speak for Gujarat more generally will not agree with everything I have said. Things I have described as impositions may well be seen by them as positive contributions to society. They will see some of my judgements on reconstruction as a general slight on their character, rather than, as I would like, a signal that things could have been done differently. Unlike me, many see the spread of tarmac and the growth of industry as signs of progress and modernisation. For them, the refineries and power stations on their shores are indicators of prosperity—not the symbols of their alienation as they sometimes appear to me. Unlike me, they will see the encouragement of certain forms of religion as the gift of divine grace and as an improvement on what was there before, rather than part of the production of an acquiescent citizenry. They may well see the consolidation of other cultural ideologies in the name of reconstruction as a benefit to the nation, rather than as the promulgation of a libertarian mandate designed to strengthen support for a narrow range of political ideas. Others will have altogether different perspectives.

Most of what is publicly known about disasters is generated by media and humanitarian organisations and governments. Such institutions commonly use compassion and other moral sentiments as justification for their actions. Their reasoning is often compelling and seductive. Disasters are made to appear as logistical problems which demand intervention and legitimate trespass. The emotive language of suffering, aid and rehabilitation is generally difficult to argue with head on: what could be wrong with 'good work'?

At one level, 'good work' has been shown to be a means for passing on ideas: spreading the moral imperative hidden within the more broadly acceptable moral imperative of humanitarianism, smuggling in their messages with bags of concrete and bundles of twisted steel. There is nothing new in this. Some of it is probably unconscious rather than rehearsed. I also hope, however, to have shown how dominant discourses about disasters allow us to believe that we understand what has happened and what is to be done. Such intellectual and moral entrapment obscures much of what actually takes place in the name of reconstruction.

If we think more broadly about what an aftermath is, or if we look at it from the perspective of those inhabiting the ruins, then the evidence from Gujarat suggests that reconstruction can be used to push particular kinds of future, politics and ways of being. Earthquakes can also bring about industrial revolutions, create proletariats, encourage religious fundamentalism and allow for other new forms of culture to emerge. Carpetbaggers and sophists may run wild. History can be reoriented, heroes promoted and demoted, old orders flattened, and new names and gods imposed.

In future, when an earthquake strikes, think of those who are suffering—but also be mindful of those who may have been waiting for such an event, and of what they might do next. Such mindfulness might also form part of a manifesto for nicer aftermaths.

After a disaster, you will not see what others see. Acknowledge and explore, rather than deny disruption. Speed should not be the only imperative. There is creativity and energy to work with. Aftermaths come in waves. Audit policy, comprehend the contradictions therein. History is important, people act because of it and to spite it. Survival is divisive, and needs to be understood as such. Earthquake amnesia is cultural in form, not natural in fact. Explanations are sociology, not divinity. Enduring change is made in the everyday, not only in the grand sweeps. Proper hope is a gift.

In time, a layer of foliage was permitted to grow in front of the 'inscription of failure', 2008, Bhuj.

NOTES

NOTE ON THE REGION

1. On the relationship between religious nationalism, neo-liberalism and private organisations in India, see Hansen (1999, 2007). On everyday nationalism in Rajasthan and Orissa, see the excellent accounts of Mathur (2008) and Chatterji (2009) respectively. On the emergence and arrangement of the neo-liberal and nationalist state in Gujarat, see Sud (2009, 2012). From a sizable literature on the political atmosphere engendered by the work of these organisations in Gujarat, see Shah (2002) and Ghassem-Fachandi (2012).
2. From 'Aims and objectives', an English-language leaflet produced by the VHP, no date.
3. *Vishwa Hindu Samachar*, April 2013.
4. Ibid., March 2013.
5. Ibid., February 2013.

INTRODUCTION

1. Fassin (2012).
2. The English term 'good work' is commonly used in Gujarat for the types of humanitarian intervention I discuss in this book. I have opted to use it frequently in the text because it captures well the innocent spirit in which many organisations with strong religious and political agendas chose to present their activities.
3. Foucault (1972: 49).
4. Formal political histories inter-related with the issues in this book are to be found in Desai (2003) and Jaffrelot (1996).
5. Influences include Neil Middleton (1998) on the politics of aid, and Linda Polman's (2011) critique of the 'circus'. A recent treatment of these issues from an anthropological perspective is found in: Riccio, Brambilla and Benadusi (2011). Influences on my understanding of development, power and the operation of bureaucracy include: Ferguson (1990), Li (2007), Mosse (2004) and Scott (1999).
6. Klein (2007).
7. The violence of 2002 gave rise to a great deal of scholarship on the history and structure of the state and communal relations. I will discuss some of this literature in Section 2.
8. The words in quotation are taken from: *Love Gujarat: A land of will and wisdom*, London: Asian Business Publications, 2011.

269

9. Debroy (2012: 16).
10. 'India shining' is an advertising slogan developed by the firm Grey Worldwide. It was used by the BJP as part of its election campaign to present a spirit of optimism in the country during 2004.
11. For analysis of HDI data in Gujarat, see: Indira Hirway and Darshini Mahadevia, *Gujarat Human Development Report 2004*, Ahmedabad: Mahatma Gandhi Labour Institute, 2004. The 2011 figures reveal that 44.6 per cent of children below the age of five suffer from malnutrition and nearly 70 per cent of children suffer from anaemia. See also Standing et al. (2010). That survey of social income and insecurity in Gujarat suggests that current government policies are ineffective.
12. Petryna (2002).
13. Wiesel (1960: 92).
14. Freud (1917).
15. On syndromes and New Orleans, see Adams, van Huttum and English (2009).
16. Lefebvre (1991).
17. For governmental and statistical accounts of the earthquake, see: Gupta et al. (2002) and Reddy (2001); see also: Pramod K. Mishra, *The Kutch earthquake: Recollections, lessons, insights*, New Delhi: National Institute of Disaster Management, 2004. The three sources together give an overview of the disaster from the perspective of senior administrators. For another important understanding of the earthquake see: V. Thiruppugazh, *Urban vulnerability reduction: Regulations and beyond*, Canberra: Australia South Asia Research Centre Working Paper, 2007/8; and idem., *Gujarat earthquake: Enormity and impact*. Gandhinagar: Gujarat State Disaster Management Authority, 2012. The author is a senior officer in the Gujarat State Disaster Management Authority and his insights are valuable.
18. For Australian figures: 'India—Further emergency assistance', Canberra: Government of Australia, 30 January 2001. EU figures given in: 'The Gujarat Earthquake: European Union swiftly pools its efforts', *Indo-EU News*, Brussels, 2001. For UK figures: *Independent evaluation: The DEC response to the Earthquake in Gujarat*, Vol. 1, London: Disasters Emergency Committee, 2001. US figures: 'India—Earthquake summary fact sheet (FY 2001)', Washington: US Agency for International Development, Bureau for Humanitarian Response, and Office of US Foreign Disaster Assistance, 28 February, 2001.
19. An additional source of valuable data on the aftermath are the five editions of a publication called *Coming Together*, compiled by Abhiyan (the major NGO in Kutch), Gujarat State Disaster Management Authority and the United Nations Development Programme. These publications discuss in great detail the working of the private sector in relation to the official policy of the state, and the problems inherent to reconstruction initiatives. The figures for BAPS, Caritas and Abhiyan are given in *Coming Together* (5th edn), p. 119. On the central role of Abhiyan as a coordinating and facilitating agency, see Panda (2002).
20. Das (2007) and Das and Kleinman (2001). Others working in post-disaster reconstruction environments have also seen the merit of the framework laid out by Das for explaining both the remaking of the everyday and the extraordinary potential of everyday existence for absorbing extreme events. Notable among these scholars are de Alwis and Hedman (2009) on the 2004 tsunami in Sri Lanka and Aceh, Hastrup (2011) on Tamil Nadu, and Samuels (2012) on Aceh.
21. Ankur Jain, 'Buried beneath debris, scam raises stink', *Times of India*, 26 January 2012.
22. BBC East Midlands, *Inside Out*, 7 January 2011. The BBC claims £140,000 was unspent and remains in a UK bank account, and £100,000 is unaccounted for.

23. The no-win, no-fee law firm Pannone took up the case on the basis of the failure of a duty of care against those who collected public funds for the school in England.
24. Merli (2010) for a discussion on theodicy, society and the 2004 tsunami in Southern Thailand.
25. This idea is found in Baudrillard (2008), on the agency of nature at Pompeii.

1. SUBLIME

1. First published as *Kritik der Urteilskraft* in 1790. I have read from Meredith's 1952 translation; see Kant (2007). I have found Lyotard (1994) useful in understanding Kant's critique of reason. There are many additional commentaries on Kant's ideas. Important is Schopenhauer's of 1818 (Schopenhauer 1969).
2. Kant wrote three papers on the earthquake shortly after the Lisbon disaster. The influence of his vicarious experience on his consideration of the sublime is obvious both in the way he carries ideas forward from these early papers and in the kinds of language he uses. On this, see also Larsen (2006) and Ray (2004).
3. Alternatives to this theoretical frame might have been 'trauma' or 'Post-Traumatic Stress Disorder' (P-TSD). Influenced by Allan Young's (1996) description of the invention of the condition, I have elected to keep my analytical terms within the sociological realm. Ravi Priya (2004) reasons that P-TSD has a cultural bias and that grief and shock in Gujarat should be understood on the basis of *karma* (the accumulated effects of good and bad deeds) and the qualities of happiness and misery. Connerton's (2011) synthesis of the literature on mourning further refined my thoughts, as has Fassin and Rechtman (2009).
4. Brown (1991: 7).

2. RETROSPECTIVE ANATOMY

1. *Kutch Mitra*, 31 January 2001.
2. Ibid.
3. My focus is not on the relief effort; however, many of the organisations that appeared in Bhuj at that time stayed on into the later phases of reconstruction. Thousands of reports, executive summaries, minutes and accounts are readily available from those organisations involved in the initial months of relief work. On relief, and the observance of Red Cross and Sphere Codes, as well as the problems and strengths of work conducted in Gujarat, see the three-part report written by a team led by the experienced Tony Vaux: *Independent evaluation: The DEC response to the earthquake in Gujarat*, Vols 1–3, London: Disasters Emergency Committee, 2001. The third volume contains the results of a survey called 'Voice for survivors', in which a team led by Mihir Bhatt of the Disaster Mitigation Institute in Ahmedabad sought general opinion on relief operations. Inconsistencies, inequalities and so forth in the distribution of aid are openly discussed. Rather more frank and raw in approach is an earlier document, probably authored by the same team: *The earthquake in Gujarat, India. Report of a monitoring visit for the DEC, March 2001*, London: Disasters Emergency Committee, 2001. This report contains eighty-four pointed paragraphs on the politics of relief, the interaction of the various agencies on the ground, and the coordination of the coordination. A piece by Uday Mahurkar and Supriya Bezbaruah ('Double disaster: Gujarat government's confused response to earthquake relief operations adds to loss and pain', *India Today*, 19 February 2001) stands out from the acres of news-

print on the earthquake. Writing just two weeks after the disaster, they hit the nail on the head at the time, and the piece has stood the test of time. They record the inability of the government to function and the eventual transfer of shocked and slothful officers. The journalism of Sheela Bhatt on Rediff.com has consistently reflected realities on the ground. Lecy (2005) is surprised to see that poverty rates have fallen in the region after the earthquake, and attributes this to the effectiveness of disaster relief rather than to the massive injection of resources.

4. *Guardian*, 30 January 2001.
5. Sheela Bhatt, 'Panic spreads as stars foretell bigger quake on Feb 3', http://www.rediff.com, 2 February 2001. Accessed 7 November 2012.

3. AFTERMATH EPISTEMOLOGY

1. See *Gujarat earthquake recovery program: Assessment report: A joint report by the World Bank and the Asian Development Bank, March 14, 2001*. The joint assessment took place between 12 and 26 February 2001. Drafts were discussed with the government of Gujarat at least four times before it was published on 14 March 2001.
2. I thank Rohan d'Souza for this typically incisive observation.
3. Also see Ashok Lahiri, Tapas K. Sen, R. Kavita Rao and Pratap Ranjan Jena, *Economic consequences of the Gujarat earthquake*, Discussion Paper No. 1, New Delhi: National Institute of Public Finance and Policy, 2001; and Krishna S. Vatsa, *The Bhuj earthquake, District of Kutch, State of Gujarat (India) January 26, 2001: A reconnaissance report. Identification of priority issues*, Alexandria, VA: World Institute for Disaster Risk Management, 2001.
4. ADB, *Completion report: India: Gujarat rehabilitation and reconstruction project*, Manila: Asian Development Bank, 2008, p. 12.
5. World Bank, *Implementation completion and results report*, Report No: ICR0000638, New Delhi: World Bank, 2009, p. 14.
6. From a vast and discordant body of literature, see Harvey (2007) on the history and development of the neo-liberal order.
7. ADB, *Completion report: India: Gujarat rehabilitation and reconstruction project*, Manila: Asian Development Bank, 2008, p. 2.
8. INPE73161; *India-Gujarat urban reform project*, Gandhinagar: Government of the State of Gujarat Urban Development and Urban Housing Department.
9. Ibid.
10. Land reforms in Gujarat have passed through various phases in the post-Independence period. For an outline of the broad contours of these, see Sud (2007).
11. ADB, *Completion report: India: Gujarat rehabilitation and reconstruction project*, Manila: Asian Development Bank, 2008, p. 4.
12. Ibid., p. 11.
13. Ibid., 2008, p. 4.
14. World Bank, *Implementation completion and results report*. Report No: ICR0000638, New Delhi: World Bank, 2009, pp. 2, 25.
15. One source puts the number of 'groups' formed as 1,111 in 606 villages (*Coming Together*, August 2002, p. 77).

4. HYPERBOLIC CAPITALISM

1. In his *Principles of political economy*, first published in 1848, Mill wrote: 'This perpetual consumption and reproduction of capital affords the explanation of what has so often excited wonder, the great rapidity with which countries recover from a state of devastation; the disappearance, in a short time, of all traces of the mischiefs done by earthquakes, floods, hurricanes, and the ravages of war. An enemy lays waste a country by fire and sword, and destroys or carries away nearly all the moveable wealth existing in it: all the inhabitants are ruined, and yet in a few years after, everything is much as it was before. This *vis medicatrix naturæ* has been a subject of sterile astonishment, or has been cited to exemplify the wonderful strength of the principle of saving, which can repair such enormous losses in so brief an interval. There is nothing at all wonderful in the matter. What the enemy have destroyed, would have been destroyed in a little time by the inhabitants themselves: the wealth which they so rapidly reproduce, would have needed to be reproduced and would have been reproduced in any case, and probably in as short a time. Nothing is changed, except that during the reproduction they have not now the advantage of consuming what had been produced previously. The possibility of a rapid repair of their disasters mainly depends on whether the country has been depopulated. If its effective population have not been extirpated at the time, and are not starved afterwards; then, with the same skill and knowledge which they had before, with their land and its permanent improvements undestroyed, and the more durable buildings probably unimpaired, or only partially injured, they have nearly all the requisites for their former amount of production. If there is as much of food left to them, or of valuables to buy food, as enables them by any amount of privation to remain alive and in working condition, they will in a short time have raised as great a produce, and acquired collectively as great wealth and as great a capital, as before; by the mere continuance of that ordinary amount of exertion which they are accustomed to employ in their occupations. Nor does this evince any strength in the principle of saving, in the popular sense of the term, since what takes place is not intentional abstinence, but involuntary privation', (Mill 1848: 94–95).
   I am aware that Mill is often seen as an inspiration for the economic policies of the political right. I take this observation from him, as somewhat distinct and separate from his broader economic and political vision.

2. See Albala-Bertrand (1993) for an economist's view of the consequences of large natural disasters with special reference to developing countries. The analysis suggests that most sectors of the economy improve; there is a rise in Gross Domestic Product and sharp rise in capital flows (ibid.: 87).

3. The policy was announced as *'Incentive Scheme 2001 for Economic Development of Kutch District', Government Resolution No. INC-10200–903–I, dated 9–11–2001*, Gandhinagar: Government of Gujarat, 2001. For the regulations on exemption from Central Excise: see *Government of India, Ministry of Finance, Department of Revenue, New Delhi, dated the 31ˢᵗ July, 2001, Notification No. 39/2001–Central Excise*, New Delhi: Government of India, 2001.

4. The deadline for new industries to commence production was originally 2003, but this was extended to 2004 and later to 2005.

5. Smaller amounts aimed at encouraging local enterprise were also available as grants. Hindsight and arrests suggest that fraudulent claims were made, but the excess of funds available contributed to the sense of plenty in the aftermath. Applications for funds to start computer centres and beauty parlours were most common.

6. Census figures for 2011 are unavailable for Anjar. In 2001, the population of Kutch was 1,583,225; in 2011, it was 2,090,313. This is an increase of over 30 per cent in a decade, a figure far higher than all other areas of Gujarat, other than the city of Ahmedabad. The percentage increase in the towns of eastern Kutch, such as Anjar, is likely to be far higher than this average given the attractions of the surrounding industry.

7. While all this was common knowledge in Kutch, it was not until May 2011 that a coalition of different interests succeeded in getting a court order for construction to be suspended in the absence of an Environmental Clearance Certificate. The Union Ministry of Environment and Forests is currently investigating claims that mangroves were destroyed, sand dunes levelled and the high-tide line moved by damming tidal creeks.

8. On this, see Pereira's astute analysis (Pereira 2009).

9. Kodrich and Laituri (2005) have shown how the online English-language Indian newspapers 'helped' in the formation of a disaster-response community based on common interests.

5. THE CARPETBAGGER

1. Published under the name of Derek Slade in 1990 by Oriflamme.

6. NOTES ON 'AFTERMATH'

1. Klein (2007).

2. Oliver-Smith (1986: 76), writing about the Peruvian earthquake and landslide of 1970. Rebecca Solnit (2010) sees the moment of post-disaster disorientation as a possible source of new politics. While I am sympathetic with the sentiment, many of the people discussed in this book also saw the moment of disaster as an opportunity to make a better world. I doubt, however, that these are the forms of utopia Solnit had in mind.

3. The first quote is from Oliver-Smith (1996: 304); the second and third are from Oliver-Smith and Hoffman (2002: 10). Aside from this insistence, this collection and an earlier volume (Oliver-Smith and Hoffman 1999) are excellent examples of why it is productive for anthropologists to study natural disasters.

4. John Locke (1632–1704) was one of the Scottish Enlightenment philosophers. He thought that humans were born without innate ideas, and that knowledge is instead determined only by experiences derived from the perceptions afforded by the senses. See Baird and Kaufmann (2008).

5. Klein (2007: 25–48) outlines this theory in a chapter provocatively entitled 'The torture lab: Ewen Cameron, the CIA and the maniacal quest to erase and remake the human mind'.

6. This ascription of disaster-like qualities to the aftermath is commonly reported. The wave of aid in Sri Lanka was called the 'second tsunami', and so forth.

7. Sorokin (1942: 156).

8. See, for example, Klein (1984) on famine relief, and d'Souza (2006) on flood control in India.

9. Analysis by the economic historian Tirthankar Roy (2008) suggests that patterns of response during the period see the destruction of state capacity, which activates anarchic unregulated markets and private institutions, until the state bounces back to take control. We see some resemblance of this pattern in Gujarat with the additional influence of the international community and the partnership of state and private interests in reconstruction.

10. The Gujarat State Disaster Management Bill was passed as Act 20 of 2003. A national disaster management bill was passed in 2005. See Ray (2005) for a critical discussion.

11. The first phrase is from Jasanoff (2010); Hacking (1990) is responsible for the second.

7. REGIME CHANGE

1. Official figures suggest 790 Muslims and 254 Hindus died. There were 223 people missing (50 less than rendered missing by the earthquake). Figures given elsewhere put the death toll at between 1,500 and 2,500.

2. In 2005, a committee led by the former Supreme Court judge U.C. Banerjee concluded the disaster was caused by an 'accidental fire'. See Ghassem-Fachandi (2012) for a recent discussion of the circumstances, stories of blame and evidence.

3. *A Government of Gujarat presentation. 2 minutes to the truth*. Compact disk. Gandhinagar: Government of Gujarat, 2002.

4. Kshatriya, Harijan, Adavasi and Muslim refer to four major socio-political groups in Gujarat, each of which is marginal in different ways and for different reasons to those who currently hold a hegemonic position. The Kshatriyas are associated with land and pastoralism and are sometimes seen as the sons of the soil; they are also associated with sacrifice and violence, and therefore are out of line with the devotional vegetarianism of those with power. Harijans are the former Untouchables, often also now called Dalits. Adavasis are often thought of as the 'indigenous' or 'pre-Hindu' population; many are classified by the state as 'Tribals'.

5. On the political strategies of the BJP during this period, see Breman (2004: 287) and Prakash (2003: 1601).

6. On this trend, see Sondhi and Mukarji (2002: 253–54).

7. 'Anti-reservation riots' were so called because they came in response to the state's policy of reserving jobs and educational places for sections of the population classified as low-ranking and backwards. On this issue, see Shah (1987).

8. This point is made by Sarkar (2002: 2873).

9. Extracts from Togadia's speech were reproduced in 'Vote on the basis of religion: Togadia', *Indian Express* (Ahmedabad City edition and the Saurashtra newsline), 19 October 2002.

10. This speech was reproduced as a pamphlet under the title 'Bharatiya Janata Party. National Executive Meeting. Presidential Address by Shri M. Venkaiah Naidu'.

11. Contrasting contributions include those from Ahmad (2002), Banerjee (2002), Berenschot (2011), Gupta (2002) and Wilkinson (2002).

12. Patel (2002). Alternative radical politics can be seen elsewhere in India in the anti-Brahmin movement in the south or the so-called 'Mandalised' movements of the Gangetic Plains, in which low-caste political lobbies have gathered strength.

13. Ahmad (2002: 1871–72).

14. Breman (2004). This argument works well for major urban centres, but has obvious limits when it comes to explaining the spread of violence to rural areas in 2002.

15. Yagnik and Sheth (2002), and expanded in Yagnik and Sheth (2005).

16. Varshney (2002: 219–38). This thesis finds little support among those with field experience in rural Gujarat, where powerbrokers are more commonly associated with retrograde instincts.

17. Mishra (2002: 86).

18. Ahmad (2002: 44).
19. See Patel (2002: 4826) on the first clause, and Sarkar (2002: 2873) on the second.
20. Also see Ahmad (2002: 1871).

8. VIEW FROM THE EAST

1. See the influential piece by Vakil and Patel (1939: 40; 1940) on the language and territory of Gujarat.
2. Majumdar's (1940) survey was also funded and published by the Gujarat Research Society. The findings are controversial and were not, as far as I can tell, much discussed in Gujarat. On the whole, the survey found elite coastal trading communities to be the most robust, Muslims fared well, and a scientific slur was placed upon popular notions of caste purity. In sum, Majumdar proposed an idea of Gujarat more or less opposite to that which the society was working to promote.
3. *Journal of the Gujarat Research Society*, 9 (3), 1947, n.p.
4. Sukheswala (1948) and Wadia (1942) conducted geographical surveys; Vakil and Patel (1939, 1940) investigated society and economy; surveys of the language were conducted by Dave (1942).
5. Here I have in mind the work of scholars such as Dirks (2001) and Raheja (1996) on ways in which colonial knowledge practices contributed to the formation of particular kinds of society. In Gujarat, the work by Shodhan (2001) carefully shows the interplay of state, religion and caste in the production of new forms of corporate social identity.
6. On this issue, see the work of Spodek (1972) and Wood (1984). These authors examine the nature of caste and traditional authority in the different regions of Gujarat, exploring the consequences of these differences for the modern politics of land and representation.
7. Maha Gujarat Parishad, *Formation of Maha Gujarat: Memorandum submitted to the States Reorganisation Commission Government of India*, Vallabh Vidyanagar: Amrit Pandya, 1954, p. 1.

9. BORDERLANDS

1. Following Schmitt (1985), Das and Poole (2004: 3–4) outline the ways in which peripheral areas become central to the interests of states.
2. For a poetic description, see Gupta (1969: 1–3).
3. Traffic in the Rann has been documented from the time of Postans (1839: 169) to that of Ibrahim (2009).
4. Ibrahim (2009) focuses on the ethnography of the borderlands between Kutch and Pakistan and the making of modern Gujarati identity. Our findings are similar.
5. On the origins, doctrines and organisation, see Williams (1984).

10. (RE)BIRTH OF AN ICON

1. Yajnik (1950: 1, 7).
2. Ibid.: 63.
3. In particular, he worked with the Arya Samaj, an organisation which worked to restore ancient values through the reform of contemporary religious practices.

4. *Indian Sociologist*, 4 (8), pp. 30, 32; 4 (9), pp. 34, 36.
5. Ibid., 4 (4), p. 14.
6. *East India (Sedition Committee, 1918) report of committee appointed to investigate revolutionary conspiracies in India*. London: His Majesty's Stationary Office, 1918, p. 12. See also Chirol (1921: 122).
7. *Indian Sociologist* vols 5 (9) to 10 (2) were issued in Paris, and 10 (8–12) were issued in Geneva; in 1920, the journal was rejuvenated and was issued for two further years. See also Fischer-Tiné (2007) for Krishnavarma's international connections.
8. The university is called Krantiguru Shyamji Krishna Verma Kachchh University.
9. See Pandya and Pandya (2003). The authors reproduce the text of a partial run of Krishnavarma's journal. Also see Vishnu Pandya's biography of Krishnavarma in Gujarati (Pandya 1985).
10. In Krishnavarma's creed, the 'Anglo-Indian' was complicit as either a supporter or beneficiary of British rule in India.
11. Yajnik (1950: 110).
12. *Indian Sociologist*, 4 (1), p. 2.
13. Ibid., 4 (3), p. 11.
14. Ibid., 1 (1), pp. 3–4.
15. The pages of his journal are oriented around a few select quotes from Spencer. This odd intellectual relationship has also been noted by the eminent A.M. Shah (2006).
16. On the details of this, see Duncan (1908: 483).
17. Spencer (1884: 46–48).
18. Spencer (1873: 186).
19. *Indian Sociologist*, 9 (10), p. 38. The quote is from Spencer's *The study of sociology* (Spencer 1873: 185).
20. Also see Kapila (2007).
21. See Spodek (1971) among others.
22. Yajnik (1950: 97).

11. VILLAGE 'ADOPTION'

1. Initial schemes were announced in: *'Package 1' Revenue Department resolution No.XLS-162001–207–(4)-S.3 and General Administration Department resolution No. EST-102001–830–KH, dated 8 February 2001*, Gandhinagar: Government of Gujarat, 2001; and: *'Package 2' Revenue Department resolution No.XLS-162001–201–(4)-S.3 and General Administration Department resolution No. EST—102001—830—KH, dated 8 February 2001*, Gandhinagar: Government of Gujarat, 2001. On the working, problems and successes of the scheme, see B.B. Patel and R. Alagh, *Response of the corporate sector to the Gujarat Earthquake of 2001*, Geneva: International Labour Office, 2003. Patel and Alagh draw particular attention to the large numbers of private organisations that eventually had to back out of the scheme; also Mahir Bhatt, *Corporate social responsibility and natural disaster reduction: Local overview of Gujarat*, Ahmedabad: Disaster Mitigation Institute, 2002. Bhatt makes interesting observations on the relationship between public and private sectors, and corporate social responsibility in Gujarat. Although based on only two weeks research in Gujarat, Koenraad Van Brabant catches perfectly what is now a historical moment of confusion and upset caused by the working of the public–private partnership scheme: *The right to information: Exploring the challenges of transparency, responsiveness and*

accountability in post-earthquake Gujarat, India, Geneva: Humanitarian Accountability Project, 2001. The report prepared by the NGO Unnati records a similar picture for the area around Bhachau: *Participatory monitoring of rehabilitation process in Kutch, 5th to 10th of September 2001*, Ahmedabad: UNNATI, 2001.

2. Figures derived from *Coming Together* (4th edn), August 2002, Appendix II.
3. Details of the variety of rural housing in Kutch are documented pictorially in fold-out sections of *Coming Together* (4th edn), August, 2002. Details of a housing satisfaction survey were published in *Coming Together* (5th edn), March 2003, pp. 25–30, and reproduced in: Jennifer Barenstein, *Housing reconstruction in post-earthquake Gujarat. A comparative analysis*, Humanitarian Practice Network Paper, London: Overseas Development Institute, 2006.
4. For a clear review of this literature, see Diya Dutta, *Elite capture and corruption: Concepts and definitions*, New Delhi: National Centre for Applied Economic Research, 2009.

12. SERVICE

1. The anthropological work on gift giving in India has been inspired by Marcel Mauss's 1925 essay on the gift (Mauss 1990). Mauss's gift involved reciprocity. Raheja (1988), however, shows how village prestations may be given without the expectation of return, as has Parry (1994) for funerary priests and Laidlaw (1995) for Jain mendicants. Unlike the Maussian gift, *dan* is that which releases the giver of social obligation. On the fine distinctions made in the religious books of Hinduism between different kinds of *dan* and gifts, see Agarwal (2010). For a recent discussion of giving and gifts, see Copeman (2011).
2. Available at: http://www.swaminarayan.org/introduction/index.htm. Accessed 7 November 2012.
3. BAPS is Gujarati in origin and ethos, and its institutions are better established in the east of the state. As recently as 1981, Raymond Williams noted that BAPS 'has not had success in reaching into Kutch because the people there have remained loyal to the Bhuj temple and to the acharaya of Ahmedabad' (Williams 1984: 54). An *acharya* is the head of a religious movement; he protects the religion, as spiritual leader and guru. There are two *acharya*s in the Swaminarayan movement. The temple in Ahmedabad (what they call Amdavad, so as to distance the historical fact that the city was founded by the Muslim Ahmed Shah) temple is the seat of the *acharya* of northern India; the idol there is Shree Nar-Narayan Dev. The temple in Vadtal is the seat of the *acharya* of southern India, where the idol is Shree Lakshmi-Narayan Dev. BAPS is an offshoot of the Vadtal temple and operates in both northern and southern divisions.
4. *Rehabilitation Package No. 1 for earthquake affected*, Gandhinagar: GSDMA, Government of Gujarat, 2001. When a village is more than 70 per cent damaged it can be relocated to sites approved by the local authorities, preferably on government-owned land close to the old site. In this policy, landless agricultural labourers were to be given plots of 100 square metres and a construction of 30 square metres; marginal farmers holding up to 1 hectare, 150 and 40 respectively, small farmers up to 4 hectares, 250 and 40, farmers holding more than 4 hectares, 400 and 50. As per the policy, BAPS translated this method of classification into the design of its new village. The weight given to landholding in this government scheme may have acted detrimentally against artisans, entrepreneurs and concrete vendors, and led to other the kinds of complication I described in Chapter 11 (*Rehabilitation Package No. 2 for earthquake affected*. Gandhinagar: GSDMA, Government of Gujarat, 2001).

The policy outlines graded rates of compensation in relation to damage, for size of property and for whether the structure was permanent or temporary (a hut). As with other rural reconstruction policies, compensation rates were pegged to the built-up area of the damaged property, up to 25, 35 and 45 square metres. This was the option those who remained in Jiyapar had opted for. In both schemes, loans were also available and, as we know, insurance was mandatory.

5. Damaged property was assessed on a scale ranging from G1 to G5, the latter being the most severely damaged. Compensation rates increased with the G number—but only G4 and G5 category buildings required full reconstruction. In principle, buildings of categories G1 to G3 were repairable. The politics of G numbers in urban areas are discussed at length in Chapter 19.

6. BAPS built 285 new houses; 76 in the old village had been classified as G4 and G5 and therefore required reconstruction.

7. A process analysed by the historian Sarkar (1999).

8. Williams (1984: xi).

9. Virmani (2010: 149–50). Virmani lives near Bhuj and was an important figure in coordinating and planning post-earthquake reconstruction in the civil society sphere.

10. See Tambs-Lyche (1997) for an outline of this division at the most general level. Spodek (1972) and Wood (1984) are best on the geographic tendencies and political consequences. Pocock (1973) wrote persuasively about the struggle between the two traditions in a village in Central Gujarat.

11. Of the houses built in the village, 43 were of type A, 173 of type B and 69 were of type C.

12. As with all other 'donor' lists, the compensation money of those with damaged property is not included.

13. Narayannagar (Jiyapar) Layout Plan, BAPS, 2002.

14. Sewa International Annual Report, April 2012–March 2013.

13. *JIHADI*, DOG AND SECULARIST

1. On this, see Reddy (2001: 31).

2. See *Kutch quake profile*, Ahmedabad: Jan Sangharsh Manch, n.d.

3. Extracts from this speech were reproduced in 'Vote on the basis of religion: Togadia', *Indian Express* (Ahmedabad City edition and the Saurashtra newsline), 19 October 2002; 'After Godhra, dogs barked, including an Italian dog: Togadia', ibid., 19 October 2002; and 'Togadia said it, and he's proud of it', ibid., 22 October 2002. I attended this speech with my friend Farhana Ibrahim. We left in silence and with sweaty palms.

4. See Ghassem-Fachandi (2012) and Jasani (2007) for the ways in which such divisions have been played out in the geography of urban Gujarat.

14. BUILDING POLITICS

1. See Copeman (2013) on the sanguinary politics of nationalist art in India.

15. INTEGRAL HUMANISM

1. Available at: http://rmponweb.org/overview/. Accessed 7 November 2012.

2. See *Commission of inquiry regarding the fact and circumstances relating to the death of Shri Deen Dayal Upadhyaya, 1969—Report*, New Delhi: Ministry of Home Affairs, 1970.
3. The contours of this philosophy are laid out most clearly in his book of the same name (Upadhyaya 1969), which is based on four lectures given in Bombay in 1965.
4. Upadhyaya (1969: 3).
5. Ibid.: 16.
6. See Bourdieu (1984) and Bourdieu and Wacquant (2004).

16. THE PLACE OF BHUJ

1. For a while, many people in Bhuj were offended by the more common term 'the Gujarat earthquake' because it was clear to them that it was in fact 'the Kutch earthquake'. The naming of disasters influences significantly the types of appeals, decisions and associations which can be put forth in the name of a disaster. In this case, however, 'the Bhuj earthquake' was an appellation which gained currency after the event, having an almost justificatory ring and often used in the literature produced by the state government. In 2011, the Institute of Seismological Research in Gandhinagar held a major international symposium on what it called the 'Bhuj earthquake'. On the first day, before the 'ice breaker' session, delegates were treated to the light and sound show at the BAPS temple in Gandhinagar.
2. These figures are taken from Gupta et al. (2002: Annexure 3). The figures are for the *taluka* or sub-district level, and therefore also include death and collapse in surrounding villages. Given that Bhachau had half the population of Bhuj, the figures are indicative of the degree of damage. I have a series of photographs taken at annual intervals from the hillock overlooking the centre of Bhachau. For quite a few years after bulldozers had levelled the ground, aside from trees and the odd house, the site was deserted. Bhachau was literally made to disappear by the disaster. The life of the town moved to what had previously been the periphery.
3. A notable exception is the Ahmedabad-based organisation Unnati, which opened offices in Bhachau and worked extremely hard to do what it thought was right in the dire conditions. See *Owner driven housing process post earthquake reconstruction programme Bhachau*, Ahmedabad: Unnati, 2006. This document was produced with hindsight, reflecting on some aspects of the organisation's experience in the town.
4. As an illustrative example, see the piece by Kuldip Nayar ('Discriminating against the distressed in a democracy', *Financial Express*, 21 February 2001), who reports widespread discrimination in the distribution of relief materials. It is tempting to ask, however, why anyone should expect the allocation of relief to be equitable at the time of disaster given that the primary distributive mechanism in India, the state, is often legally discriminatory and famously imperfect during the most peaceable of times. Furthermore, private organisations inevitably continue to operate, when possible, through pre-existing networks of patronage and knowledge, which are necessarily partisan. That shock at the notion of discrimination appears so commonly after disasters raises questions about concepts of 'exception', 'humanity' and 'justice' which come into play at such times.
5. For a discussion of changing relations between the *bhayad* of Kutch, see McLeod (2007). Also see Rushbrook Williams (1958) for a general account of how the internally warring *bhayad* of Kutch was, in part, pacified by colonial military intervention in the early nine-

teenth century. As I imply in this chapter, there is a deep relationship between indigenous and colonial knowledge practices on the one hand and the production of contemporary social categories and modes of understanding on the other.

6. Ogilvy (1855).
7. Raikes (1855).
8. Lumsden (1855).
9. Charles Walters (British Library, India Office Records, F/4/1149, 1827); also the account produced by James Burnes first produced for private circulation among his friends in 1829. The text appears to have been printed for public consumption in the same or following year in Bombay. The work was published in his native Scotland in 1830. For ease of reference, I have used a recent reprint (Burnes 2004).
10. See Postans (1839).
11. Accounts of Watson (1876) and Burton (1851) are noteworthy.
12. Anon. (1880).
13. British Library, India Office Records F/4/1149, 1827.
14. Anon. (1880: 136).
15. Rushbrook Williams (1958: 113).

17. WHERE TO START?

1. On these decisions and what Pombal did in the end in Lisbon, see Paice (2008).

18. PLANNERS

1. The agenda of the FIRE(D) project and the methods of working are laid out in: *Indo-US Financial Institutions Reform and Expansion (FIRE) Project—Debt Market Component: A New Approach to Providing Urban Environmental Infrastructure and Services*, New Delhi: FIRE(D) Project Office, 1999. For an account of EPC's initial work in Bhuj, see: 'Indo–US Financial Institutions Reform and Expansion Project—Debt Market Component FIRE(D) 2002'. *Initiative for Planned and Participatory Reconstruction*. No. 29, New Delhi: FIRE(D) Project Office, 2002.
2. See *Gujarat State Disaster Management Act*, Gandhinagar: Government of Gujarat, 2003.
3. See *2001 Rehabilitation Package No. 5 For earthquake affected. Government Resolution General Administration Department No: EST-102001–830–KH, dt. 08–02–2001*, Gandhinagar: Government of Gujarat, 2001.
4. See B.R. Balachandran, *The reconstruction of Bhuj: Case study: Integration of disaster mitigation into planning and financing urban infrastructure after an earthquake*, Washington: World Bank, 2003, p. 99.
5. See *2001 Rehabilitation Package No. 5 For earthquake affected. Government Resolution General Administration Department No: EST-102001–830–KH, dt. 08–02–2001*, Gandhinagar: Government of Gujarat, 2001.
6. On planning mechanisms in Gujarat, see Shirley Ballaney, *Town planning mechanism in Gujarat, India*, Washington: World Bank, 2008. The author was part of the EPC team in Bhuj.
7. See *2001 Rehabilitation Package No. 5 For earthquake affected.*

19. G NUMBERS

1. *Draft Development Plan (Final report for submission under Section 16 of the Gujarat Town Planning and Urban Development Act, 1976)*, Ahmedabad: Environmental Planning Collaborative (EPC), Babtie Consultants (India) Pvt. Ltd, JPS Associates and Theotech Engineers, 2001. Here I discuss select aspects of the way in which the plan was conceived and implemented. The draft plan EPC produced for Bhuj aimed to improve the lot of the town as a whole. EPC dissected Bhuj into categories: an economy, a pattern of land use, a network of roads and water bodies, a series of open spaces and heritage sites, an informal sector, as well as solid waste and water management facilities. The relationship between these sectors was examined in order to determine how each could be improved to make the town more prosperous, efficient and easier to govern. Many of the proposals made in the plan were taken forward by the state, and by some private sector organisations. Also see Balachandran (2010) and Tyabji (2006) on the planning of Bhuj.

20. THE UNBEARABLE INTENSITY OF REDUCTION

1. The sociologist Ino Rossi (1993) has also seen the particular importance of the changing relationship between individual and collective action in the aftermath of earthquakes—in this case in southern Italy.

21. NOSTALGIA

1. For a discussion of the origins and uses of the term 'nostalgia', see Davis (1979).
2. These ideas are derived from a nostalgic scheme devised by the sociologist Bryan Turner (1987).
3. These refer to different months of the Hindu calendar. Ashad falls in June/July and marks the start of the monsoon in Kutch. In much of the rest of Gujarat, New Year falls after Diwali and is synonymous with the first day of the month of Kartik (October/November), which marks the start of a new accounting year. Most Hindus in other parts of India mark the New Year in April.
4. There is noteworthy irony here because, as we will see in Chapter 30, Pragmulji's ancestors were pitted against MacMurdo as he led the political colonisation of their kingdom. Now, nearly two centuries later, his testimony is called upon by the ancestors of the colonised to make a case against the post-colonial state. The shift also reflects the ways in which the rulers of Kutch gradually became sympathetic to colonial ways of seeing.
5. In literature this is a distinction also made by Lerner (1972: 245–46).
6. Nora (1989: 13).

22. HISTORY MAKING

1. The list of works on provincial history in both Gujarati and English is long (see Simpson 2011). Pre-eminent is the collection by Rathod (1949), on the history of Kutch, with an emphasis on the Ramayana traditions. His personal library was considerable and is today housed in a private museum in Bhuj. Antani (2005) is an administrator in the government's Bhuj Museum and has written a standard history of Kutch. Jadia (1999) was also an administrator in the same museum, and has written a popular book on the history of

Kutch with an emphasis on musicology. Jethi (2008) is curator of the privately run Aina Mahal Palace Museum in Bhuj. His account, also translated into French, is loyal to the rulers of Kutch.

2. For an insider's account of the relationship between the rulers and their deities, see K.S. Dilipsinhji's (2004) rich exploration of the traditions of Bhuj.

3. The gazetteer for Kutch includes the story of the king of Bhuj and the fifty-two yard celestial serpent known as *gujan* or *shersnaag*, 'city snake' (Anon. 1880: 216).

4. Letter from the Darbar Gadh to the chairman of Bhuj Urban Development Authority, 7 July 2001 (copy in possession of this author); also reproduced in: *Draft Development Plan (Final report for submission under Section 16 of the Gujarat Town Planning and Urban Development Act, 1976)*, Ahmedabad: Environmental Planning Collaborative (EPC), Babtie Consultants (India) Pvt. Ltd, JPS Associates and Theotech Engineers, 2001.

23. RITUALS OF RECONSTRUCTION

1. In some ways these rehabilitation institutions were too good an idea because they ignored much of what was there already. Bhuj had and has a huge number of associations, clubs and offices representing caste, religious and special interest groups (the Laughter Club meeting on the bank of the lake always lifted my spirits). The terms of funding and the sociological awareness of those working on rebuilding Bhuj were largely such that these important associational influences were disregarded as 'communal' or 'caste-ist', or their significance was unrecognisable to the outside planner or social worker. This was unfortunate, for the energy and organisation of these institutions could have been directly engaged in acts of reconstruction.

2. *Bhuj Town Planning Schemes. Report on Public Consultations, January 1, 2003*, Ahmedabad: Environmental Planning Collaborative, 2003.

3. Letter from the Additional Assistant Engineer to the Incharge Officer, EPC (copy in possession of this author); also reproduced in: *Draft Development Plan (Final report for submission under Section 16 of the Gujarat Town Planning and Urban Development Act, 1976)*, Ahmedabad: Environmental Planning Collaborative (EPC), Babtie Consultants (India) Pvt. Ltd, JPS Associates and Theotech Engineers, 2001.

4. *Mansara, Mayamata, Samrangana* and *Rajavallabha*. For a discussion, see Sachdev and Tillotson (2002).

25. SLOW DEATH

1. The quote is from Halbwachs (1992: 73; see also 1980). Halbwachs is often treated as a figure of historical note, while others characterise his project as a parallel venture to those of Bergson (2004) and Freud (1924). His work is often dismissed for his reliance on the super-collective mind, derived from his teacher Emile Durkheim. However, in my view, he actually points to the limits of the concept of a super-collective organic mind by showing how such a thing exists only in individual and group interactions. For sure, there are constructive criticisms of his analysis, including his zealous separation of autobiographical and historical memory and his anguished conceptualisation of family and peasantry. In addition, and perhaps more importantly, as Connerton (2004: 39) demonstrates, Halbwachs pays little attention to the 'characteristics of transfer' between individual and collective memory.

2. Lifton (1968: 518), as discussed in the Introduction.

26. VALUES OF CITIZENSHIP

1. I discuss this survey in Simpson (2007).
2. This structure was originally built outside the old town to allow Sunni Muslims to come together in annual prayer in order to escape the social divisions which characterised their daily lives.

27. ALL IS GOOD?

1. Recent historians such as Goldberg (1989), Larsen (2006), Paice (2008), Shrady (2009) and Wootton (2000) contribute to placing the Lisbon earthquake and its debates in proper context. Kendrick (1955) remains the classic account of the English sources; Brown (1991: 23–55) is succinct on the philosophical response to the disaster.
2. Originally published in 1697 (Bayle 1826).
3. Originally published in 1710 (Leibniz 2009).
4. Originally published in 1734 (Pope 1994).
5. Originally published in 1765 (de Beausobre 1758).
6. Quoted in Kendrick (1955: 18).
7. See the work of Rozario (2007) and Van de Wetering (1982).
8. See Bode's brilliant analysis (Bode 1989: 251–441).
9. Voltaire, 'Poem on the Lisbon disaster; or an examination of the axiom "All is well"', written in 1756 (Voltaire 1912: 255–63).
10. Kendrick (1955: 184). I have drawn on Kendrick's work in the following paragraphs; also see Wootton (2000: 95–122) on the context of the debate between Rousseau and Voltaire.
11. This is a point well made by Russell Dynes (2005), one of the pioneers of modern disaster research.
12. Voltaire (1912: 263).

28. EXPLANATION

1. Paice (2008).

29. INHABITATION

1. See the report *In bad faith? British charity and Hindu extremism*. London: AWAZZ, South Asian Watch Ltd, 2004.
2. *Terrorism and community relations: Sixth report of session 2004–05: Vol. 3 Oral and additional written evidence*. House of Commons papers 165–III 2004–05. Norwich: Stationery Office, 2005.
3. Mukta (2000) offers an analysis of the display at the temple in Neasden and some of the things she heard guides tell visitors. She also shows how BAPS directly furthers the cause of what she calls the 'Hindu right' in the UK.
4. See, e.g., Barakat and Zyck (2011) on Lebanon; and Jennifer Barenstein. *Housing reconstruction in post-earthquake Gujarat. A comparative analysis*. Humanitarian Practice Network Paper. London: Overseas Development Institute, 2006.
5. Here I have in mind participation in the design and function of a village overall rather than the features of individual houses.

284

6. For a clear articulation of this view, see Boana (2009) on housing reconstruction in Sri Lanka following the tsunami of 2004.

7. This is the view of Pieterse (2001); see also Jennifer Duyne. 'Challenges and risks in post-tsunami housing reconstruction in Tamil Nadu', *Humanitarian Exchange*, 33: 35–36, 2006.

8. See the argument and concluding literature review of Teddy Boen and Rohit Jigyasu. 'Cultural considerations for post disaster reconstruction post-tsunami challenges', *Asian Disaster Management News*, 11(2): 10–11, 2005.

9. A compatible conclusion is reached by Sanderson at al., who surveyed some of the housing constructed in Gujarat ten years on and concluded: 'good post-disaster housing is a product of three factors: durability, i.e. it can withstand future shocks and stresses to a reasonable degree; adaptability, considering the wider and longer-term concerns regarding materials used, ownership and usage; and finally, people, i.e. the active engagement and interest of those for whom the houses are intended' (Sanderson et al. 2011: 14).

30. SHOCKS OF COLONIALISM

1. See 'Treaties, Agreements, etc., Entered into Between the Honourable East India Company and the Kutch State, between 26th of October 1816 and 8th of October 1851', in *Selections from the Bombay Records of the Bombay Government*, No. 15 (new series). Bombay: Bombay Education Society's Press, 1855. For a more detailed account of the politics of the treaties with Kutch during this period, see McLeod (2007) and Rushbrook Williams (1958).

2. The account is provided by Burnes (2004 [1829]: 59), based on conversations with a Major Noble who accompanied the mission from Anjar to Bhuj.

3. Burnes (2004 [1829]: 66).

4. Perhaps he was enjoying an aperitif at the earthquake moment. We know from his diaries (Ghosh 1977) he enjoyed a glass of wine in the evening. MacMurdo does not say, but the time and his mood were right.

5. Ibid.: 92.

6. Ibid.: 98.

7. Ibid.: 99–100; this significant point is also made by Captain Ballantyne, who arrived in Anjar from Bhuj the day after the earthquake ('Extracts from letters of Captain Ballantyne, Agent in Kattiwar for his H.S. the Guicwar, concerning the earthquake', attached as an appendix to MacMurdo 1820: 111).

8. Ibid.: 102.

9. Ibid.: 103.

10. Letter dated 17 June 1819 (British Library, India Office Records, F/4/620).

11. Postans (1839: 59).

12. MacMurdo (1820: 106).

13. Ibid.: 106.

14. Postans (1839: 88–89).

15. Petition from Mohamed Saleh Kazee of Ahmedabad (British Library, India Office Records, F/4/620).

16. Rushbrook Williams (1958: 212).

17. Rushbrook Williams (1958: 232).

18. Burnes (2004 [1829]: 72).

19. A translation of a letter from Aanandjee Narrainjee to Seth Hansraj of Mandvi to the chief secretary to the government in Bombay on 1 May 1820 simply states: 'Captain MacMurdo marched from Hakwad to Teiker (or Leiker) where the whole of the remaining villages were settled with, and marching from there came to Warrarwar where he died about 10 or half past 10 o'clock am. Melancholy indeed is the circumstance but the will of God be done' (Maharashtra State Archive, Mumbai, Political Department, 1820–1821, *Mixed Volumes*, Vol. 25/1).

20. MacMurdo's mausoleum remains reasonably well cared for. Debris in and around the site suggest that offerings continue to be made there on a regular basis.

21. The words are taken from an inscription Postans suggests could be found near all five gates of the city. I know it to be present in the heavily fortified tower adjacent to MacMurdo's bungalow. 'After the worship of Guneesa and Ashapura, then be honour to Hujeepal and Mahadeo-raee. In the year of Vicram, 1875, in the month Jet, on the ninth of the dark half, an earthquake happened, at which time the fort of Anjar was destroyed; but during the minority of the illustrious Maharaj Rao Daisulijee, the Regency ordered its re-erection; and in the beginning of the month Assar, in the year of Vicram, 1882, the work was commenced, the subjects were made happy, and the city was rendered flourishing' (Postans 1839: 84).

22. 'The holy city of Anjar was struck by an earth quake on the ninth day of the dark half of the month Jyeshtha (June 16, 1819) when the bastion Verisal kotho, the armoury, the shelf to keep cannons and the compound collapsed. Instructed by the King of Kings, Mehta Morarji Ladha Manager of Anjar, with the help and ideas of master mason Devraj Hirji of Bhuj and architect Lal Limbani of Anjar, completed reconstruction work on Monday the 5th day of the bright half of the first month of Jyestha'.

23. The 'angel of destruction' is from Postans (1839: 97).

24. MacMurdo (1820: 104).

25. Postans (1839: 85).

31. EARTHQUAKE DIASPORA

1. Bilham (1999) has built up an archive of material related to the 1819 earthquake, combining literary and geological evidence.

2. Burnes (1835).

3. Locusts and drought visited Kutch in 1811 and 1812 (Carnac 1819: 296–303). The resulting crop shortage reduced the population of Kutch by half (Anon. 1880: 40). In 1813, Kutch was infested with bubonic plague. In 1819, there was an outbreak of cholera, followed by famine, pestilence and intestinal boils (LeGrand 1856: 448). In 1819, as we know, a horrid earthquake struck, which was accompanied by what was probably a small tsunami. In 1823, further crop failures and rumours of an invasion from Sindh contributed to the reduction of the population (Anon. 1880: 165). In 1824, there was drought and famine (Masselos 1996: 29–32). Throughout the 1840s and 1850s, there were further crop failures and infestations of pests, which continued intermittently until the turn of the twentieth century.

32. NEHRU'S VILLAGE (TWICE)

1. '3,365 houses wrecked', *Times of India*, 9 August 1956, p. 1.

286

2. 'Prompt steps to aid "quake-stricken": RS. 75,000 sanctioned by Kutch govt', ibid., 5 August 1956, p. 10.
3. 'Slow pace of relief work in Kutch: Official machinery blamed', ibid., 30 July 1956, p. 1.
4. 'Prompt steps to aid "quake-stricken": RS. 75,000 sanctioned by Kutch govt', ibid., 5 August 1956, p. 10. On Rajkot prisoners (in Sabarmati Jail in Ahmedabad), see 'Prisoners' donation', ibid., 24 August 1956, p. 5.
5. Untitled article, ibid., 22 August 1956, p. 3.
6. Untitled classified advertisement, ibid., 23 October 1956, p. 2.
7. 'Constructing buildings in quake zones: Call to devise suitable designs', ibid., 13 September 1956, p. 3.
8. 'Houses will be quake-proof: Anjar re-building', ibid., 29 November 1956, p. 5.
9. 'Mr. Nehru visits Anjar town: Quake victims assured permanent resettlement', ibid., 19 August 1956, p. 1.
10. 'Opposition parties fomenting trouble: Mr. Nehru's charge: Call to eschew violence', ibid., 20 August 1956, p. 1.
11. 'Rehabilitation centre', ibid., 20 August 1956, p. 7.
12. 'Help from all parts of country and abroad made construction of self-contained unit possible', ibid., 5 July 1958, p. 8.
13. 'The changing face of Kutch: Trade revival pressed', ibid., 15 July 1958, pp. 6 and 11.
14. 'RS. 30–lakh plan submitted: Loans and subsidies', ibid., 30 July 1956, p. 1.

33. PLANNING TO FORGET

1. Letter from Group 2001 to the chief minister of Gujarat, dated 16 March 2001 (copy in possession of this author).
2. See Chatelain et al. (2008: 818).
3. See Rastogi et al. (2011: 67). The paper was presented at a high-profile international symposium on the 'Bhuj earthquake' held in Gandhinagar in 2011. The event was endorsed by the chief minister of Gujarat. The abstract is readily available online, although the main body of the paper is behind a pay wall. I have not been able to find a single reference to this paper in the press in Gujarat. GSDMA granted permission for the publication of the paper.

34. MEMORY

1. This story is documented by Oliver-Smith (1986).
2. A wonderful example is given by the historian K.S. Inglis (1992), who shows how a monument in Cambridge, England, which was originally constructed to mark victory in war has been gradually transformed into a memorial to those who died in war.
3. An argument spelled out at length in Simpson and Corbridge (2006).
4. Winter (1995: 50–53).

AFTERWORD

1. Maurice Blanchot (2005: 3), as quoted at the start of Section 7.
2. I thank Maria Paz Peirano for pointing this out, and for introducing me to the work of Jose Luis Torres Leiva, Sebastian Lelio, Nicolas Lopez, Leopoldo Castedo and others.

3. Just before the earthquake, similar rumours of Hindu victimhood were recorded at the BAPS (Bochasanwasi Shri Akshar Purushottam Swaminarayan Sanstha) temple in London. Since its inception in the early nineteenth century, the Swaminarayan movement (of which BAPS is a splinter) has campaigned for the abolition of female infanticide in western India. A guide at the temple's exhibition is reported as having explained the practice as a way of saving girls from kidnap by Muslims. On this issue, see Mukta (2000: 462), and Bhatt and Mukta (2000) for general context. In fact, historical literature conclusively demonstrates that infanticide was a method that elite Hindu castes deployed to avoid the high cost of dowry payments associated with getting girls married. The literature on the topic is significant. Notable nineteenth-century sources include Cave-Brown (1857), Morr (1811) and Wilson (1855); more recent literature by Indian scholars includes Mehta (1966) and Nath (1973).

4. I have in mind Edgar Morin's (1971) classic study of rumour in Orleans, where paranoia and hysteria combine to make tales of unpleasant things in the face of alienating social change.

REFERENCES

Adams, Vincanne, Taslim van Hattum and Diana English. 2009. 'Chronic disaster syndrome: Displacement, disaster capitalism, and the eviction of the poor from New Orleans'. *American Ethnologist*, 36 (4): 615–36.

Agarwal, Sanjay. 2010. *Daan and other giving traditions in India: The hidden pot of gold*. New Delhi: AccountAid.

Ahmad, Imtiaz. 2002. 'The state of lies and the lies of the state'. In M.L. Sondhi and Apratim Mukarji (eds), *The black book of Gujarat*, pp. 37–46. New Delhi: Manak Publications.

Ahmad, Riaz. 2002. 'Gujarat violence: Meaning and implications'. *Economic and Political Weekly*, 37 (20): 1870–3.

Albala-Bertrand, J.M. 1993. *Political economy of large natural disasters: With special reference to developing countries*. Oxford: Clarendon Press.

Anon. 1880. *Gazetteer of the Bombay Presidency*, Vol. 5: *Cutch, Palanpur, Mahi Kantha*. Bombay: Government Central Press.

Antani, Naresh. 2005. *Kachchh kala ane ithias: Lekha sangraha* [Kutch art and history: Collection of essays]. Bhuj: Srimati Ila Naresh.

Baird, Forrest E., and Walter Kaufmann. 2008. *From Plato to Derrida*. Upper Saddle River, NJ: Pearson Prentice Hall.

Balachandran, B.R. 2010. 'Planning the reconstruction of Bhuj'. In Shirish Patel and Aromar Revi (eds), *Recovering from earthquakes: Response, reconstruction and impact mitigation in India*, pp. 159–203. New Delhi: Routledge.

Banerjee, Sumanta. 2002. 'Gujarat carnage and a cynical democracy'. *Economic and Political Weekly*, 37 (18): 1707–8.

Barakat, Sultan, and Steven A. Zyck. 2011. 'Housing reconstruction as socio-economic recovery and state building: Evidence from southern Lebanon'. *Housing Studies*, 26 (1): 133–54.

Baudrillard, Jean. 2008 [1990]. *Fatal strategies*. Cambridge, MA: MIT Press.

Bayle, Pierre. 1826 [1697]. *An historical and critical dictionary (selected and abridged)*. London: Hunt and Clarke.

Berenschot, Ward. 2011. *Riot politics: Hindu–Muslim violence and the Indian state*. London: Hurst.

Bergson, Henri. 2004 [1896]. *Matter and memory*. Mineola: Dover Publications.

Bhatt, Chetan, and Parita Mukta. 2000. 'Hindutva in the West: Mapping the antinomies of globalization'. *Ethnic and Racial Studies*, 23 (3): 407–41.

Bilham, Roger. 1999. 'Slip parameters for the Rann of Kachchh, India, 16 June 1819, earthquake, quantified from contemporary accounts'. In I.S. Stewart and C. Vita-Finzi (eds), *Coastal tectonics*, pp. 295–318. London: Geological Society.

Blanchot, Maurice. 2005. *The writing of the disaster* (trans. Ann Smock). Lincoln: University of Nebraska Press.

Boana, Camillo. 2009. 'Housing anxiety and multiple geographies in post-tsunami Sri Lanka'. *Disasters*, 33 (4): 762–85.

Bode, Barbara. 1989. *No bells to toll: Destruction and creation in the Andes*. New York: Scribners.

Bourdieu, Pierre. 1984. *Homo academicus*. Stanford: Stanford University Press.

Bourdieu, Pierre, and Loïs Wacquant. 2004. 'Symbolic violence'. In Nancy Scheper-Hughes and Philippe Bourgois (eds), *Violence in war and peace: An anthology*, pp. 272–4. Oxford: Blackwell.

Breman, Jan. 2004. *The making and unmaking of an industrial working class: Sliding down the labour hierarchy in Ahmedabad, India*. New Delhi: Oxford University Press.

Brown, Robert H. 1991. *Nature's hidden terror: Violent nature imagery in eighteenth-century literature*. London: Camden House.

Burnes, Alexander. 1835. 'A memoir on the eastern branch of the river Indus giving an account of the alterations produced to it by an earthquake in 1819, also a theory of the Runn, and some conjectures on the route of Alexander the Great, drawn up in the years 1827–28'. *Journal of the Royal Asiatic Society*, 3: 550–88.

Burnes, James. 2004 [1829]. *Sketch of the history of Cutch from its first connexion with the British Government in India to the conclusion of the treaty of 1819*. New Delhi: Asian Education Servies.

Burton, Richard Francis. 1851. *Sindh, and the races that inhabit the valley of the Indus*. London: W.H. Allen.

Carnac, J.R. 1819. 'Some account of the famine in Gujerat in the years 1812 and 1813'. *Transactions of the Bombay Literary Society*, 1: 296–303.

Cave-Browne, John. 1857. *Indian infanticide: Its origin, progress, and suppression*. London: W.H. Allen.

Chatelain, Jean-Luc, Bertrand Guiller and Imtiyaz A. Parvez. 2008. 'False site effects: The Anjar case, following the 2001 Bhuj (India) earthquake'. *Seismological Research Letters*, 79 (6): 816–19.

Chatterji, Angana P. 2009. *Violent gods: Hindu nationalism in India's present—narratives from Orissa*. New Delhi: Three Essays Collective.

Chirol, V. 1921. *India old and new*. London: Macmillan.

Connerton, Paul. 2004 [1989]. *How societies remember*. Cambridge: Cambridge University Press.

———2011. *The spirit of mourning: History, memory and the body*. Cambridge: Cambridge University Press.

Copeman, Jacob. 2011. 'The gift and its forms of life in contemporary India'. *Modern Asian Studies*, 45 (5): 1051–94.

———2013. 'The art of bleeding: Memory, martyrdom, and portraits in blood'. *Journal of the Royal Anthropological Institute*, 19 (special issue): S149–S171.

Das, Veena. 2007. *Life and words: Violence and the descent into the ordinary*. Berkeley: University of California Press.

Das, Veena, and Arthur Kleinman. 2001. 'Introduction'. In Veena Das (ed.), *Remaking the world: Violence, social suffering and recovery*, pp. 1–30. Berkeley: University of California Press.

Das, Veena, and Deborah Poole. 2004. 'State and its margins: Comparative ethnographies'. In Veena Das and Deborah Poole (eds), *Anthropology in the margins of the state*, pp. 3–34. Oxford: James Currey.

Dave, T.N. 1942. 'Linguistic survey of the borderlands of Gujarat'. *Journal of the Gujarat Research Society*, 4 (4): 262–72.

Davis, F. 1979. *Yearning for yesterday: A sociology of nostalgia*. New York: Free Press.

de Alwis, Malathi, and Eva-Lotta Hedman. 2009. *Tsunami in a time of war: Aid, activism and reconstruction in Sri Lanka and Aceh*. Colombo: International Centre for Ethnic Studies.

de Beausobre, Louis. 1758 [1765]. *Essai sur le bonheur, or reflexions philosophiques sur les biens et les maux de la vie humaine*. Amsterdam: J.H. Schneider.

Debroy, Bibek. 2012. *Gujarat: Governance for growth and development*. New Delhi: Academic Foundation.

Desai, Radhika. 2003. *Slouching towards Ayodhya: From Congress to Hindutva in Indian Politics*. New Delhi: Three Essays Collective.

Dilipsinhji, K.S. 2004. *Kutch in festival and custom*. New Delhi: Har-Anand Publications.

Dirks, N.B. 2001. *Castes of mind: Colonialism and the making of modern India*. Princeton: Princeton University Press.

d'Souza, Rohan. 2006. *Drowned and dammed: Colonial capitalism and flood control in eastern India*. New Delhi: Oxford University Press.

Duncan, D. 1908. *Life and letters of Herbert Spencer*. New York: Appleton and Co.

Dynes, Russell R. 2005. 'The Lisbon Earthquake of 1755: The first modern disaster'. In Theodore E.D. Braun and John B. Radner (eds), *The Lisbon Earthquake of 1755: Representations and reactions*, pp. 34–49. Oxford: Voltaire Foundation.

Fassin, Didier. 2012. *Humanitarian reason: A moral history of the present*. Berkeley: University of California Press.

Fassin, Didier and Richard Rechtman. 2009. *The empire of trauma: An inquiry into the condition of victimhood*. Princeton: Princeton University Press.

Ferguson, James. 1990. *Anti-politics machine: Development, depoliticization, and bureaucratic power in Lesotho*. Cambridge: Cambridge University Press.

Fischer-Tiné, Harald. 2007. 'Indian Nationalism and the "world forces": Transnational and diasporic dimensions of the Indian freedom movement on the eve of the First World War'. *Journal of Global History*, 2 (3): 325–44.

Foucault, Michel. 1972. *The archaeology of knowledge, and the discourse on language* (trans. A. Sheridan Smith). New York: Pantheon.

Freud, Sigmund. 1917. 'Mourning and melancholia'. In *On the history of the psycho-analytic movement, papers on metapsychology and other works*, pp. 237–58. London: Hogarth Press.

———1924. 'The aetiology of hysteria'. In *Collected papers*, Vol. 1: *Early papers, On the history of the psycho-analytic movement*, pp. 183–219. London: Hogarth Press.

Ghassem-Fachandi, Parvis. 2012. *Pogrom in Gujarat: Hindu nationalism and anti-national violence in India*. Princeton: Princeton University Press.

Ghosh, Suresh Chandra. 1977. *The peninsula of Gujarat in the early nineteenth century*. New Delhi: Sterling Publishers.

Goldberg, Rita. 1989. 'Voltaire, Rousseau, and the Lisbon Earthquake'. *Eighteenth Century Life*, 13 (2): 1–20.

Gupta, Dipankar. 2002. 'Limits of tolerance: Prospects of secularism in India after Gujarat'. *Economic and Political Weekly*, 37 (46): 4615–20.

Gupta, Hari Ram. 1969. *The Kutch affair*. Delhi: U.C. Kapur.

Gupta, L.C., M.C. Gupta, Anil Sinha and Vinod K. Sharma. 2002. *Gujarat earthquake 26ᵗʰ of January, 2001*. New Delhi: National Centre for Disaster Management.

Hacking, Ian. 1990. *The taming of chance*. Cambridge: Cambridge University Press.

Halbwachs, Maurice. 1980. *The collective memory* (trans. F.J. Ditter and V.Y. Ditter). New York: Harper and Collins.

———1992. *On collective memory* (trans. L.A. Coser). Chicago: University of Chicago Press.

Hansen, Thomas Blom. 1999. *The saffron wave: Democracy and Hindu nationalism in modern India*. Princeton: Princeton University Press.

———2007. *Wages of violence*: Naming and identity in postcolonial Bombay. Princeton: Princeton University Press.

Harvey, David. 2007. *A brief history of neo-liberalism*. Oxford: Oxford University Press.

Hastrup, Frida. 2011. *Weathering the world: Recovery in the wake of the tsunami in a Tamil fishing village*. Oxford: Berghahn.

Ibrahim, Farhana. 2009. *Settlers, saints and sovereigns: An ethnography of state formation in western India*. New Delhi: Routledge.

Inglis, K.S. 1992. 'The homecoming: The War Memorial Movement in Cambridge, England'. *Journal of Contemporary History*, 27 (4): 583–605.

Jadia, P. 1999. *Kachchh: An introduction to the historical places, embroideries, arts and crafts etc. of Kachchh*. Bhuj: Radhey Screen Printing.

Jaffrelot, Christophe. 1996. *The Hindu nationalist movement and Indian politics, 1925 to the 1990s*. London: Hurst.

Jasani, Rubina. 2007. 'Violence, reconstruction and Islamic reform: stories from the Muslim "ghetto"'. *Modern Asian Studies*, 42 (2/3): 431–56.

Jasanoff, Sheila. 2010. 'Beyond calculation: A democratic response to risk'. In Andrew Lakoff (ed.), *Disaster and the politics of intervention*, pp. 14–41. Columbia: Columbia University Press.

Jethi, P.J. 2008. *Kutch: People and their handicrafts*. Bhuj: Nayana P. Jethi.

Kant, Immanuel. 2007 [1952]. *Critique of judgement* (trans. James Creed Meredith). Oxford: Oxford University Press.

Kapila, Shruti. 2007. 'Self, Spencer, swaraj: Nationalist thought and critiques of Liberalism, 1890–1920'. *Modern Intellectual History*, 4 (1): 109–27.

Kendrick, T.D. 1955. *The Lisbon earthquake*. New York: Lippincott.

Klein, Ira. 1984. 'When the rains failed: Famine, relief, and mortality in British India'. *Indian Economic and Social History Review*, 21 (2): 185–214.

Klein, Naomi. 2007. *The shock doctrine: The rise of disaster capitalism*. New York: Metropolitan Books.

Kodrich, Kris, and Melinda Laituri. 2005. 'The formation of a disaster community in cyber-space: The role of online news media after the 2001 Gujarat Earthquake'. *Convergence*, 11 (3): 40–56.

Laidlaw, James. 1995. *Riches and renunciation: Religion, economy, and society among the Jains*. Oxford: Clarendon Press.

Larsen, Svend Erik. 2006. 'The Lisbon Earthquake and the scientific turn in Kant's philoso-phy'. *European Review*, 14 (3): 359–67.

Lecy, Jesse D. 2005. 'Aid effectiveness after the Gujarat Earthquake: A case study of disaster relief'. *Journal of Development and Social Transformation*, 4: 5–15.

Lefebvre, Henri. 1991 [1947]. *The critique of everyday life*. London: Verso.

LeGrand, Jacob George. 1856. 'Historical, geographical, and statistical memoirs on the province of Kattywar; and on the districts of Babriawar and Okhamundul; also a report on the iron of Kattywar'. In *Selections from the Records of the Bombay Government*, 37 (new series), pp. 1–108. Bombay: Bombay Education Society's Press.

Leibniz, G.W. 2009 [1710]. *Theodicy: Essays on the goodness of God, the freedom of man and the origin of evil*. London: Cosimo.

Lerner, L. 1972. *The uses of nostalgia: Studies in pastoral poetry*. London: Chatto and Windus.

Li, Tanya Murray. 2007. *The will to improve: Governmentality, development, and the practice of politics*. Durham, NC: Duke University Press.

Lifton, Robert Jay. 1968. *Death in life: The survivors of Hiroshima*. London: Weidenfeld and Nicolson.

Lumsden, J.G. 1855 [1843]. 'Observations by Mr J.G. Lumsden, Political Agent in Kutch, explanatory of the principles on which an annexed map of that province has been prepared by him, showing the possessions of His Highness the Rao and the dependent chiefs, &c. in Kutch'. In *Selections from the Records of the Bombay Government*, 15 (new series), pp. 187–96, map. Bombay: Education Society's Press.

Lyotard, Jean-François. 1994. *Lessons on the analytic of the sublime: Kant's critique of judgment* (trans. Elizabeth Rottenberg). Stanford: Stanford University Press.

MacMurdo, James. 1820. 'Papers relating to the earthquake which occurred in India in 1819'. *Transactions of the Literary Society of Bombay*, 3: 90–116.

Majumdar, D.N. 1940. *Race elements in cultural Gujarat*. Lucknow: Gujarat Research Society.

Masselos, Jim. 1996. 'Migration and urban identity: Bombay's famine refugees'. In Sujata Patel and Alice Thorner (eds), *Bombay: Mosaic of modern culture*, pp. 25–58. Bombay: Oxford University Press.

Mathur, Shubh. 2008. *The everyday life of Hindu nationalism: An ethnographic report*. New Delhi: Three Essays Collective.

Mauss, Marcel. 1990 [1922]. *The gift: Forms and functions of exchange in archaic societies* (trans. W.D. Halls). London: Routledge.

McLeod, John. 2007. '"A numerous, illiterate, and irresponsible Bhayat": The Maharaos of Kutch, their nobles and the British Paramount Power, 1816–1947'. *Journal of Imperial and Commonwealth History*, 35 (3): 371–91.

Mehta, Makrand. 1966. 'A study of the practice of female infanticide among the Kanbis of Gujarat'. *Journal of the Gujarat Research Society*, 28 (1–4/109–112): 57–66.

Merli, Claudia. 2010. 'Context-bound Islamic theodicies: The tsunami as supernatural retribution versus natural catastrophe in southern Thailand'. *Religion*, 40 (2): 104–11.

Middleton, Neil. 1998. *Disaster and development: The politics of humanitarian aid*. London: Pluto.

Mill, John Stuart. 1848. *Principles of political economy, with some of their applications to social philosophy*. London: J.W. Parker.

Mishra, Satish. 2002. 'Gujarat: A case study of the tyranny of power'. In M.L. Sondhi and Apratim Mukarji (eds), *The black book of Gujarat*, pp. 79–86. New Delhi: Manak Publications.

Morin, Edgar. 1971. *Rumour in Orleans*. New York: Pantheon Books.

Morr, Edward. 1811. *Hindu infanticide: An account of the measures adopted for suppressing the practice of the systematic murder by their parents of female infants; with incidental remarks on other customs peculiar to the natives of India.* London: Johnson & Co.

Mosse, David. 2004. *Cultivating development: An ethnography of aid policy and practice.* London: Pluto.

Mukta, Parita. 2000. 'The public face of Hindu nationalism'. *Ethnic and Racial Studies,* 23 (3): 442–66.

Nath, Viswa. 1973. 'Female infanticide and the Lewa Kanbis of Gujarat in the nineteenth century'. *Indian Economic and Social History Review,* 10 (4): 386–404.

Nora, Pierre. 1989. 'Between memory and history: *Les lieux de mémoire*'. *Representations,* 26: 7–25.

Ogilvy, T. 1855 [1834]. 'Miscelleneous information connected with Kutch; furnished to Mr Ogilvy, Political Agent in that province, on the 17th November 1850, by His Highness the Rao'. In *Selections from the Records of the Bombay Government,* 15 (new series), pp. 197–208. Bombay: Education Society's Press.

Oliver-Smith, Anthony. 1986. *The martyred city: Death and rebirth in the Andes.* Albuquerque: University of New Mexico Press.

———1996. 'Anthropological research on hazards and disasters'. *Annual Review of Anthropology,* 25: 303–28.

Oliver-Smith, Anthony and Susanna M. Hoffman (eds). 1999. *The angry earth: Disaster in anthropological perspective.* New York: Routledge.

———2002. 'Introduction: Why anthropologists should study disasters'. In Susanna M. Hoffman and Anthony Oliver-Smith (eds), *Catastrophe and culture: The anthropology of disaster.* pp. 3–22. Oxford: James Currey.

Paice, Edward. 2008. *Wrath of god: The great Lisbon earthquake of 1755.* London: Quercus.

Panda, Smita Mishra. 2002. 'Kutchch Nav Nirman Abhiyan: An evolving network of NGOs in Gujarat, India'. *Gender, Technology and Development,* 6 (2): 313–17.

Pandya, Vishnu. 1985. *Pandit Shyamji Krishnavarma.* Rajkot: Praveen Pushtak Bundar.

Pandya, Vishnu and Arati Pandya. 2003 [1997]. *Azadi jangnu patrakaratva: Landanma Indian Sociologist* [Journalism of the Freedom Struggle: *Indian Sociologist* in London]. Ahmedabad: Samantar Prakashan.

Parry, Jonathan P. 1994. *Death in Benares.* Cambridge: Cambridge University Press.

Patel, Girish. 2002. 'Narendra Modi's one-day cricket: What and why?' *Economic and Political Weekly,* 37 (48): 4826–37.

Peel, J.D.Y. 1971. *Herbert Spencer: The evolution of a sociologist.* New York: Basic Books.

Pereira, Alvaro S. 2009. 'The opportunity of disaster: The economic impact of the 1755 Lisbon earthquake'. *Journal of Economic History,* 69 (2): 466–99.

Petryna, Adriana. 2002. *Life exposed: Biological citizens after Chernobyl.* Princeton: Princeton University Press.

Pieterse, N.J. 2001. *Development theory deconstructions/reconstructions.* London: Sage.

Pocock, David. 1973. *Mind, body and wealth: A study of belief and practice in an Indian village.* Oxford: Blackwell.

Polman, Linda. 2011. *The crisis caravan: What's wrong with humanitarian aid?.* London: Picador.

Pope, Alexander. 1994 [1734]. *Essay on man and other poems.* New York: Dover Thrift Editions.

Postans, Marianna. 1839. *Cutch or random sketches taken during a residence in one of the northern provinces of western India interspersed with legends and traditions.* London: Smith, Elder and Co.

Prakash, Aseem. 2003. 'Re-imagination of the state and Gujarat's electoral verdict'. *Economic and Political Weekly*, 38 (16): 1601–10.

Raheja, Gloria. 1988. *The poison in the gift: Ritual, prestation, and the dominant caste in a North Indian village*. Chicago: University of Chicago Press.

————1996. 'Caste, colonialism and the speech of the colonised: Entextualisation and disciplinary control in India'. *American Ethnologist*, 23 (3): 494–513.

Raikes, S.N. 1855. 'Memoir and brief notes relative to the Kutch State'. In *Selections from the Records of the Bombay Government*, 15 (new series), pp. 1–88. Bombay: Education Society's Press.

Rastogi, B.K., A.P. Singh, B. Sairam, S.K. Jain, F. Kaneko, S. Segawa, and J. Matsuo. 2011. 'The possibility of site effects: The Anjar case, following past earthquakes in Gujarat, India'. *Seismological Research Letters*, 82 (1): 59–68.

Rathod, R.S. 1949. *Kachchhnu Sanskruti darshan* [Introduction to the culture of Kutch]. Ahmedabad: N.S. Mandir.

Ravi Priya, Kumar. 2004. '"Survivors" suffering and healing amidst changing socioeconomic forces in two years of post-earthquake Kachchh'. *Psychology in Developing Societies*, 16 (1): 41–60.

Ray, C.N. 2005. 'A note on the Disaster Management Bill, 2005'. *Economic and Political Weekly*, 40 (47): 4877–9, 4881.

Ray, Gene. 2004. 'Reading the Lisbon Earthquake: Adorno, Lyotard, and the contemporary sublime'. *Yale Journal of Criticism*, 17 (1): 1–18.

Reddy, L.R. 2001. *The pain and the horror: Gujarat earthquake*. New Delhi: APH.

Riccio, Bruno, Chiara Brambilla and Mara Benadusi (eds). 2011. *Disasters, development and humanitarian aid: New challenges for anthropology*. Rimini: Guaraldi.

Rossi, Ino. 1993. *Community reconstruction after an earthquake: Dialectical sociology in action*. Westport, CT: Praeger.

Roy, Tirthankar. 2008. 'State, society and market in the aftermath of natural disasters in colonial India: A preliminary exploration'. *Indian Economic Social History Review*, 45 (2): 261–94.

Rozario, Kevin. 2007. *The culture of calamity: Disaster and the making of modern America*. Chicago: University of Chicago Press.

Rushbrook Williams, L.F. 1958. *The black hills: Kutch in history and legend: A study in Indian local loyalties*. London: Weidenfeld and Nicolson.

Sachdev, V., and G. Tillotson. 2002. *Building Jaipur: The making of an Indian city*. New Delhi: Oxford University Press.

Samuels, Annemarie. 2012. 'Remaking neighbourhoods in Banda Aceh: Post-tsunami reconstruction of everyday life'. In Matthew Clarke, Ismet Fanany and Sue Kenny (eds), *Post-disaster reconstruction: Lessons from Aceh*, pp. 210–23. London: Earthscan.

Sanderson, David, Anshu Sharma and Juliet Anderson. 2011. 'NGO permanent housing 10 years after the Gujarat earthquake: revisiting the FICCI–CARE Gujarat rehabilitation programme'. *Environment and Urbanization*, 24 (1): 1–15.

Sarkar, Sumit. 1999. 'Christianity, Hindutva and the question of conversions'. In K.N. Panikkar (ed.), *The concerned Indian's guide to communalism*, pp. 215–44. New Delhi: Viking.

Sarkar, Tanika. 2002. 'Semiotics of terror: Muslim children and women in Hindu Rashtra'. *Economic and Political Weekly*, 37 (28): 2872–6.

Schmitt, Carl. 1985 [1922]. *Political theology: Four chapters on the concept of sovereignty* (trans. G. Schwab). Cambridge, MA: MIT Press.

Schopenhauer, Arthur. 1969 [1818]. *The world as will and representation* (trans. E.F.J. Payne). New York: Dover Publications.

Scott, James. 1999. *Seeing like a state: How certain schemes to improve the human condition have failed.* New Haven: Yale University Press.

Shah, A.M. 2006. '*The Indian Sociologist*, 1905–14, 1920–22'. *Economic and Political Weekly*, 41 (31): 3435–9.

Shah, Ghanshyam. 1987. 'Middle class politics: Case of anti-reservation agitations in Gujarat'. *Economic and Political Weekly*, 22 (19–21): AN155–AN161, AN163, AN165, AN167, AN169–AN172.

————2002. 'Contestation and negotiations: Hindutva sentiments and temporal interests in Gujarat elections'. *Economic and Political Weekly*, 37 (48): 4838–43.

Shodhan, Amrita. 2001. *A question of community: Religious groups and colonial law.* Kolkata: Samya.

Shrady, Nicholas. 2009. *The last day: Wrath, ruin and reason in the Great Lisbon Earthquake of 1755.* London: Penguin.

Shylendra, H.S. 2001. 'Are earthquake deaths overestimated? Assessment for Kutch villages'. *Economic and Political Weekly*, 36 (9): 722–3.

Simpson, Edward. 2007. 'State of play six years after Gujarat earthquake'. *Economic and Political Weekly*, 42 (11): 932–7.

————2011. *Society and history of Gujarat since 1800: A select bibliography of the English and European language sources.* New Delhi: Orient Blackswan.

Simpson, Edward and Stuart Corbridge. 2006. 'The geography of things that may become memories: The 2001 earthquake in Kachchh-Gujarat and the politics of rehabilitation in the pre-memorial era'. *Annals of the Association of American Geographers*, 96 (2): 566–85.

Solnit, Rebecca. 2010. *A paradise built in hell: The extraordinary communities that arise in disasters.* London: Penguin.

Sondhi, M.L., and A. Mukarji (eds). 2002. *The black book of Gujarat.* New Delhi: Manak.

Sorokin, Pitirim. 1942. *Man and society in calamity: The effects of war, revolution, famine, pestilence upon human mind, behaviour, social organisation and cultural life.* New York: Dutton.

Spencer, Herbert. 1873. *The study of sociology.* New York: Appleton & Co.

————1884. *The principles of ethics*, Vol. 2. London: Williams and Norgate.

Spodek, Howard. 1971. 'On the origins of Gandhi's political methodology: The heritage of Kathiawad and Gujarat'. *Journal of Asian Studies*, 30 (2): 361–72.

————1972. '"Injustice to Saurashtra": A case study of regional tensions and harmonies in India'. *Asian Survey*, 12 (5): 416–28.

Standing, Guy, Jeemol Unni, Renana Jhabvala and Uma Rani. 2010. *Social income and insecurity: A study in Gujarat.* New Delhi: Routledge.

Sud, Nikita. 2007. 'From land to the tiller to land liberalisation: The political economy of Gujarat's shifting land policy'. *Modern Asian Studies*, 41 (3): 603–38.

————2009. 'The Indian state in a liberalizing landscape'. *Development and Change*, 40 (4): 645–65.

————2012. *Liberalization, Hindu nationalism, and the State: A biography of Gujarat.* New Delhi: Oxford University Press.

Sukheswala, R.N. 1948. 'Geological evolution of Maha-Gujarat'. *Journal of the Gujarat Research Society*, 10 (2): 53–79.

Tambs-Lyche, Harald. 1997. *Power, profit, and poetry: traditional society in Kathiawar, western India.* New Delhi: Manohar.

Tierney, Kathleen, Christine Bevc and Erica Kuligowski. 2006. 'Metaphors matter: Disaster myths, media frames, and their consequences in Hurricane Katrina'. *Annals of the American Academy of Political and Social Science*, 604 (1): 57–81.

Turner, B.S. 1987. 'A note on nostalgia'. *Theory, Culture and Society*, 4 (1): 147–56.

Tyabji, Azhar. 2006. *Bhuj: Art, architecture and history*. Ahmedabad: Mapin Publishing in association with Environmental Planning Collaborative.

Upadhyaya, Deendayal. 1969. *Integral humanism*. New Delhi: Bharatiya Jana Sangh.

Vakil, C.N., and M.H. Patel. 1939. 'The social and economic structure of greater Gujarat'. *Journal of the Gujarat Research Society*, 1 (1): 39–54.

———1940. 'Social and economic structure of greater Gujarat, IV: Industrial development of Gujarat'. *Journal of the Gujarat Research Society*, 2 (3): 139–48.

Van de Wetering, Maxine. 1982. 'Moralizing in Puritan natural science: Mysteriousness in earthquake sermons'. *Journal of the History of Ideas*, 43 (3): 417–38.

Varshney, Ashutosh. 2002. *Ethnic conflict and civic life: Hindus and Muslims in India*. New Haven: Yale University Press.

Virmani, Sandeep. 2010. 'Compounding disasters—first natural, then man-made: Failed interventions we can learn from'. In Shirish Patel and Aromar Revi (eds), *Recovering from earthquakes: Response, reconstruction and impact mitigation in India*, pp. 142–58. New Delhi: Routledge.

Voltaire. 1912. *Toleration and other essays by Voltaire* (trans. Joseph McCabe). New York: G.P. Putnam's Sons.

Wadia, D.N. 1942. 'The geological evolution of Gujarat'. *Journal of the Gujarat Research Society*, 4 (4): 215–19.

Watson, J.W. 1876. *History of Gujarat*. Bombay: Government Central Press.

Wiesel, Elie. 1960. *Night*. New York: Hill and Wang.

Wilkinson, Steven I. 2002. 'Putting Gujarat in perspective'. *Economic and Political Weekly*, 37 (17): 1579–83.

Williams, Raymond B. 1984. *A new face of Hinduism: The Swaminarayan religion*. Cambridge: Cambridge University Press.

Wilson, John. 1855. *History of the suppression of infanticide in western India under the government of Bombay, including notices of the provinces and tribes in which the practice has prevailed*. Bombay: Smith and Taylor.

Winter, Jay. 1995. *Sites of memory, sites of mourning: The Great War in European cultural history*. Cambridge: Cambridge University Press.

Wood, John R. 1984. 'British versus princely legacies and the political integration of Gujarat'. *Journal of Asian Studies*, 44 (1): 65–99.

Wootton, David. 2000. 'Introduction'. In *Voltaire, Candide and related texts* (trans. David Wootton), pp. viii–xxxiii. Indianapolis, IN: Hackett Publishing.

Yagnik, Achyut, and Suchitra Sheth. 2002. 'Whither Gujarat? Violence and after'. *Economic and Political Weekly*, 37 (11): 1009–11.

—2005. *The shaping of modern Gujarat: Plurality, Hindutva and beyond*. New Delhi: Penguin.

Yajnik, Indulal. 1950. *Shyamaji Krishnavarma: Life and times of an Indian revolutionary*. Bombay: Lakshmi Publications.

Young, Allan. 1996. *The harmony of illusions: Inventing post-traumatic stress disorder*. Princeton: Princeton University Press.

INDEX